PHOTOSHOP 6
DOWN & Dirty TRICKS

SCOTT KELBY

The Adobe® Photoshop® 6
Down and Dirty Tricks
Team

PRODUCTION EDITOR
Chris Main

COPY EDITOR
Richard Theriault

TYPESETTING
Janet Bechtle

CREATIVE DIRECTOR
AND COVER DESIGN
Felix Nelson

STOCK IMAGES
The stock images in this book
are courtesy of PhotoDisc.
www.photodisc.com

PUBLISHED BY
New Riders Publishing

Copyright © 2001 by New Riders Publishing

FIRST EDITION: May 2001

International Standard Book Number: 0-7357-1147-X

Library of Congress Catalog Card Number: 2001088953

05 04 03 02 01 7 6 5 4 3 2 1

Interpretation of the printing code: The rightmost double-digit number is the year of the book's printing; the rightmost single-digit number is the number of the book's printing. For example, the printing code 01-1 shows that the first printing of the book occurred in 2001.

Composed in Myriad and Minion by New Riders Publishing

Printed in the United States of America

Trademarks

Warning and Disclaimer

www.downanddirtytricks.com

ACKNOWLEDGMENTS

This book would not have been possible without the tireless efforts and support of some very special people. First, I'd like to thank my wonderful, beautiful, and absolutely amazing wife and business partner Kalebra. Her constant support, understanding, energy, patience, and hilarious sense of humor made writing this book a really wonderful experience. She's part editor, part target audience, part coach, and part wonder woman, and I couldn't have done it without her. She's the kind of woman love songs are written for, and nobody knows better than I how lucky I am to have her.

I want to thank two very special people on my creative team: Felix Nelson and Chris Main. I want to thank Felix for his creative input in this book. Every time I thought I had come up with a great technique, Felix would walk into my office, look at it, and suggest one little thing that would take the whole project to another level. He's an amazing talent, a pleasure to work with, and this book is much better because he was a part of it. My "main man" Chris Main did an outstanding job of editing, creating, designing, capturing, and keeping everything organized and on track through the whole project, and I wouldn't have dared to try it without him. They're the kind of team that makes you feel that you can tackle any project, and I'm indebted to them both for all their help and enthusiasm for this book.

I want to thank my other business partners and good friends Jim Workman and Jean A. Kendra. They've totally supported all my crazy ideas and never pulled an "I told you so" when some of those ideas hit the ground with a thud. They never lost faith in "that whole vision thing" and gave me lots of freedom to design, create, and teach, and I can't thank them enough.

I especially want to thank Richard Theriault (or Dicky T as we like to call him) for coming to my rescue (once again) on 20 minutes notice, and busting his butt for weeks on end. He never does anything without putting his heart into it, and this book was no exception. He's an editor's editor, a first class wordsmith, and a great friend. Many thanks DT—you've done it again!

I want to give a very special thanks to my father Jerome Kelby. I realized many years ago that I have been blessed with an unfair advantage in life by having been raised by such a wonderful dad. I've never met anyone more charming, more ethical and forthright, more loving, more generous, more crazy, or more fun. And I've never met a man I've admired more. There's no denying it—he's my hero.

I want to thank my three-year-old son Jordan for keeping me in great spirits by coming in every day and telling me, "I want to work with you, Daddy," and typing a few random keystrokes on my keyboard; and for the many mental breaks he gave me when he'd come in and say, "Daddy, do you want to play with my cars?" (or trains, or space shuttle, or Buzz Lightyear). He's already taught me a lot, and I continue to learn more from him every day. I just love that little guy.

I'm grateful to my brother Jeff for having such confidence in me, for joining our team, and having such a positive influence in my life. To Doug Gornick for teaching me so much about Photoshop over the years and reminding me of how much there is still yet to learn. To my good friend Bill Lindsay, who was one of the catalysts for my being in this business. To Dave Gales, an amazing man, mentor, friend, and pastor of the best small church in this hemisphere. To the people who've attended my seminars, bought my training videos, read *Photoshop User* magazine and constantly kept asking me "When are you going to write a book?"

Thanks to all my friends at Adobe who've helped me so much over the years—Terry White, Barbara Rice, Rye Livingston, Kevin Connor, and Jill Nakashima. Thanks to Chris Smith at KW Media Group for kickin' so much butt that I didn't mind him going to Cancun while we finished the book. He's da man! To Mark Monciardini for his help and cool tips. To Julie Stephenson whose hard work keeps those cards and letters comin'. To my Web team who make it all look so easy: Kleber Stephenson, Tommy Maloney, and Jon Gales. To my good friend John Graden who has taught me so much about so many things. And most importantly to God for leading me to the woman of my dreams, for giving me a family I adore, for allowing me to make a living doing what I love, for always being there when I need Him, and for blessing me with such a wonderful, fulfilling, and happy life.

ABOUT THE AUTHOR

Scott Kelby

 Scott is Editor-in-Chief of *Photoshop User* magazine and President of the National Association of Photoshop Professionals, the trade association for Adobe Photoshop users worldwide. Scott is also Editor-in-Chief of *Mac Today* magazine, a print magazine for graphic designers using Macintosh, and is President and CEO of KW Media Group, Inc., a Florida-based software training and publishing company.

He's one of the co-authors of the book *Maclopedia, the Ultimate Reference on Everything Macintosh* from Hayden Books, and *Adobe Web Design and Publishing Unleashed,* from Sams.net Publishing. Some of Scott's Photoshop work appears in the book *Adobe Photoshop: Creative Techniques,* also from Hayden.

Scott is an Adobe Certified Expert in Photoshop, the training director for the Adobe Photoshop Seminar Tour, Technical Chair and Educational Director of PhotoshopWorld (the annual convention for Adobe Photoshop users), and is a speaker at graphics tradeshows and events nationwide. Scott is also featured in a series of Photoshop, Illustrator, and Web design video training tapes and has been training graphics professionals across the country since 1993.

Scott lives in the Tampa Bay area in Florida with his wife Kalebra and his three-year-old son Jordan. For more background info, visit www.scottkelby.com.

TABLE OF CONTENTS

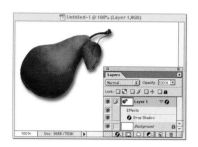

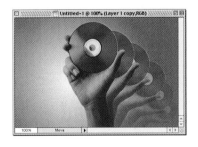

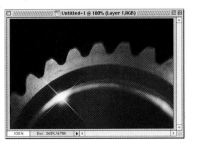

TABLE OF CONTENTS

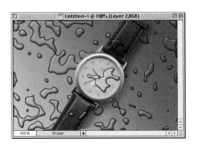

INTRODUCTION

As the author, I'm supposed to tell you something in this introduction to make you want to buy this book, so how's this? "You've just purchased the coolest Adobe® Photoshop® book ever written." Now I don't want you to think that my obvious bias doesn't make me a good judge of Photoshop books. I've read 'em al!. OK, I haven't read them all, but I've read most of them. At least a bunch of them, perhaps as many as a "whole mess of them," and there are some fantastic books out there. With probably 100 Photoshop books on the shelves right now, what makes this the coolest Photoshop book ever written? Is it the most complete Photoshop book? Nope. Will it teach you all the important techniques that you'll need to know to become a Photoshop expert? Afraid not. This book is designed to do just one thing—teach you the effects that will blow your clients away, make you loads of money, and give you the most fun you've ever had using Photoshop—all *without* having to be a Photoshop expert. *That's* what makes this the coolest Photoshop book ever. No years of study, no complex mathematical concepts to master, no baloney. All fun stuff, no bad stuff. None.

You'll be absolutely amazed at how easy these tricks are once you know the secrets.

After reading this book, regardless of your level of experience, you'll be able to create those same incredible Photoshop special effects that otherwise would take years to learn. You'll be absolutely amazed at how easy these tricks are once you know the secrets, and they're all here, including those closely guarded "insider tips" and down and dirty tricks of the trade. I'll tell you right now, you're going to have a blast with this book.

Is this book for me?

Yes. (I was just going to end the paragraph there, but my editor wouldn't let me.) It's always been my contention that most people would love to fly a big jet airliner. They'd love to sit in the pilot's seat, roll down the runway, pull the wheel back, and climb into the sky. But the years of study and training (and luckily, a host of FAA regulations) keep most people from ever having that thrill. They love the idea of flying a big jet, they just don't want to do what it takes to become a pilot. Flying, good; studying for years, bad. I've talked with numerous Photoshop users who feel the same way. They want to do all the incredible effects, they want to make everyone's jaw drop, they want to know the cool tricks, but they don't want to spend years learning it all from the ground up. If that sounds like you, this book is for you. If that sounds nothing like you—if you enjoy all the minutiae, all the technical aspects, and if you feel you need all the background details on everything you do before you even do it, this book (I really hate to say this) probably isn't for you. You'll notice I said "probably"; I hate to close the door on a potential sale.

How to use this book

This book isn't one to read in bed. This is one to read while you're sitting in front of your computer. If you read it anywhere else, after just a few pages, you're going to jump up, boot your computer, and start trying some of these effects, so you may as well save yourself the time and sit in front of your computer right from the start.

You don't have to begin at Chapter One and read this like a novel (however, if you decide to read this like a novel, dim the lights, put on some classical music, and set out a few candles. It won't really enhance your understanding of the book, but you'll feel like you're in a Folgers® commercial). This is designed as a "jump in anywhere" book. You can start on page 120 and you'll be able to complete that effect as easily as the effect on page one. Of course, there isn't an effect on page one, but if there was.... Anyway, you should go to the effects that interest you most and start there. Jump around. Live a little. And if you've been using Photoshop for years, don't let it throw you because I spell everything out. For example, instead of just saying "create a new layer," I say, "Create a new layer by clicking on the New Layer icon at the bottom of the Layers palette." I do that because I want everyone to be able to open the book to any page and start creating. Most books start off with a few chapters that explain the Photoshop basics, how to use the tools, etc., but I didn't. I couldn't wait to get to the effects (and I figured you didn't want to wait either), so I started with them on the first page of Chapter One and didn't stop until my head exploded. I thought that if you wanted to learn all about Photoshop, you'd buy one of those "learn all about Photoshop" books. If you bought this book, you want to do cool stuff *now!*

...if you wanted to learn all about Photoshop, you'd buy one of those "learn all about Photoshop" books. If you bought this book, you want to do cool stuff now!

Getting testy

I wanted any Photoshop user, at any level of experience, to be able to easily recreate the techniques contained in this book, so we tested them using people who don't regularly use Photoshop. In fact, some of them have never used Photoshop at all. I figured it this way: If someone who doesn't use Photoshop can recreate these effects, surely someone with any experience will breeze right through them. Here's what I did: I would write a step-by-step tutorial for an effect, then I would get someone at my office (usually someone from the business department) and make them sit down and try to recreate the effect (after a while, they'd see me coming and try to hide). I would sit behind them and watch them go through each project. If they got stuck, I'd find out why, then I'd go back and tweak the text to make sure people that bought the book wouldn't run into that same problem. After these tweaks, I'd have someone who was already familiar with Photoshop recreate the effect (from the edited text), and when it worked perfectly, only then would I let it go to the editor. So even if you don't always understand what's happening along the way, when you get to the end, it'll look just like it does in the book.

Other cool stuff

The original title for this book was *Photoshop 6 Down and Dirty Tips and Tricks* but it sounded kinda clunky, so I took the word *Tips* out to make the title shorter. I took the word out, but I left all the tips in. So besides tons of step-by-step projects, you'll find sidebars with tips that relate to those effects. Sometimes a tip doesn't actually relate to a specific effect, but I couldn't find a good place to put it, so I stuck it there, and sometimes it's just a random comment from me. I tried to keep the swearing to a minimum.

Is this book for Mac, PC, or both?

Adobe Photoshop enjoys immense popularity on both platforms, and I want this book to enjoy immense popularity on both platforms, so it covers both the Mac and PC versions of Photoshop. I have to admit, it was pretty easy, because Photoshop is identical on both the Macintosh and PC platforms, so I really didn't have to do very much to make it cross-platform. However, even though the software is the same, the keyboards on the Mac and PC are slightly different. It's really just three keys that have one name on a Mac and a different name on a PC. Throughout the book, every time I give a keyboard shortcut, I give both the Macintosh and PC keyboard shortcuts.

Why I wrote this book

Since 1993, I've been lucky enough to train many thousands of Photoshop users across the country through my live seminars. Although they come to learn Photoshop, it's a learning experience for me too. It isn't enough for me just to know Photoshop, I have to learn what it is that people from all different backgrounds and disciplines want to learn most about Photoshop. So I asked a lot of questions along the way and met a lot of really great people. One thing I learned early really stuck with me. There was one area that everybody seemed to have great interest in: learning the tricks of the trade. Learning how to do those jawdropping special effects that make you, and your clients, look great. Luckily for me, I was just like them. I wanted to learn all those cool tricks too, and the first Photoshop session I ever taught was in Ft. Lauderdale, Florida, and it was called "Photoshop Down and Dirty Tricks." It turned out to be the most popular session of the entire seminar because it was the exact thing people had been telling me they wanted to learn. I went on to produce my own Photoshop video called (you guessed it) *Photoshop Down and Dirty Tricks*. It was a huge success, and I later went on to do 12 other Photoshop videos on specific topics, including *Photoshop Down and Dirty Tricks Part II*. Then came my column in *Photoshop User* magazine called "Scott Kelby's Down and Dirty Tricks." This book is just a natural extension of what I love doing best in Photoshop—down and dirty tricks. That probably explains why I had such a great time writing it. This book takes some of my favorite Photoshop techniques from my live seminars, my column in *Photoshop User,* and my videos and combines them all into one resource. It's the book that I wish I could've found when I was trying to learn these types of effects, and I'm thrilled to be able to bring it to you.

This is the book I wish I could have found when I was trying to learn all these cool effects.

Time to get jiggy with it

I did some research, and found that the Latin word "jiggy" actually means "Launch Photoshop," and when used in conjunction with "with it," it means "begin the tutorial." That's a 100% fabrication, but I just couldn't start the book with "Let's get started." So sit back, pour yourself a nice glass of Courvoisier, and begin to unlock a world of Photoshop delights that dare not speak its name. OK, that's a bit dramatic, but I do know this—you're about to have an awful lot of fun as you learn some of the coolest down and dirty tricks on the planet. Now go forth and do cool stuff.

Wait! One more thing...

Check out this book's companion Web site at **www.downanddirtytricks.com.** It's full of stuff. The kind of stuff you'd find on an author's Web site. Stuff like giant full-color pictures of me. Some looking thoughtful, others looking wistful, some looking dazed and confused. Plus, I thought I'd put some extra tips up there and anything else I could think of to keep it from looking like a big blank page. So stop by. Keep refreshing the page over and over again, so it looks like I'm getting a lot of hits. That's the least you can do. ;-) OK, *now* you can go forth and do cool stuff.

1

I have always felt that Photoshop soft drop shadows are a lot like grated Parmesan cheese—there aren't

Standing in the Shadows of Love
Basic Drop Shadows

many things you can add them to that they won't make better. Soft drop shadow effects are great for adding realism and depth to your projects, and personally, I love 'em, so I use them fairly often. OK, more than fairly often, I use them liberally. I'll never forget a quote I read from Photoshop design guru Glenn Mitsui in the excellent book Photoshop Studio Secrets *by Deke McClelland and Katrin Eismann. When asked about shadows, Glenn summed it up quite eloquently, I thought, with this comment, "My motto is simple. No shadows bad; plenty shadows good." I couldn't agree more. This chapter teaches you the classic drop shadow effects so you'll never be caught with a flat-looking image again. Go forth, and shadow plenty!*

What does Lock Transparent Pixels do?

Lock Transparent Pixels (known as Preserve Transparency in previous versions) is a complicated name for a simple thing. Here's a quick explanation that will help: When you have an object on a layer, everything but that object is transparent, meaning you can see through to the layers behind it. If you put a background of daises on a layer beneath it, you will see those daisies surrounding your object. When you turn Lock Transparent Pixels on, you're telling Photoshop to "leave those transparent areas alone; just affect my object."

For example, open an image that has an object on its own layer (a watch, a ball, etc.). Go under the Edit menu and choose Fill. Click OK and the entire layer fills with your foreground color. Press Command-Z (PC: Control-Z) to undo your fill. Now turn on Lock Transparent Pixels and try that fill again. This time it only fills your object, not the whole layer. Why? Because you protected (preserved) the transparent areas from being filled; therefore, it could only fill your object. Makes sense now, eh?

Drop Shadows (The Do-It-Yourself Manual Version)

I know what you're thinking, "Why do I have to learn the old method when Photoshop has a built-in drop shadow effect?" It's because there are times when the automatic version just won't do the trick. Trust me—knowing this technique will prove invaluable. OK, it won't be invaluable, but it can't hurt.

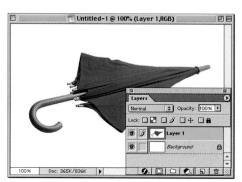

STEP ONE: Open a new document in RGB or Grayscale mode. Open an image that has an object that you want to add a drop shadow to. Select the image (using one of Photoshop's selection tools) and drag-and-drop that image (using the Move tool) into your blank document. It will appear on its own layer (as shown above).

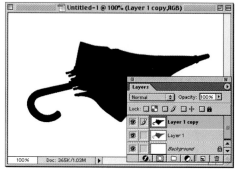

STEP TWO: In the Layers palette, make a copy of this layer by dragging the layer to the New Layer icon at the bottom of the Layers palette (it's the second icon from the right. It looks like a page with a corner turned up). Press the letter "d" to set your foreground color to black. Then press Shift-Option-Delete (PC: Shift-Alt-Backspace) to fill your object with black.

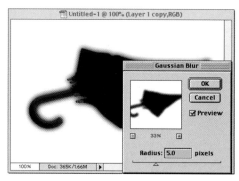

STEP THREE: Go under the Filter menu, under Blur, and choose Gaussian Blur. When the dialog box appears, enter 5 for the Radius and click OK. (Technically, there's no right or wrong number you can enter here—the higher the number, the blurrier your drop shadow will be. It's really up to you to decide how blurry to make your shadow.)

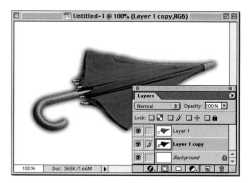

STEP FOUR: In the Layers palette, click-and-hold on the top layer (Layer 1 copy) and drag it behind your original layer (Layer 1). This moves the shadow layer behind the object (which is nice, because in real life most shadows appear behind the object rather than in front of it. Sorry, that's just me being a wise . . . guy).

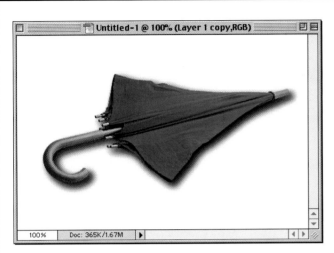

STEP FIVE: Switch to the Move tool (you might as well get used to the keyboard shortcut—just press the letter "v"), then drag your blurry shadow layer down and to the right (I think moving it down and to the right is a federal law, but I can't swear to it). This is called "offsetting the shadow." You could also move it, say, up and to the left as if the light source was lying on the floor beaming upward, but that's dangerous—somebody could trip, fall, and break a hip or something.

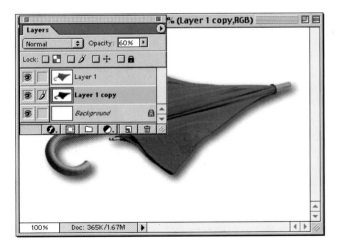

STEP SIX: The last step is to lower the opacity of the shadow layer in the Layers palette. Try something in the 60–70% range. If you leave it set at the default setting of 100%, you'll get an unrealistic all-black shadow (most shadows are gray). Test it yourself. Raise your hand over your keyboard and look at the shadow—is it a big black handprint you can't see through or a semi-transparent gray shadow? Gotcha!

QUICK TIP
You can change the opacity of a layer without using the Opacity field on the Layer palette or touching the pop-down opacity slider. Just type in the amount of opacity you'd like on your keyboard. For example, if you'd like a 56% opacity for your current layer, type 56 on your keyboard. If you want nice round percentages, type the first number. For example, if you'd like an opacity level of 70%, type the number 7, because just typing one number will get you 10% increments. If you want an exact opacity amount (like 73%), you have to type the 73 quickly—or you'll get 70% then 30%.

Get better shadows when four-color printing
If your project is going to be printed on a four-color printing press, you should change the blend mode of your shadow layer from Normal to Multiply. This is accomplished in the pop-up menu just below the name tab in the Layers palette. By default, it's set to Normal. This means that anything on this layer will cover everything on the layers beneath it when the opacity is set at 100%. But because of the way the Multiply blend mode interacts with the colors beneath it, you can get better, more realistic-looking soft drop shadows.

However, if the background behind your shadow is pure white, you can ignore this step—it only helps when the shadow is being printed over a background that contains color.

How far should I offset my shadow?

Every time you create a drop shadow, you'll be faced with a decision—how far away to position the shadow from the object. There's no set distance for the amount of offset, so this is a call you'll have to make. Just remember that the farther away the shadow appears from the object, the higher off the background the object will appear. So if you want the object to appear very near the background, say 1/2" off the background, keep the shadow close (like the default setting). If you want the background to appear farther below (like an inch or two), you'll have to increase the amount of distance. For special effects, it's not uncommon to see a shadow literally inches away from the object, which makes the object look as if it's far above the background. So, in short, it's your call.

Automated Drop Shadows (A Layer Effects)

Now that you've paid your dues, it's time to lie back and enjoy life. Yes, my friends, you've earned the right to use automatic drop shadows. They're so easy to use, you'll find yourself adding drop shadows to things that have no business having drop shadows.

STEP ONE: Open a new document in RGB or Grayscale mode. Open an image that has an object that you want to add a drop shadow to. Select the image (using one of Photoshop's selection tools), and drag-and-drop that image (using the Move tool) into your blank document. It will appear on its own layer (as shown above).

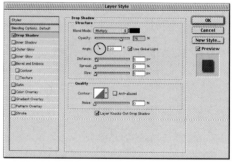

STEP TWO: Go under the Layer menu, under Layer Style, and choose Drop Shadow. The Drop Shadow dialog box (shown above) will appear, and you'll see a drop shadow applied to your image as well (the preview is live on screen, so as long as this dialog box isn't covering your image, you'll be able to see the shadow applied to your image).

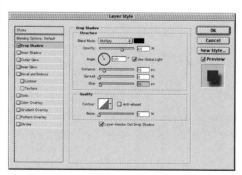

STEP THREE: The first issue to deal with is the distance (how far the shadow will appear from the object). Rather than typing in a number and using the "trial and error" method for getting the right distance, move your cursor outside the dialog box into your image window and click-and-drag the shadow where you want. That's a pretty sweet feature.

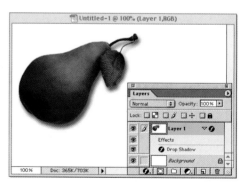

STEP FOUR: The default settings for the Drop Shadow effect are, well, perhaps not the greatest (that's being kind). I usually increase the Size (amount of blur) to around 10 to make the shadow softer, and I usually lower the Opacity to 65%. Click OK to complete the drop shadow effect.

Reverse White Shadow

This is a great effect for anyone doing a lot of black-and-white work (like newspapers, newsletters, etc.), because it gives you a nice Photoshoppy effect without having to rely on color.

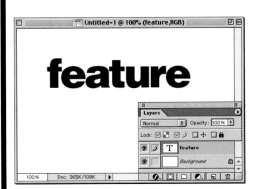

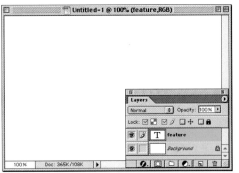

STEP ONE: Press the letter "d" to set your foreground color to black. Use the Type tool to create your type, then press the letter "x" to swap your foreground and background colors, making your foreground color white.

STEP TWO: Press Shift-Option-Delete (PC: Shift-Alt-Backspace) to fill your text with white. Your screen should look like the example above. (I know, it's not the most exciting screen capture, but that's what white text on a white background looks like.)

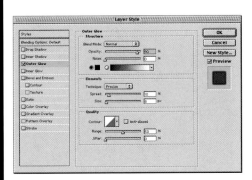

STEP THREE: Go under the Layer menu, under Layer Style, and choose Outer Glow. When the dialog box appears, click on the square beige color swatch to bring up the Color Picker. Change the color to black and click OK in the Color Picker to lock in black as your glow color.

STEP FOUR: Change the blend mode to Normal, set the Opacity to 90%, change the Technique to Precise, increase the Spread to 10, and increase the Size to 8. When you click OK, the image appears on screen as white text with nearly a black glow around the letters (as shown above).

Rotating through the Layer Effects

After you open any one of the Layer Style dialog boxes (like Drop Shadow or Glow), you can use a keyboard shortcut to switch to other effects: press Command-1, 2, 3, 4, etc. (PC: Control-1, 2, 3, 4, etc.) to step through the different Layer Effects. *(Note: when you're talking about one particular effect, like the Drop Shadow, it's referred to as a Layer Effects. But once you have more than one effect, they're called Layer Styles.)* You will notice, however, that the controls are grayed out for the particular effect that you switched to. You still need to click on the check box in the Styles list on the left to make the dialog box active.

You can reopen the dialog box for any layer that has a Layer Effect applied by double-clicking directly on the little *f* icon that appears before the effect's name in the Layers palette. The dialog box will open to the last settings used for your particular effect.

If you double-click on the little *f* icon to the right of the layer's name, it brings up the Layer Style Blending Options dialog box.

Why you have to rasterize your Type layer

During the project shown at right, you have to convert your Type from an editable Type layer into a regular Photoshop image layer in order to complete the effect. This conversion process is called "rasterizing your Type layer" (known as "rendering" in previous versions of Photoshop).

The reason you have to rasterize your Type layer is that Type layers are special vector-based layers that enable you to re-edit your type, including changing type faces and even changing type sizes at any time—as long as it remains a Type layer. That's all great; however, there is a tradeoff—you can't apply any filters to these Type layers until you convert them into Photoshop image layers (which are made up of pixels). So don't make this conversion until you check all of your spelling for typos and that the font and size are just what you want, because once you convert, you'll have to start from scratch if you have a typo. To rasterize your Type layer, go under the Layer menu, under Rasterize, and choose Type.

Zoom Shadows

This particular effect is very popular in digital video, and I've seen it in dozens of TV commercials. In this effect, the shadow has the zoom effect applied so heavily that you can barely distinguish what the shadow type says, but since the original type is nearby, it makes it an easy visual match.

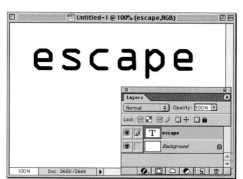

STEP ONE: Create your type (it will appear on its own layer).

STEP TWO: Make a copy of your Type layer by dragging it to the New Layer icon. Then go under the Layer menu, under Rasterize, and choose Type to convert your Type layer copy into an image layer.

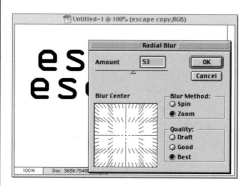

STEP THREE: Go under the Filter menu, under Blur, and choose Radial Blur. For Blur Method, choose Zoom and raise the Amount to at least 25 (you can experiment and go higher if you like. If it's too blurry, you can always undo and try again.)

STEP FOUR: Lower the opacity of the zoomed layer and switch to the move tool by pressing the letter "v." Move the zoomed layer quite a bit above (or below) your type. Remember, don't worry so much about the readability of the shadow text, because the original clean text is in front of it. Visually, they'll know what the shadow is supposed to say.

Painting Drop Shadows

This is the real "Down and Dirty" way to create drop shadows, and you get to use a paint blend mode that is so smart, it actually knows where your image is and lets you paint around it. Just grab a soft-edged brush, lower your opacity, change one little option, and start painting right "under" your image.

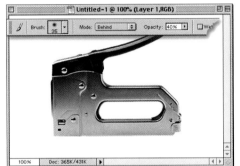

STEP ONE: Open an image that has an object on its own layer (or open a background image, select the object with one of Photoshop's selection tools, then press Shift-Command-J [PC: Shift-Control-J] to put the object on its own layer).

STEP TWO: Click on the Paintbrush tool. Go up to the Options Bar and lower the Opacity setting to 40%, then change the mode from Normal to Behind.

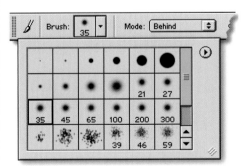

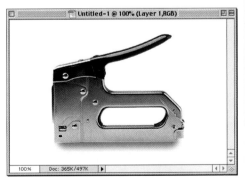

STEP THREE: In the Options Bar, click on the downward facing triangle next to the currently selected brush and a flyout menu of brushes will appear. Choose a medium-sized, soft-edged brush. (Note: Hard-edged brushes are on the top row and soft-edged brushes are on the next two rows. The number below the brush is its diameter measured in pixels.)

STEP FOUR: Draw along the edge of the object where you want your shadow to fall (hold the Shift key for a straight line). Make sure your brush extends a bit into your object. (Don't worry, you won't actually paint on the object—the Behind mode puts your painted shadow behind the object. Eerie, ain't it?)

Blend modes for tools

By now, you're probably familiar with layer blend modes. If not, what they do, in short, is determine how the current layer interacts with the layers beneath it. In Normal mode (the default), any solid object on that layer covers up anything beneath it in other layers. When you change the blend mode of a layer, it will take into consideration the layers beneath it when it blends with those layers—often in very annoying and displeasing ways (depending on which layer mode you choose). Some are helpful; others are, well, pretty awful.

In the example at left, we changed the Paintbrush tool's blend mode to a mode that lets us paint behind the image.

After you select one of Photoshop's paint tools, you can rotate through the various blend modes by pressing Shift-+ (the Shift key and the plus sign) to get a visual representation of how the blend modes work. If you don't have a Paint tool selected, it will step through your currently active layer's blend modes.

Converting paths to selections

In this example, we converted our path (created with the Pen tool) to a selection by pressing Command-Return (PC: Control-Enter). This instantly converts your path to a selection. However, you can have a lot of control over how your path becomes a selection, including adding feathering to your selection, if you use the Make Selection command rather than just hitting Enter.

To find the Make Selection command, go to the Paths palette (under the Window menu, choose Show Paths). When the palette appears, go to the palette's pop-down menu (at the top-right corner of the palette) and choose Make Selection. A dialog box will appear. To add feathering (softening just the edges) to your selection, simply type a number in the Feather Radius field and click OK.

Drawing Precise Shadows

Here's another drop shadow method that works well when you need a precise shadow. This method lets you use the Pen tool to draw exactly where the shadow should be, giving you total control over every step of the way.

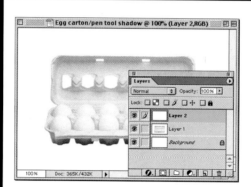

STEP ONE: Open the document that contains the image you want to add a drop shadow to. Put the object on its own layer. Add a new blank layer above your object layer by clicking on the New Layer icon at the bottom of the Layers palette (it's the second icon from the right).

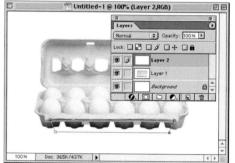

STEP TWO: Press the letter "p" to switch to the Pen tool. Click the Pen tool once where you want your shadow to start, then continue clicking to form the shape you want your shadow to have. When you reach the point where you started, a small circle will appear in the lower right-hand corner of the Pen tool's icon, telling you that you've come "full circle." Click once to connect your path.

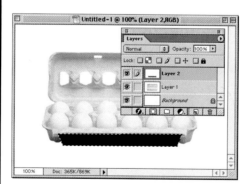

STEP THREE: To turn your path into a selection, press Command-Return (PC: Control-Enter), and it will turn your path into a selection. Press the letter "d" to set your foreground color to black. Fill your selection with black by pressing Option-Delete (PC: Alt-Backspace). Press Command-D (PC: Control-D) to deselect.

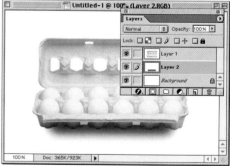

STEP FOUR: Lastly, soften the shadow by going under the Filter menu, under Blur, and choosing Gaussian Blur. Lower the opacity of the shadow layer to 70%, then drag it below the object layer (in the Layers palette) to complete the effect.

Colorizing Drop Shadows

Although most of the drop shadows in this book (and probably almost any other book) are black, you can create special effect drop shadows if you want to. An easy way to do that is to colorize the drop shadow itself.

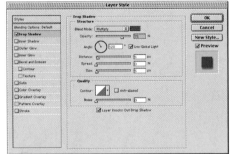

STEP ONE: Open a new document in RGB mode. Open an image that has an object in it that you want to add a color drop shadow to. Select the image (using one of Photoshop's selection tools) and drag-and-drop that image (using the Move tool) into your blank document. It will appear on its own layer (as shown above).

STEP TWO: Go under the Layer menu, under Layer Style, and choose Drop Shadow. The Drop Shadow dialog box (shown above) will appear. To change the color of the shadow, click on the black color swatch to bring up the Color Picker. When the Color Picker appears, choose the color you'd like your shadow to be, and click OK to lock in that color.

STEP THREE: Choose the distance you'd like your color shadow to be offset from your object. Rather than typing a number in the Distance field, move your cursor outside the dialog box into your image window, and drag the shadow where you want it.

STEP FOUR: You might want to increase the Size (amount of blur) to at least 10 (use a higher figure for high-res images) and lower the opacity to around 65% (it's your call on what to set the opacity to). Click OK to complete the effect.

Using the Eyedropper tool inside the Color Picker

In the effect at left, you're colorizing a drop shadow by using the Color Picker inside the Drop Shadow dialog box. But did you know that while the Color Picker dialog box is open, you can move your cursor outside the dialog box, and it changes into the Eyedropper tool (no really, I swear), and you can then click on a color in any open document and sample that color? Try it, it's pretty handy.

2

A few years back, I made myself a promise. If I ever wrote my own book, I wouldn't be bound by the conventions of

Shadow Dancing
Advanced Drop Shadow Techniques

those before me. I would break out from the mold—from the constraints that society has imposed upon us to fulfill a dream that few would ever ponder, and even fewer dare attempt. Yes I would be the one who would write not one, but two—yes two—chapters on creating soft drop shadows.

Am I wrong to take what is a seemingly harmless effect, and elevate it to a level that is deserving of both a basic and an advanced chapter? Perhaps. But ask yourself this, "Is there really anything more satisfying than having someone look at your art, and rather than trying to contemplate your motivation, rather than trying to get inside your head, rather than trying to sense your anguish, they just look at you dead in the eye and say, 'Hey man, nice drop shadow.'" I think that says it all. Let us begin.

Free Transform: the keyboard shortcut brain teaser

Most of the time when we use the Free Transform function, we Control-click (PC: Right-click) inside the Free Transform bounding box and choose our desired transformation from the handy pop-up menu. This way, we only have to remember one keyboard shortcut—Control-click (PC: Right-click). But in actuality, there are keyboard shortcuts for almost every Free Transform function (except for rotate—just move your cursor outside the bounding box then move your mouse to rotate). Here's the list just in case you feel like learning them:

- Hold the Command key (PC: Control key) and drag a corner square handle to distort your object.
- Hold Shift and drag a square handle on any corner for proportional scaling of your object.
- Hold Shift-Option-Command (PC: Shift-Alt-Control) and grab a top or bottom square handle and drag outward to add a perspective effect.
- Hold Option-Command (PC: Alt-Control), grab the center handle, and drag right or left to skew.

Perspective Front Shadow

This is an effect that's been around for a while, but the particular version you'll learn here was inspired by a promo spot I saw for Fox Television's hit TV show *The X Files*. I also saw a version of this effect in the movie poster for *The Talented Mr. Ripley*. If he did this effect, he *is* talented.

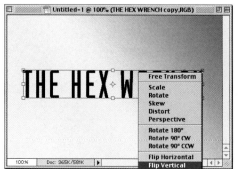

STEP ONE: Open a new document and create your type. I put a light gray to nearly white gradient in the background, but it's not necessary. In the Layers palette, drag your Type layer to the New Layer icon at the bottom of the Layers palette (it's the second icon from the right) to make a copy of your layer.

STEP TWO: Press Command-T (PC: Control-T) to bring up the Free Transform function. Control-click (PC: Right-click) directly inside the Free Transform bounding box, and a pop-up list of possible transformations will appear. Choose Flip Vertical from this list. Don't press Return (PC: Enter) yet.

STEP THREE: Drag your flipped layer downward until the bottoms of the letters of both sets of text nearly touch. Now press Return (PC: Enter) to complete your transformation. Go under the Layer menu, under Rasterize, and choose Type to convert your flipped Type layer into an image layer.

STEP FOUR: Press Command-T (PC: Control-T) to bring up the Free Transform function again. Control-click (PC: Right-click) directly inside the Free Transform bounding box and choose Perspective. Grab the bottom left or right adjustment handle and drag outward to create the perspective effect.

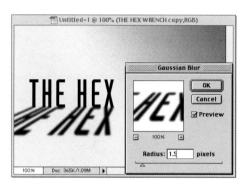

STEP FIVE: Next, grab either the top left or right adjustment handle and drag inward to accentuate the effect, and press Return (PC: Enter) to complete the transformation. Go under the Filter menu, under Blur, and choose Gaussian Blur. Add a slight 1.5-pixel blur to lightly soften the shadow.

STEP SIX: Switch to the Rectangular Marquee tool and drag a rectangular selection around the end (closest to you) of your shadow, extending about $1/3$ of the way into your shadow (as shown above). Go under the Select menu and choose Feather. In the Feather Selection dialog box, choose 10 pixels as your Feather Radius. Click OK.

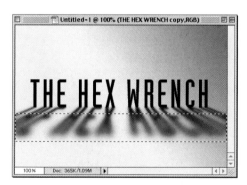

STEP SEVEN: Go under the Filter menu, under Blur, and choose Gaussian Blur. Apply a 2-pixel blur. Deselect by pressing Command-D (PC: Control-D). Draw another, deeper selection around your shadow that is about $2/3$ of the way to the base of your type (as shown above), then apply another 2-pixel Gaussian Blur.

STEP EIGHT: Lastly, draw one last selection around your shadow that is about $3/4$ of the way to the base of your type, and then apply one last 2-pixel Gaussian Blur. What this does is make your type appear more blurry as it moves away from the base of the type—just like a shadow would in real life. Deselect to complete the effect.

Getting out of a transformation

While you're using the Free Transform function, if you suddenly decide you don't want to transform your object after all, just press the Escape key on your keyboard to leave Free Transform. If you've made a transformation you don't like, you can undo your last step by pressing Command-Z (PC: Control-Z) while you're still in Free Transform.

Also, while you're in Free Transform, you can move your object by placing your cursor inside the bounding box (your cursor changes to an arrow) and dragging the box to a new location.

When you're transforming your object, you can lock in your transformation by either pressing Return (PC: Enter) or double-clicking within the bounding box.

COOL TIP: If you want to transform an object AND put a copy of it on its own layer at the same time, add the Option key (PC: Alt key) to the Free Transform keyboard shortcut, making it Option-Command-T (PC: Alt-Control-T).

Making copies of layers

In this example, we make a copy of the layer by dragging the layer (in the Layers palette) to the New Layer icon at the bottom of the Layers palette. But there are other ways of creating copies of layers. The fastest is probably just to press Command-J (PC: Control-J). This makes an instant duplicate of your current layer.

Another way is to take the Move tool, hold the Option key (PC: Alt key), click within your image on the layer you want to copy, and drag. As you drag, you'll see that a new layer copy has been created in the Layers palette.

Another method is to go under the Layer menu and choose Duplicate Layer. A dialog box will appear that enables you to name your newly copied layer and to choose whether you want this new layer to appear in your current document or in another open document, or you can choose to have it become a new document itself.

As a shortcut, you can Control-click (PC: Right-click) on your layer (in the Layers palette) and a pop-up menu will appear where you can choose Duplicate Layer.

Perspective Cast Shadow

This twist on the classic drop shadow effect adds realism in two ways: (1) it casts a shadow that is more realistic to what an actual light source would cast, and (2) the shadow is not as soft near the object, and it gets softer as it moves away—just like in real life.

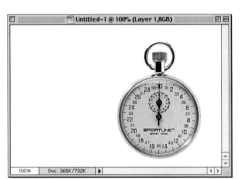

STEP ONE: Put an object on its own layer. Make a copy of that layer by dragging it to the New Layer icon at the bottom of the Layers palette. Press the letter "d" to change the foreground color to black, then press Shift-Option-Delete (PC: Shift-Alt-Backspace) to fill your object copy with black.

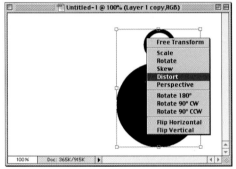

STEP TWO: Press Command-T (PC: Control-T) to bring up the Free Transform function. Control-click (PC: Right-click) directly inside the Free Transform bounding box and a pop-up list of possible transformations will appear. Choose Distort from this list.

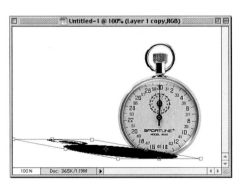

STEP THREE: In this step, you need to make the copy filled with black lie almost flat on the ground, so grab the top center adjustment point and drag it downward (as shown above). Press Return (PC: Enter) to complete your transformation.

STEP FOUR: Make sure your foreground color is still set to black and the background color is set to white by pressing the letter "d." Then switch to the Gradient tool by pressing the letter "g." Look in the Options Bar to make sure your currently selected gradient is Foreground to Background.

STEP FIVE: In the Layers palette, click on the Lock Transparent Pixels check box for your shadow layer. Drag the Gradient tool from one end of your shadow to the other. You want the gradient to start with black at the base of your object and change to white as your shadow extends away from the object.

STEP SIX: Turn off the transparency lock on your shadow layer. Go under the Filter menu, under Blur, and choose Gaussian Blur. When the dialog box appears, enter 2 for Blur Radius and click OK. In the Layers palette, drag Layer 1 copy below Layer 1. This puts the shadow behind your object.

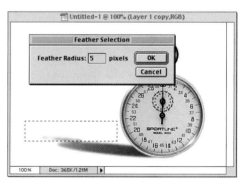

STEP SEVEN: To add more realism, you can create a perspective blur, where the shadow is less blurry near the object and becomes softer the further away it gets (like in real life). To do this, use the Marquee selection tool to draw a rectangle that covers the top $1/4$ of your cast shadow. Go under the Select menu and choose Feather. Add a 5-pixel feather to soften the transition. Then go under the Filter menu, under Blur, and choose Gaussian Blur. Add a 2-pixel blur, and then deselect by pressing Command-D (PC: Control-D).

STEP EIGHT: With the Marquee selection tool, draw a selection that covers the top half of your cast shadow. Apply another 3-pixel Gaussian Blur, and then deselect. Draw a new Marquee tool selection that covers $3/4$ of your shadow (almost to the base) and apply another Gaussian Blur to finish the effect. This creates a 10-pixel blur around the furthest areas of the cast shadow, an 8-pixel blur around the top half, a 5-pixel blur around a $1/4$ of the distance away from the base, and only a slight 2-pixel blur up close.

Making selections in a straight line

In this example, we used the Rectangular Marquee tool, but if you need to draw a selection that includes straight lines but is not a rectangle or a square, you can use the Polygonal Lasso. It draws straight lines from point to point as you click. To access the Polygonal Lasso tool, simply press the letter "L" (which switches you to the regular Lasso tool), click-and-hold in the document where you want your selection to start, press the Option key (PC: Alt key) then release the mouse to temporarily switch to the Polygonal Lasso. Just click in your document where you want to create a straight line. As long as you hold the Option/Alt key, it remains the Polygonal tool. When you release the Option key, it turns into an active selection. If you want to continue drawing with the regular Lasso tool without closing the selection, click-and-hold before releasing the Option/Alt key.

Putting selections on their own layers

In this example, we make a selection and put the selected area on its own layer by pressing Shift-Command-J (PC: Shift-Control-J). This performs the same function as going under the Layer menu, under New, and choosing Layer via Cut.

Layer via Cut cuts out your selection from the background image and moves it to its own layer (leaving a big white space in the layer below). If you want to move your selection to its own layer WITHOUT cutting (and leaving a knockout where you cut), leave out the Shift key and instead just press Command-J (PC Control-J). This is the same as going under the Layer menu, under New, and choosing Layer via Copy (which leaves your original selected area intact on the layer below and places an exact duplicate of your selection on the layer above).

Shadows that Climb the Wall

Here's an effect where you cast a shadow for an object, and when the shadow meets a wall (or other object, such as the train in the image below), it climbs the wall like it might in real life under certain lighting conditions.

STEP ONE: Open the document that contains the image that you want to add a drop shadow to. Select the object (in this case, two people) and put the object on its own layer by pressing Shift-Command-J (PC: Shift-Control-J).

STEP TWO: Copy this layer by dragging it to the New Layer icon in the Layers palette. Press "d" to set your foreground to black. Press Shift-Option-Delete (PC: Shift-Alt-Backspace) to fill your copy with black. Press Command-J (PC: Control-J) to copy this filled layer.

STEP THREE: Press the letter "v" to choose the Move tool. Move the shadow image slightly down and towards the wall in the image. Use the Polygonal Lasso to draw a selection right along the edge where your shadow meets the wall, and continue your selection until you've selected the entire shadow from that point down on the ground (as shown above). Press Delete (PC: Backspace), then Command-D (PC: Control-D) to deselect.

STEP FOUR: Click on Layer 1 copy in the Layers palette and Press Command-T (PC: Control-T) to bring up Free Transform. Control-click (PC: Right-click) in the bounding box and choose Distort from the pop-up menu. Bring the top center adjustment point down towards the wall to align it to the bottom of the first shadow. Bring the bottom center point up to align the bottom of the shadow with the bottom of your object.

STEP FIVE: Once again, use the Polygonal Lasso to draw a selection along the edge of your shadow where the ground meets the wall, and continue your selection until you've selected the entire shadow from that point upward on the wall (as shown above).

STEP SIX: Press Delete (PC: Backspace), then Command-D (PC: Control-D) to deselect. Go under the Filter menu, under Blur, and choose Gaussian Blur. For Radius enter 3 or 4 and click OK. Lower the opacity of this layer to 50%.

STEP SEVEN: In the Layers palette, click on your original shadow layer. Apply the same Gaussian Blur as in the previous step by pressing Command-F (PC: Control-F), and lower the opacity of this layer to 50% as well.

STEP EIGHT: Lastly, in the Layers palette, drag both shadow layers below your object layer to complete the effect.

Making your Actions palette less cluttered

After you create a number of actions, your Actions palette can start to look a bit cluttered (and confusing). That's why Adobe created Button Mode, which hides all of the Actions' controls, nested folders, and annoying stuff like that and puts all your actions just one button-click away. You can access Button Mode in the Action palettes pop-down menu.

You can also visually organize your actions by color. Just double-click on any action, and you'll see a pop-up list of colors you can use to visually segment your actions. When you're in Button Mode, the button takes on that color. You could, for example, make all your prepress actions one color, drop shadow actions another, and so on to group your actions by color for easy access.

Ruler guide trick

Any time that you drag out a guide from your ruler, you can change its orientation as you drag it (just in case you meant to grab a horizontal guide and instead you accidentally grabbed a vertical guide. Hey, it could happen). To change the guide from vertical to horizontal (or vice versa), press the Option key (PC: Alt key) while you're dragging, and it'll switch to the other orientation. Release the key and it switches back. That way, you can position it exactly how you like it before releasing the mouse button.

Inner Shadow Depth Effect

I saw this effect in *ESPN Magazine*, and it's pretty darn slick. It's a creative use of Photoshop's Layer Effects and gradients, and the way the artist at ESPN put it together is very clever. After you learn the effect, you can apply the basic premise to a number of variations of your own.

STEP ONE: Open a new document in RGB mode and create a new layer. Press Command-R (PC: Control-R) to turn on the rulers. From the top ruler, pull a guide down about $1/2$" from the top, then drag down another guide about 1" past your first guide. Switch to the Elliptical (round) Marquee tool. Hold the Shift key and draw a circle on the left side, starting at the top guide and stopping at the bottom guide. Continue holding the Shift key, move to the far right, and draw another circle (as shown above).

STEP TWO: Press Shift-M to switch to the Rectangular Marquee tool. Hold the Shift key and draw a rectangle between the two circles, starting from the top center of the left one to the bottom center of the right. This creates the pill shape for the button. Remove the guides by pressing "v" and dragging them back to the top ruler. Choose a light blue (like Pantone 283) for your foreground color and press Option-Delete (PC: Alt-Backspace) to fill with this color.

STEP THREE: Press the letter "d" to set your foreground color to black, then press "t" to switch to the Type tool. Type the words "THE MAGAZINE" in a sans serif italic typeface. Set your type so that it's almost as large as your pill shape. Go under the Layer menu, under Rasterize, and choose Type to convert your Type layer into an image layer. Press Command-T (PC: Control-T) to bring up Free Transform. Drag the top and bottom anchors to stretch your type so that it touches the top and bottom of the pill shape (as shown above). Press Return (PC: Enter).

STEP FOUR: Hold the Command key (PC: Control key), and in the Layers palette click once on your pill layer (Layer 1) to select the pill shape (don't actually change layers, just Command-click on the pill layer to load it as a selection). Then go under the Edit menu and choose Stroke. For Width, choose 8 pixels, and for Location, choose Inside. Click OK to put a thick stroke around the pill, making the letters and the stroke appear as one unit. You might have to use a larger or smaller stroke than 8 pixels to make the stroke touch the type. Now deselect.

STEP FIVE: Click on the Gradient tool, and in the Options Bar up at the top, click once on the gradient sample. When the Gradient Editor appears, create a gradient that goes from teal (like Pantone 328) to light blue (like Pantone 283) back to teal again. In the Name field, name your gradient "Teal Gradient," then click New to add this gradient to your gradient presets. Click OK to close the Gradient Editor. In the Layers palette, turn Lock Transparent Pixels on, then drag your new Teal Gradient from the left side of the pill to the right side (the result is shown above).

STEP SIX: Go under the Layer menu, under Layer Style, and choose Outer Glow. Click on the color swatch and set your color to black. Change the blend mode to Normal, change the Technique to Precise, increase the Spread to 10, and increase the Size to 8 (higher for high-res images). Click OK. Hold the Command key (PC: Control key), and in the Layers palette, click once on your pill layer (Layer 1) to put a selection around it. Press Command-E (PC: Control-E) to merge your two layers together (your selection should still be visible). Go under the Select menu and choose Inverse. Hit Delete (PC: Backspace) to remove the bleed from over the outer glow, leaving the shadows showing only on the inside of the pill (as shown above). Deselect to complete the effect.

QUICK TIP
To remove a ruler guide, use the Move tool to drag it back to the ruler it came from.

Quick change for your ruler measurements

If you want to quickly change your ruler's unit of measurement, hold the Control key (PC: Right-click) and click directly on one of Photoshop's rulers. A pop-up menu will appear where you can choose your desired unit of measurement.

Another method (to use when you're charging by the hour) is to double-click directly on one of Photoshop's rulers. The Units & Rulers Preferences dialog box will appear, where you can choose your desired measure-ment unit from the Rulers pop-up menu.

Dragging layers between documents

In Step Two , we open a second image and drag-and-drop it on top of a background image in another document. By default when you do this, the image you're dropping lands wherever you release your mouse. So if you drag it over and let go of the mouse button right away, chances are your image will be off to the left or right a bit.

To get your image to be perfectly centered when you drag from one document to another, all you have to do is hold the Shift key as you drag. Your dragged layer will then appear centered within your target document.

Adding Depth with Shadows inside Selections

Sometimes there just isn't an object to add a shadow to (which is sad). So here's how to use a simple selection to enable you to add shadows to a background or multiple images by painting a soft brush stroke inside a selection. This keeps your shadow inside that selection. Try it—then it'll all make sense.

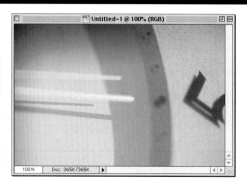

STEP ONE: Open your background image, and open an image that you want to add on top of the background image.

STEP TWO: Press Command-A (PC: Control-A) to Select All, and use the Move tool to drag-and-drop your second image onto your background image. (Note: You can do this same effect without adding another image; it works the same way. I'm just adding a second image for some visual contrast.)

STEP THREE: Press the letter "L" to switch to the Lasso tool. Press Shift-L until the Polygonal Lasso tool appears (used for drawing straight line selections). Draw a triangle selection (as shown above). This effect will work with other types of selections as well, so if you don't want to draw a triangle, you can use the Rectangular Marquee tool and draw a square, if you prefer.

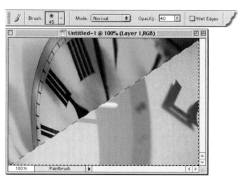

STEP FOUR: Press Delete (PC: Backspace) to remove the part of the top image that is inside your selected area. Press the letter "b" to switch to the Paintbrush tool. In the Options Bar, lower the Opacity to 40%, and choose a soft-edged brush from the brushes' flyout menu.

Drop shadow paint strokes

In this effect, we're using a soft-edged brush to create the impression of a drop shadow, and it works pretty well.

But there are other sets of brushes you can use, including one called "Drop Shadow Brushes" that you can load into Photoshop's flyout brushes menu with just one click. Here's how: In the Options Bar, click on the downward-facing triangle next to the currently selected brush and a flyout menu of brushes will appear. Click on the right-facing triangle in the brushes' flyout to reveal a pop-down menu of options. The bottom section of this menu lists sets of brushes you can load into your brushes menu by simply choosing them. Choose Drop Shadow Brushes and click OK, and these new brushes will be added to your brushes' flyout palette. Are these shadow brushes any good? I really don't want to say.

STEP FIVE: Click the Paintbrush once inside your selection where you want your shadow to begin. You'll want to put about 50% of the brush inside the selected area—the other 50% should extend beyond the selection into the other image. Hold the Shift key down, then move your cursor to where you want your shadow to end, and click again. When you do this, Photoshop will automatically draw a straight brush stroke (shadow) between the two points.

STEP SIX: That's the basic technique: By drawing a selection, you don't have to worry about accidentally painting your shadow on the other image (or other parts of the same image). Let's take this a step further to add more shadows. Use the Polygonal Lasso tool to draw another triangular selection (as shown above). After it's selected, press Command-I (PC: Control-I) to invert the selected area.

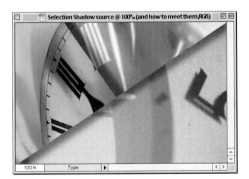

STEP SEVEN: Repeat Step Five to create a new shadow on the inside of your selected area (the completed shadow is shown above). Deselect by pressing Command-D (PC: Control-D). You can see that the image now has multiple levels of depth.

STEP EIGHT: You can enhance the feeling of depth by adding more elements (such as the type that we added here) below the layers with shadows.

Which tool are you using?

If you're new to Photoshop, here's a tip that might make learning Photoshop's tools easier: In the bottom left-hand corner of your document window, there's an Info bar that can display file size information, scratch disk space, or other details about your document. While you're still learning, you may find it helpful to change the readout in this Info bar to give you the name of the tool you're using. This is especially helpful when you're trying to locate specific tools to use for the projects in this book.

To change your Info bar readout, click-and-hold on the right-facing triangle to the right of the Info bar and a pop-up list will appear with your choices. Choose Current Tool from the list, and it will now display your currently chosen tool. As you click through the tools in the palette, each tool's name will appear in the Info bar.

Creating Custom Layer Effects Drop Shadows

Don't you wish there was a way to create your own default settings for the Layer Effects Drop Shadow? You know, one with enough blur and offset to look like a decent shadow? Well, here's a way to do that by creating your own custom Layer Style that you can access from the Styles palette with just one click.

STEP ONE: Open any document with an object on its own layer (it doesn't really matter what it looks like; we just need an object on a layer, so don't sweat it).

STEP TWO: Go under the Layer menu, under Layer Style, and choose Drop Shadow (or just click on the little *f* icon at the bottom of the Layers palette and choose Drop Shadow, as shown above).

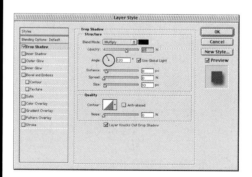

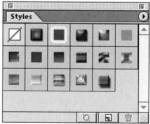

STEP THREE: In the Drop Shadow dialog box, I generally increase the Size (blur amount) to at least 10 and the Distance amount to around 8, and I lower the Opacity to 65%, but you can choose any settings you prefer to get just the drop shadow you want. When it looks good to you, click OK.

STEP FOUR: Go under the Window menu and choose Show Styles to make the Styles palette visible.

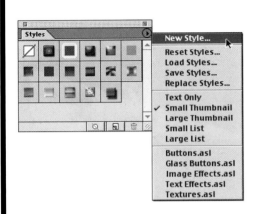

STEP FIVE: In the Styles palette's pop-down menu, choose New Style. This will bring up the New Style dialog box.

STEP SIX: In the New Style dialog box, give your style a name. Make sure the check box for Include Layer Effects is turned on and click OK. This adds your custom drop shadow to your Styles palette as the last swatch in the palette.

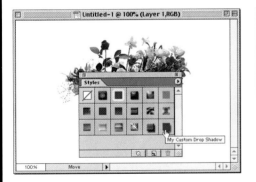

STEP SEVEN: Now open an image (on its own layer) that you want to apply your custom drop shadow to.

STEP EIGHT: All you have to do now is click on the thumbnail icon in the Styles palette that represents the custom drop shadow that you created (by default, when you create a Style, it appears as the last swatch in the palette). So click on it to apply your custom shadow and to complete the technique of creating your own style.

Other ways to create Styles

In the tutorial at the left, you're creating a Style by choosing New Style from the Styles palette pop-down menu. But you can also create Styles directly from the Layer Effects dialog box (it's actually called the Layer Style dialog box, but I didn't want you to confuse it with the Styles palette. Though, in re-reading my last sentence, I probably did just that—made it confusing. Sorry 'bout that). Anyway, as I said, you can create Styles from the Layer Style (Effects) dialog box. After you create your combination of effects (styles, what-ever), click on the New Style button in the upper right-hand corner (just below Cancel) and the New Style dialog box will appear where you can name your style. This new style will be added to the Styles palette just as if you created it from the Styles palette itself.

Easy-to-remember keyboard shortcuts

In the technique shown on this page, you wind up using Group with Previous to keep your shadows within the layer directly beneath them. The keyboard shortcut is easy to remember because it uses the same keyboard shortcut almost all other Adobe products use to "Group" objects together. It's Command-G (PC: Control-G). Adobe has gone to great lengths to keep you from having to learn a new set of keyboard shortcuts for each Adobe application, so once you learn one application's shortcuts, chances are you can apply them to other Adobe applications. Many of Photoshop's shortcuts are based on Adobe Illustrator shortcuts, so if you know those, you're well on your way. So keep that in mind when working in Photoshop. If you don't know the keyboard shortcut, ask yourself what that shortcut would be in Illustrator, and chances are you'll be right. However, if you're used to CorelDRAW … you're out of luck.

Grouping Shadows Effect

This trick enables you to take a drop shadow and mask it into an object on the layer directly beneath it. This is helpful if your shadow winds up casting on something it shouldn't (like the sky). The uncomfortably odd collage below attempts to show why you'd need this technique. Notice, I said that it "attempts."

STEP ONE: Open a background image as the base of your collage.

STEP TWO: Now open two other images that you want to add to the collage. Drag them onto your background image, giving you three layers: a background layer, an object just above it (in this case, a sign) and another object above that (in this case, a muscle guy).

STEP THREE: Choose the front-most image (muscle guy), and apply a drop shadow by choosing Drop Shadow from the *f* icon's pop-up menu at the bottom of the Layers palette. Position your shadow so it clearly casts onto the sign. The problem is that it also casts onto the sky and beach behind him, which ruins this borderline realistic, yet oddly curious collage. (OK, it isn't realistic at all. Work with me, will ya?)

STEP FOUR: The Layer Effects Drop Shadow is attached directly to the layer you applied it to, but you'll need to remove the shadow and put it onto its own separate layer. To do that, go under the Layer menu, under Layer Style, and choose Create Layer. This puts the drop shadow on its own layer. (Note: The shadow is still casting onto the sign and the sky behind him.)

STEP FIVE: To mask this shadow into the sign on the layer beneath it, go to the Layers palette, click on the shadow layer, and press Command-G (PC: Control-G), which is the shortcut for Group with Previous. This forces the shadow to appear just within the sign and keeps it from casting onto the background.

STEP SIX: Press the letter "v" to switch to the Move tool, and drag the sign around (here, I dragged it upward and to the left). Notice how the shadow stays within the sign, regardless of where it's moved. You can also adjust the shadow layer's position, too, by switching to the shadow layer and dragging it in your image. To undo this grouping effect, press Shift-Command-G (PC: Shift-Control-G).

QUICK TIP

There's a keyboard shortcut that you can use for Free Transform's Distort function instead of Control-clicking (PC: Right-clicking) inside the Free Transform bounding box. You just hold the Command key (PC: Control key), then grab either the top or bottom center handle and drag to the left or right (whew!) to distort your image.

Getting rid of white edge pixels in collaged images

In the technique shown on these pages, when I brought muscle guy into the image, he had a tiny white halo around his arms, hair, and neck. This leftover fringe came from the original image that I took him from, which had a white background. When I selected him, it brought some of the fringe along too.

I was able to quickly get rid of that white fringe around the edge by going under the Layer menu, under Matting, and choosing Defringe. I used the default 1-pixel setting, clicked OK, and it immediately removed the white edge fringe. It does this by creating a new edge pixel that is a combination of the background and the edge of your object. If you try a 1-pixel Defringe and it's not enough, undo it, and try a 2-pixel Defringe.

3

I'll never forget the night I fell in love with type effects. It was a dark and stormy night. The kind of night that makes you feel like if you went outside, it would be dark and stormy. It was before the proliferation of

ABC, Easy as 1-2-3
Cool Type Effects

desktop computers, and I was typing away on my IBM Selectric typewriter. Suddenly, a shot rang out (not really—it just seemed like that should be there).

I was writing a manuscript for a treatment of a play that would eventually become a novel that would never see the light of day. In other words, I was bored, so I was playing around with a typewriter. Then it hit me, "What this typewriter needs is a special key that would create a soft-edged shadow behind the type, then add a slight beveled effect, with some metallic-looking highlights. Yeah, and maybe some beams of light bursting through the tiny 12-point Pica type, with a zoom blur extending through the letters." Then I thought, "Nah," and I went downstairs and made myself a sandwich. I never really thought about it again until version 2.5 of Photoshop. By then, it was too late—my IBM Selectric went in the trash and the rest, my friends, is history. Did I tell you about the time I dreamed up the original idea for microwave ovens? Well, it was a dark stormy night...

To rasterize or not to rasterize?

In Step One, we have you rasterize your Type layer. This takes away the ability to go back into your type and change the spelling, leading, tracking, or spacing. So why would you do this? Well, if you're thinking of applying any sort of filter (from the Filter menu), you'll have to. That's because Type layers are different than Photoshop image layers. They're scalable vector-based layers (kind of Adobe Illustrator type), and they stay that way (totally editable, scalable, etc.) until you convert them from this vector Type format into a regular pixel-based layer. This is called rasterizing (in earlier versions of Photoshop, it was called "rendering"). In the example at right, we can't add perspective to our Type layer; it must be rasterized first (in fact, it was grayed out in the pop-up menu until we rasterized the layer). Basically, here's the rule: If you want to run a filter or do 'most anything funky to your type, you're going to have to rasterize it first.

Adding 3D Depth to Type

This is pretty nice technique for giving your type a 3D effect without having to rely on a separate 3D application. Basically, you're using Motion Blur and Threshold to create the "block" effect behind your type. When you combine the block and your type it creates the illusion of depth. It's just so…deep.

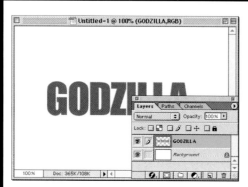

STEP ONE: Create a new 5" x 3" document in RGB mode at 72 ppi. Click on the Foreground color swatch and choose a bright foreground color. Switch to the Type tool, click once in your document, type some text, and click the check button in the Type Options Bar. Go under the Layer menu, under Rasterize, and choose Type to convert your Type layer into an image layer. Press the letter "v" to switch to the Move tool.

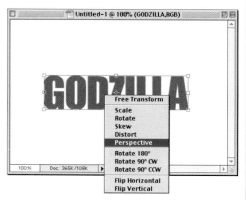

STEP TWO: Press Command-T (PC: Control-T) to bring up the Free Transform tool. Press the Control key (PC: Right-click) and click-and-hold inside your text. A contextual pop-up menu will appear. Choose Perspective from this menu and release the mouse button.

STEP THREE: Click-and-hold on the upper-right control point and drag straight up to create the wide part of the perspective effect. Next, click on the upper-left control point and drag straight down to add even more perspective effect. Press Return (or Enter) to complete your perspective transformation.

STEP FOUR: Make a copy of the layer with your text by dragging it to the New Layer icon at the bottom of the Layers palette. Press the letter "d" to set your foreground color to black, then fill with black by pressing Shift-Option-Delete (PC: Shift-Alt-Backspace).

STEP FIVE: Next, go under the Filter menu, under Blur, and choose Motion Blur. When the dialog box appears, change the Angle setting to 30° and the Distance to 35 (that's what we used in this example; you can change these numbers as you like). Then click OK.

STEP SIX: Press Command-Left Bracket ([) (PC: Control-Left Bracket) to move this blurred layer behind your text layer. Then press Command-E (PC: Control-E) to merge this layer with the Background layer (it must be merged with the background for this effect to work).

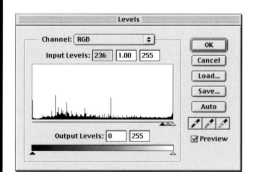

STEP SEVEN: Press Command-L (PC: Control-L) to bring up the Levels dialog box. Drag the shadow point (the black upward facing triangle on the far left, just under the graph) to the far right, almost to the very end (as shown above). This takes away the soft edges created by the Motion Blur and creates the blocky 3D shadow effect. Click OK.

STEP EIGHT: Click on your text layer and press the letter "v" to get the Move tool. Drag your text down and to the left until it aligns with the baseline of your 3D shadow (as shown above).

CONTINUED

How to move your layers without touching them

OK, the title up there is a little misleading: You can't move them without touching them, but you can move them around in the Layers palette without clicking on them by using the following keyboard shortcuts:

• To move your current layer down in the Layers palette, press Command-Left Bracket (PC: Control-Left Bracket).

• To move your current layer up in the Layers palette, press Command-Right Bracket (PC: Control-Right Bracket).

Now, if you really want to move a layer around within your image without using the mouse, just switch to the Move tool and use the arrow keys on your keyboard.

Controlling your tracking

Tracking is the space between a group of letters or words (kerning is the space between just two letters).

To visually (rather than numerically) set the tracking tighter (removing space between a group of letters), take the Type tool and highlight your text, then press Option-Left Arrow (PC: Alt-Left Arrow) to tighten. Press Option-Right Arrow (PC: Alt-Right Arrow) to add space between a selected group of letters or words.

QUICK TIP
To show/hide your Layers palette, press F7 on your keyboard.

STEP NINE: This is an optional step, but to add more realism you could colorize the 3D shadow. In the Layers palette, click on the Background layer. Switch to the Magic Wand tool by pressing the letter "w," and click once on your 3D shadow to select it.

STEP TEN: Choose a foreground color that is a much darker shade than your original text color (in this case, you'd choose a dark shade of green), and press Option-Delete (PC: Alt-Delete) to fill the 3D shadow with dark green. If you want to put your 3D shadow on its own layer (rather than remaining on the background layer), press Shift-Command-J (PC: Shift-Control-J). If not, then just deselect by pressing Command-D (PC: Control-D).

Quick Neon

This effect combines two Layer Effects to create an instant neon effect. I used this effect on text (as shown below), but it works equally as well on EPS line art that you place into Photoshop.

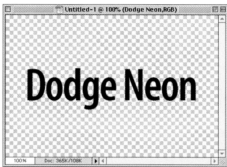

STEP ONE: Open a new document (RGB mode) and fill the background with black by first pressing the letter "d" then Option-Delete (PC: Alt-Backspace). Use the Type tool to create your text (use at least 60-point or larger type). This creates black text on a black background.

STEP TWO: To see your black type, you have to hide the black background layer by going to the Layers palette and clicking on the Eye icon in the first column beside the Background layer. After you position your text, click on the Background layer's Eye icon again to make the black background visible.

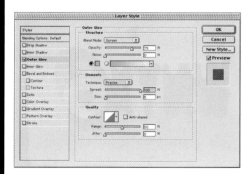

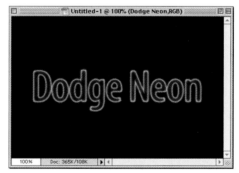

STEP THREE: Go under the Layer menu, under Layer Style, and choose Outer Glow. Click on the color swatch and choose a neon-like color (magenta, purple, yellow, etc.). In the dialog box, change the Technique to Precise. Don't click OK yet. In the Styles list on the left, click on the name Inner Glow and change the Technique to Precise. Don't click OK yet.

STEP FOUR: Now, click on the color swatch and change the color to match the neon-like color you chose earlier, then click OK to complete the effect. (Note: these settings work well on low-res, 72-ppi images. For high-res, 300-ppi or higher images, you need to increase the Size setting in both Layer Style dialog boxes to 20 to get the same effect).

Importing artwork from Adobe Illustrator

There are at least five different ways to import artwork created in Adobe Illustrator, but frankly, there's only one GOOD way to do it. In Adobe Illustrator, save the file as an EPS, switch to Photoshop, open the document you want to import your artwork into, and go under the File menu and choose Place. Choose your saved EPS Illustrator artwork and click OK. A bounding box will appear with a preview (if you saved it with a preview), and you can scale the image to any size you'd like (it's still EPS vector artwork at this point). When you get it to the exact size you like, press the Return or Enter key, and only then will it rasterize and become a pixel-based Photoshop image. When it rasterizes, it takes on the exact resolution and color mode of the document it was imported into. That's all there is to it.

Alternatives to the Type Mask tool

The Type Mask tool creates selections in the shape of type, rather than type itself (like the regular Type tool). If you prefer to use the regular Type tool to create a type-shaped selection, you can. In fact, I prefer it because you can really see what your type is going to look like.

Just create your type as usual, hold the Command key (PC: Control key), and click once on the Type layer's name in the Layers palette. This puts a selection around your type. Now you can drag your Type layer into the trash can at the bottom of the Layers palette. So what are you left with? That's right, a selection in the shape of your type—exactly like what the Type Mask tool would've done.

Combining Gradients, Strokes, and Shadows

This effect makes great use of Photoshop's Layer Effects, including one of my favorite features from the 6.0 upgrade—the ability to apply a gradient as a stroke. Of course, I couldn't just stop at that; I had to keep piling on the effects until I had enough Photoshop stuff on there to increase my client's invoice. Kidding. Kind of.

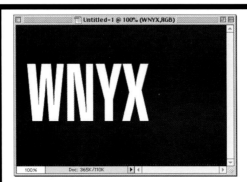

STEP ONE: Open a new document in RGB. Press the letter "d" to set your foreground color to black, and fill with black by pressing Option-Delete (PC: Alt-Backspace). Press the letter "x" to switch your foreground color to white, then use the Type tool to create your type (I used Helvetica Ultra Compressed). Choose Inner Shadow from the Layer Style pop-up menu at the bottom of the Layers palette (it's the little ƒ icon).

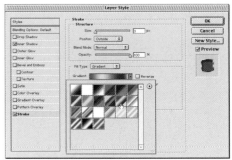

STEP TWO: The Inner Shadow default settings work fine, but don't click OK yet. While you're in the dialog, click on the word Stroke in the list of Styles on the left side to bring up its options (as shown above). For Position, choose Outside; for Fill Type, choose Gradient; for Style, choose Reflected; and for Angle, choose 107. Then choose the Copper gradient preset from the Gradient Picker (above), then click OK.

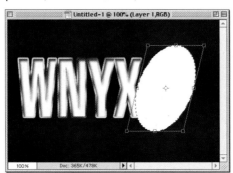

STEP THREE: Create a new layer by clicking on the New Layer icon in the Layers palette. Choose the Elliptical Marquee tool and draw a tall oval just to the right of your text. Fill your oval with white by pressing Option-Delete (PC: Alt-Backspace). Press Command-T (PC: Control-T) to bring up Free Transform. Hold the Command key (PC: Control key), grab the bottom center point, and drag to the left to skew your oval (as shown above).

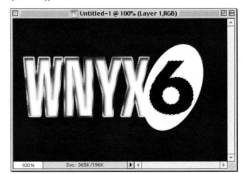

STEP FOUR: Click Return (PC: Enter) to lock in your transformation. Press the letter "d" to make black your foreground color. Get the Type tool and type in "6" (I used the font Futura Bold). Position your "6" within the oval. Hold the Command key (PC: Control key) and click on your "6" layer to put a selection around it. In the Layers palette, click on the oval layer beneath, and press Delete (PC: Backspace) to knock out the "6" from the oval.

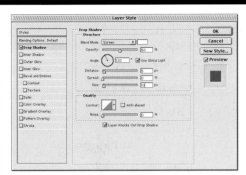

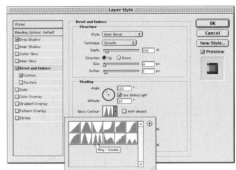

STEP FIVE: Press Command-D (PC: Control-D) to deselect, then drag your "6" layer into the trash can to delete it. On the oval Layer, choose Drop Shadow from the Layer Style pop-up menu at the bottom of the Layers palette (it's the little *f* icon). In the Drop Shadow dialog box, change the color of the shadow to white (by clicking on the color swatch). Change the Blend Mode to Screen, lower the Opacity to 50%, and increase the Size to 10. While you're in this dialog, click on Bevel and Emboss in the list of Styles on the left side to bring up its options.

STEP SIX: Click on the Contour check box just below the name Bevel and Emboss in the Styles list. Lower the Size to 4 and set Soften to 1. Under the Shading section of the dialog box, change the Altitude to 39 and set the Opacity of the Highlight Mode to 100%. Then click the down-facing triangle next to the Gloss Contour sample to reveal the flyout menu of contour presets. Choose the preset named "Ring – Double" (as shown above). While you're still in this dialog, click on the word Satin in the list of Styles to bring up its options.

A faster way to rasterize your Type layer

Tired of digging through the Layer menu to rasterize your type? Here's a shortcut: Go to the Layers palette, hold the Control key (PC: Right-click), and click-and-hold on your Type layer. A contextual pop-up menu will appear where you can choose Rasterize Layer. No more digging!

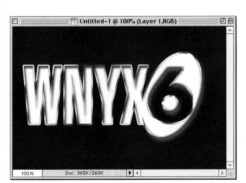

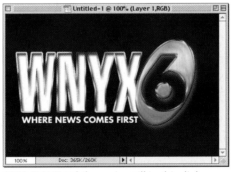

STEP SEVEN: Change the Blend Mode in the Satin dialog to Overlay, then click the down-facing triangle next to the Contour sample to reveal the flyout menu of contour presets. Choose the preset named "Ring." Next, click on Color Overlay in the Styles list on the left. Change the Color to Pantone 1375, change the Blend Mode to Overlay, and lower the Opacity to 90%.

STEP EIGHT: While you're still in this dialog, click on the Style Gradient Overlay. In the dialog, click on the down-facing triangle to bring up the Gradient Picker, and choose the default Copper gradient (as we did in Step Two). For Angle, choose -75; then click OK. Lastly, to complete the effect, I added the words "Where News Comes First" using the Type tool in the font Futura Bold.

Cool gradient trick

As you know, if you make a selection and drag the Gradient tool through it, it fills your selection with a gradient. But did you know that if you make multiple selections and drag the Gradient tool across all of them at once, it will treat them as one big selection? Try it—it's pretty slick.

Gradient Glow with Bevel

I saw this effect in a print ad for what (in my personal opinion) is probably the greatest live performance on the planet. It's called Mystère from Cirque du Soleil, and it's performed nightly at the Treasure Island Hotel and Casino in Las Vegas. My thanks to NAPP Senior Designer Felix Nelson who helped me figure this one out.

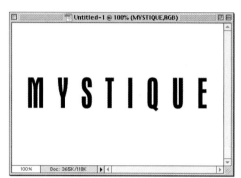
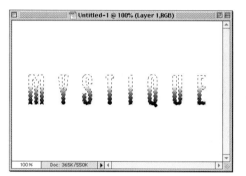

STEP ONE: Open a new document in RGB mode. Press the letter "t" to select the Type tool and then enter your text. This effect seems to work well with tall, thin typefaces. Go under the Layer menu, under Rasterize, and choose Type. Create a new layer by clicking on the New Layer icon at the bottom of the Layers palette.

STEP TWO: Hold down the Command key (PC: Control key) and click on the text layer to put a selection around your type. Click on the Eye icon in the Layers palette to the left of the text layer to make that layer invisible. Click on the Gradient tool, and in the Options Bar, choose Foreground to Background as the gradient. Press "d" to reset your foreground color to black, then drag the Gradient tool a short distance through the center of your selection from bottom to top (as shown above).

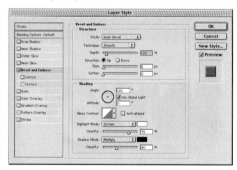

STEP THREE: Under the Select Menu, under Modify, choose Expand. Enter 1 pixel, then press OK. Create a new layer by clicking on the New Layer icon in the Layers palette. Create another gradient fill by dragging from the top to the bottom of the text (the opposite direction that you dragged on your original text layer). Drag this new layer behind Layer 1. Go to the Layer menu, under Layer Style, and choose Bevel and Emboss. Type in the settings shown above.

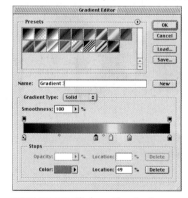

STEP FOUR: Click on the Background layer, then press Command-D (PC: Control-D) to deselect. Press Command-I (PC: Control-I) to invert this layer. Click in the gradient sample in the Gradient Options Bar to bring up the Gradient Editor. Create a gradient like the one above, type in a name, and then click New.

STEP FIVE: Create a new layer by clicking on the New Layer icon in the Layers palette. Hold down the Command key (PC: Control key), and click on the text layer to make it an active selection. Under the Select Menu, under Modify, choose Expand. Type in 7 pixels, then press OK. Drag the Gradient tool from the top to the bottom of the selection, then press Command-D (PC: Control-D) to deselect.

STEP SIX: Under the Filter menu, under Blur, choose Gaussian Blur. Type in 9 pixels, then press OK (use a higher number for high-res images). Duplicate Layer 3 by dragging it to the New Layer icon, then move this layer above Layer 1. Change the Layer blend mode to Overlay, and lower the Opacity to 30%. We used the Type tool to add the "Circus of the Sun" text below the type effect.

QUICK TIP
To visually increase the space between lines of text (called leading), highlight your type, then press Option-Down Arrow (PC: Alt-Down Arrow) to increase the space and Option-Up Arrow (PC: Alt-Up Arrow) to decrease the space.

Type sizing

Rather than typing in numbers to increase the size of your type, you might prefer to do it visually (rather than numerically). Here's how: After you create your type, highlight it with the Type tool, then press Command-T (PC: Control-T) to bring up the Character palette. Click once inside the font size field, then use the Up Arrow key to increase the text one point at a time. To visually increase the type size 10 points at a time, just add the Shift key with the Up Arrow. To decrease in 10-point increments, press Shift-Down Arrow. (Note: You don't have to highlight the size field in the Character palette, just click inside it once).

Is there a faster way than this?

Yes. Actually there are two ways (if not more), but only the second is faster. The first requires you to have Adobe Illustrator (or FreeHand, or CorelDRAW) so that you can put your type on a path in that application, save it as an EPS, and use Photoshop's Place command (under the File menu) to import the type on a path.

The other way is to buy the Photoshop plug-in Extensis PhotoGraphics, which lets you apply type to a circle or a path, plus a whole mess (bunch, batch?) of other features from right within Photoshop itself. You can download a fully working demo of PhotoGraphics from Extensis' Web site at www.extensis.com.

Putting Type on a Circle

I first saw this technique about a year ago in an online tutorial by Roxanne Etheridge at the PixArt Web site (www.ruku.com) and more recently at NAPP member Mark Monciardini's site (www.designsbymark.com). This really is an amazingly simple technique, but it does take a few minutes to complete.

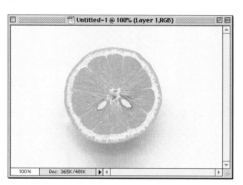

STEP ONE: Open the image you want to place circular type around. (Note: You can apply this technique to a blank document by drawing a circular selection and adding a 1-pixel black stroke to it as a guide for the rotation of your text.)

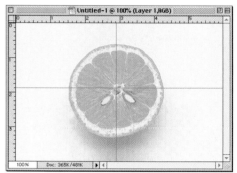

STEP TWO: Press Command-R (PC: Control-R) to make your rulers visible. Drag a guide down from the top ruler and place it in the center of your circular object, then drag another guide from the left side ruler and place it in the center also, giving you one horizontal and one vertical guide, both centered on your object.

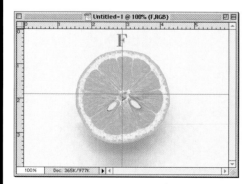

STEP THREE: Using the Type tool, create the first letter of the word that you want to wrap around the top of your circle. Click on the Move tool in the Toolbar to make it active, and move the letter to the very top center of your circle.

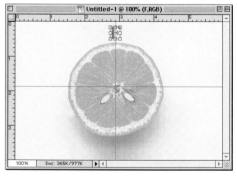

STEP FOUR: Press Command-T (PC: Control-T) to bring up the Free Transform function. When the Free Transform bounding box appears, you'll see square handles on each corner and on the sides and a target directly in the middle. Hold the Shift key, then click directly on this center target and drag it downward until it is in the center of your circle (at the point where the horizontal and vertical guides intersect).

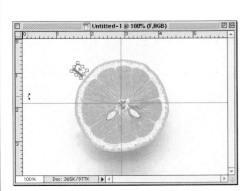

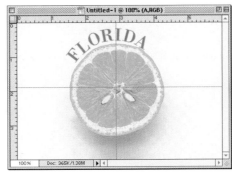

STEP FIVE: Now move your cursor back up, but keep it just outside the bounding box. You will see that your cursor changes into a two-headed arrow. This is the Rotate function. Now simply click-and-drag to the left, and you'll notice that as you rotate, your type follows the shape of your circle (that's because you placed the center point at the center of your circle; it's rotating around that center point).

STEP SIX: When you get the type where you like it, press Return (or Enter). If you hold the Shift key while rotating, it will snap to an invisible grid as you drag, which can help you with proper spacing, but you might find it adds too much space between the letters. It's your call. Keep repeating this process of creating a letter, clicking on the Move tool, placing the letter on top of the circle, bringing up Free Transform, dragging the center point down to the cross hairs, and rotating the letter into place until your top word is completed.

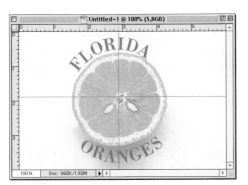

STEP SEVEN: To place a word at the bottom of the circle, follow the same exact steps, except start by centering the first letter of the word at the bottom of the circle.

STEP EIGHT: If, after you create your words, they aren't exactly centered (which is quite likely), go to the Layers palette and link the letters of a word together by clicking in the second column beside each layer. Once they're linked together (a Link icon will appear next to each letter), click on the Move tool, and press Command-T (PC: Control-T) to bring up Free Transform.

CONTINUED

Formatting ®, ™, and other symbols in Photoshop

To visually adjust the baseline shift (great for adjusting trademark and registration mark symbols) highlight the character you want to affect and press Shift-Option-Up Arrow (PC: Shift-Alt-Up Arrow) to move the character above the baseline, and of course, use the same shortcut with the Down Arrow to move text below the baseline (for things like H_2O).

Accessing Free Transform functions

Although we're constantly accessing Free Transform functions like Skew, Scale, Flip Horizontal, etc., from either the pop-up menu or by use of a keyboard shortcut, you can access these functions by going under the Edit menu, under Transform.

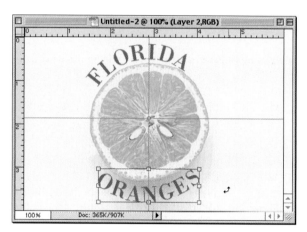

STEP NINE: Move the center point of the Free Transform bounding box back to the center where the guides intersect, then start rotating your letters around the circle. Press Return (or Enter) when it's lined up correctly.

STEP TEN: Once the type is aligned and you've checked for typos, you can rasterize each layer and then merge all the letters on the top of the circle together by making just those layers visible and choosing "Merge Visible" from the Layers palette's pop-down menu.

QUICK TIP
You can colorize your type from within either the Character palette or from the Options Bar (while the Type tool is selected) by clicking on the color swatch to bring up the Color Picker. Choose your new color and click OK. Your type will now appear in the color you've selected. You can also select individual letters and colorize them as well by highlighting them with the Type tool and choosing a color.

Beveled Outline Effect

Here's a quick type effect that you can create using Layer Effects. In this particular example, you're going to colorize your final effect using a multi-color gradient, but you can skip that part if you like and just start the effect with the foreground color of your choice for a solid color effect.

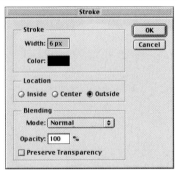

STEP ONE: Open a new document in RGB mode and create some type (thick bold typefaces work best for this effect). Hold the Command key (PC: Control key), then click once on the Type layer's name in the Layers palette to put a selection around the type. While it's selected, click the New Layer icon at the bottom of the Layers palette.

STEP TWO: Go under the Edit menu and choose Stroke. When the dialog box appears, enter 6 for your Width (choose a higher number for high-res images). Under Location, choose Outside and click OK to stroke your selection with your foreground color. Deselect by pressing Command-D (PC: Control-D), then drag your original Type layer into the trash can to delete it.

STEP THREE: Go under the Layer menu, under Layer Style, and choose Bevel and Emboss. Increase the Depth to 300%. Your image should look the capture above, but don't click OK yet. In the Bevel and Emboss dialog box, in the list of Layer Styles on the left side of the dialog, click directly on the name Gradient Overlay to bring up its options (don't click the check box, click on its name. Just clicking the check box will apply the effect, but it will not bring up the Gradient Overlay dialog).

STEP FOUR: Click on the downward-facing triangle next to the gradient sample and the Gradient Picker will appear. Choose a colorful gradient by clicking on it. Then, in the Layer Styles list on the left side, click on the check box for Drop Shadow to add a soft drop shadow to complete the effect.

Avoiding Type tool confusion

As you've learned by now, I like to switch tools by pressing their keyboard shortcut (rather than traveling all the way over to the Tool palette). It just saves so much time that it doesn't make sense to move your mouse all the way across the screen each time you need a different tool. However, when using Photoshop 6.0's Type tool, it can get confusing. That's because when you have the Type tool and you press a key on your keyboard, Photoshop thinks you want to type (not switch tools), which makes perfect sense. That's why, if you want to switch tools when you're using the Type tool, you need to click on the tool in the palette, rather than typing the keyboard shortcut. You'll notice that in some of these tutorials, after you create your type, I have you click on the Move tool (rather than pressing the letter "v") so that you can bring up commands like Free Transform. If I didn't and you had the Type tool chosen and pressed the letter "v," it would just type a letter "v." Makes sense now, eh? Eh? Oh come on, it makes sense.

Kerning shortcuts

Increasing or decreasing the space between two letters is called *kerning*, and Photoshop lets you kern your type either numerically or by using a keyboard shortcut (which is much better because kerning should be done by eye). To visually kern tighter (remove space between two letters) click your cursor between two letters that you want to kern (just click, don't highlight), then press Option-Left Arrow (PC: Alt-Left Arrow) to tighten. Press Option-Right Arrow (PC: Alt-Right Arrow) to add space between the two letters.

Backlit Beams of Light

This effect is very popular on TV and in digital video where there are a number of plug-ins that let you achieve similar effects. This one uses Photoshop's built-in filters. Special thanks to Felix Nelson for developing this technique and sharing it with me, so I could share it with you.

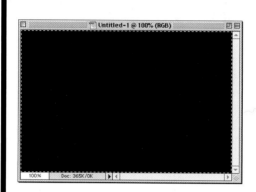

STEP ONE: Open a new document in RGB mode. Press the letter "d" to reset your foreground color to black, then fill your background layer with black by pressing Option-Delete (PC: Alt-Backspace).

STEP TWO: Use the Type tool to create your type. It will appear on its own layer, but it may not be visible because of the black background. To reveal your type, so you can position it where you want, hide the Background layer by going to the Layers palette and clicking on the Eye icon in the first column next to the Background layer.

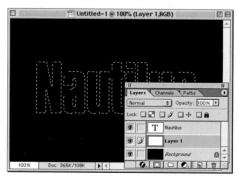

STEP THREE: Make the Background layer visible again by clicking in the first column. In the Layers palette, create a new blank layer by clicking on the New Layer icon at the bottom of the Layers palette. Drag this new layer just below your Type layer. Hold the Command key (PC: Control key), go to the Layers palette, and click once on your Type layer to make a selection around your type.

STEP FOUR: Go under the Select menu, under Modify, and choose Expand. Enter 5 pixels and click OK. Press the letter "d," then the letter "x" to make white your foreground color. Then press Option-Delete (PC: Alt-Backspace) to fill your expanded selection with white.

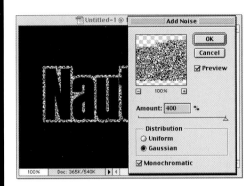

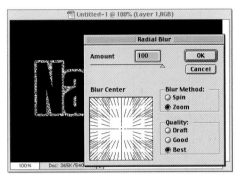

STEP FIVE: Go under the Filter menu, under Noise, and choose Add Noise. Enter an Amount of 400, turn on the Gaussian option and the Monochromatic option, and click OK.

STEP SIX: Press Command-D (PC: Control-D) to deselect. Go under the Filter menu, under Blur, and choose Radial Blur. In the Blur dialog box, choose 100 for Amount, Zoom for Blur Method, and Best for Quality. Click OK.

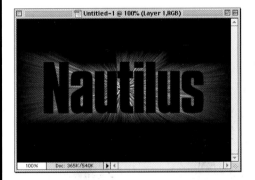

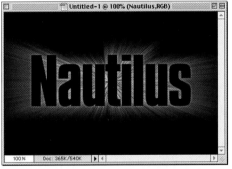

STEP SEVEN: At this stage, your image should look like the one above. Now, press Command-L (PC: Control-L) to bring up the Levels dialog box. Press the Tab key once and type in 0.64 in the middle Input Levels field. Press Tab again, type in 200, and click OK to intensify the effect.

STEP EIGHT: Press Command-F (PC: Control-F) to run the Radial Blur filter again. In the Layers palette, click on your Type layer, go under the Layers menu, under Layer Style, and choose Outer Glow. Click on the beige color swatch to bring up the Color Picker. Choose white as your glow color and click OK. Change the blend mode to Normal, then click OK in the Outer Glow dialog box.

CONTINUED

Using the Radial Blur in Best mode means "coffee break"

In this effect, we use Zoom as the Blur Method for our Radial Blur in Step Six. If you do this effect on a low-res image (like 72 ppi), it'll take a minute or two, maybe less. However, if you run a Radial Zoom Blur on a high-res, 300-ppi image, you have time to grab a cup of coffee. In fact, depending on your computer, you might have time to run out for lunch. This is one slooooooooow filter. It's doing a lot of that "Mr. Science"-type math, so it takes forever (in computer terms, forever is anything more than two minutes. A lifetime is 30 minutes). This filter sometimes takes a lifetime. Sorry 'bout that.

Precise placement of the Lens Flare center

You can precisely control the location of the Lens Flare center by going to the Info palette and clicking on the cross hair in the lower left-hand side of the palette. This brings up a pop-up menu of measurement values. Choose Pixels (for Web Design) or Inches (if you're lazy like me), then put your cursor over the exact spot where you want your Lens flare to appear in your image. If you look in the Info palette, you'll see the exact position in inches. Write it down (or remember it), then go to the Lens Flare dialog box and Option-click (PC: Alt-click) once in the Lens Flare preview window. A "Precise Flare Center" dialog will appear where you can input the X and Y coordinates you wrote down (remembered?) earlier. Click OK, and your Lens Flare will appear—right on the spot!

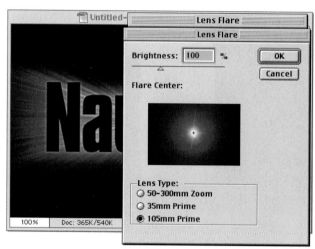

STEP NINE: In the Layers palette, click on the Background layer. Go under the Filter menu, under Render, and choose Lens Flare. For brightness, choose 100; for Lens Type, choose 105mm Prime. In the Flare Center preview window, drag the cross hair to the center, then click OK. In the Layers palette, click on Layer 1 (your beams of light layer), then press Command-F (PC: Control-F) to run the Lens Flare filter on this layer.

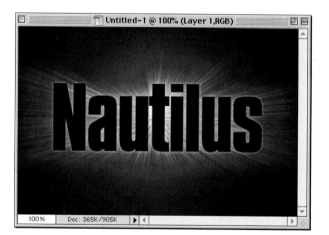

STEP TEN: Press Command-U (PC: Control-U) to bring up the Hue/Saturation dialog box and click on the Colorize check box. Slide the Hue slider to 214, Saturation to 41, and click OK to give your beams of light a blue tint to complete the effect. As an optional step, press Command-T (PC: Control-T) to bring up Free Transform. Hold the Command key (PC: Control key) and drag any handle to distort the beam for some really slick twists on this effect.

QUICK TIP
To zoom in on the preview image in a filter dialog box, hold the Command key (PC: Control key) and click within the preview window. To zoom out, Option-click (PC: Alt-click) in the preview window. (Note: This does not work in all of the filter dialog boxes, namely the Artistic, Brush Strokes, or the Sketch filters. These were once the Aldus Gallery effects that Adobe added to Photoshop).

Quick Grunge Type

What do you do when you're hired to do a logo for an inline skate company, a rock band from Seattle, or a CD jewel case cover? Use this. This technique takes beautifully crafted type, created by artisans with painstaking attention to detail, and turns it into something shattered and torn. You gotta love that.

STEP ONE: Open a new document (either in RGB or Grayscale mode), and use the Type tool to create some type.

STEP TWO: You're going to apply a filter to your type, so you'll have to convert this layer from an editable Type layer into a Photoshop image layer. Go under the Layer menu, under Rasterize, and choose Type to convert your Type layer into an image layer.

STEP THREE: In the Layers palette, turn Lock Transparent Pixels on by pressing the Forward Slash key (/).

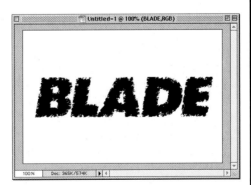

STEP FOUR: Go under the Filter menu, under Brush Strokes, and choose Sprayed Strokes. In the Sprayed Strokes dialog box, lower the Stroke Length, then click OK. For a more intense effect, repeat the filter by pressing Command-F (PC: Control-F). If you want jaggier type, turn off Lock Transparent Pixels and run the filter again.

Making the Glow Layer Effects work

Have you ever applied the Outer Glow or Inner Glow Layer Effects and didn't see the glow appear on screen—even after you increased the Size to 20 or 30 pixels? That's because, by default, the blend modes for the Glow Layer Effects are set to Screen. In many cases, depending on what you have on the layers beneath your Glow layer, you won't be able to see the glow at all. The way around it? Just change the Blend Mode (in the Glow Layer Effects dialog boxes) from Screen to Normal. Then increasing the Size and Spread amount will make a visible difference.

Don't confuse clipping groups with clipping paths

The layer's term "clipping group" is often confused with the well-known path's term "clipping path," but the two are entirely different. OK, they're not entirely different in what they do: a clipping group puts your image inside type (or anything black) on the layer beneath it, so you could say it clips off everything outside the type. A clipping path is created with the Pen tool, and you can choose to save this path with your document, so when you import your image into another application (like QuarkXPress, Adobe InDesign, Adobe Illustrator, etc.), everything outside the path is clipped off. This is most often used for clipping off the white backgrounds that appear behind objects.

In short, it'll help if you remember that a clipping group is a layer technique, while a clipping path is a path created with the Pen tool that is used mostly in print for silhouetting images from their backgrounds.

Putting an Image into Type (Clipping Group)

This technique lets you take any image and place it inside type that you've set on the layer directly beneath it. This is a pretty flexible effect because you can reposition your image inside the type after you create it, and if for some reason, you don't like the results, you can undo the effect.

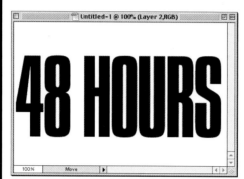

STEP ONE: Open a new document in RGB mode. Press the letter "d" to set your foreground color to black. Create some large display-sized type (tall thick typefaces work well for this effect).

STEP TWO: Open the image you want to put inside your type. Switch to the Move tool by pressing the letter "v," then click-and-hold on this image and drag-and-drop it into your original document. This should give you three layers: (1) your Background layer, (2) your Type layer, and (3) a layer with the image that you want clipped into your type.

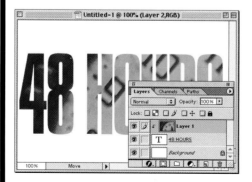

STEP THREE: Make sure your top layer (the image) is active (click on it in the Layers palette) then press Command-G (PC: Control-G) and your image will now appear inside your type.

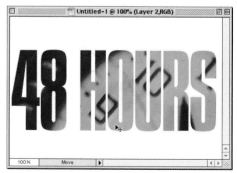

STEP FOUR: You can now reposition your image within your type by clicking-and-dragging with the Move tool. To undo this effect, press Shift-Command-G (PC: Shift-Control-G).

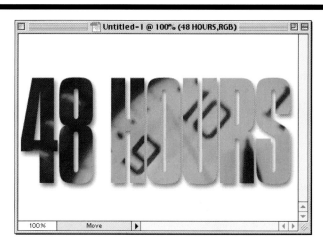

STEP FIVE: In most cases, it helps if you add a drop shadow to your Type layer to better define the edges of your letters (plus, it looks cool). Click on the Type layer (in the Layers palette), then add the drop shadow by choosing Drop Shadow from the Layer Style pop-up menu at the bottom of the Layers palette (it's the little *f* icon).

STEP SIX: This effect doesn't just work on type, it works on anything black that you put below your image. Try this: Undo your clipping group and delete your Type layer. Create a new layer, switch to a hard-edged brush, and use the Paintbrush tool to paint a black blob in the middle of your layer. Then drag this black blob layer below your image, click on your image layer, then press Command-G (PC: Control-G) to group them. Here's a neat trick: Switch to the blob layer, get a soft-edged brush, and start painting directly on the blob and watch how it affects your image. Pretty sweet!

QUICK TIP
You don't have to use type to create this effect—anything that's filled with black on the layer below your image will do the trick. I've seen people use a scan of a client's logo and clip an image into it. As long as it's black, it'll work, so don't be afraid to use paintbrush strokes, scans, etc. on the layer below your image.

The letter by letter version

A popular version of this effect is to put a different image into each letter of your type. I've seen a lot of companies do this—they take their name and put a different image that represents one of their products or a facet of their company in each letter.

This is very easy to do, but it's a little more time consuming (if you use a long word, it can be very time consuming). Here are a couple of tips if you decide to go this route:

(1) Use large thick typefaces. The thicker the better.

(2) Use tall rectangular images. I usually crop all of my images to be tall and rectangular before I begin adding them to my main document.

(3) When you're trying to position your image over a letter, lower the opacity of that layer so that you can see the letter's outline on the layer below it. This little tip will keep you from going postal.

(4) Then just press Command-G (PC: Control-G) to put your image within the letter. Then, on to the next letter.

The old "Bring up the last filter dialog box" trick

If you've applied a filter and you want to reapply the same filter with different settings, there's a keyboard shortcut for just that. You can bring up the dialog box for the last filter you ran, with the same settings you last used, by pressing Option-Command-F (PC: Alt-Control-F).

If you want to reapply the last filter using the exact same settings, just press Command-F (PC: Control-F).

Multiple Inlines/Outlines Type Effect

This is a popular technique in Adobe Illustrator, but Photoshop can pull off the same effect. We can even take it a step further (thanks to soft drop shadows) in Photoshop and make it an even cooler little effect.

STEP ONE: Open a new RGB document. Set your foreground color to the color you want your type (I used Pantone 116), then use the Type tool to create some large type (72 points or larger).

STEP TWO: At the bottom of the Layers palette, click-and-hold on the little *f* icon to bring up the Layer Style list. Choose Stroke from this list to bring up the Layer Style Stroke dialog box.

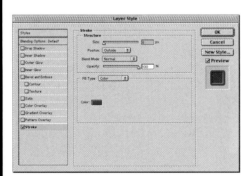

STEP THREE: Increase the Size to 8. Click on the color swatch, and when the Color Picker appears, click on the Custom button to bring up the Pantone Color Picker. Type in 2728 to choose Pantone 2728 and click OK to put a blue stroke around your Type layer.

STEP FOUR: Hold the Command key (PC: Control key) and in the Layers palette, click once on the Type layer to put a selection around your type. In the Layers palette, create a new layer by clicking on the New Layer icon at the bottom of the Layers palette.

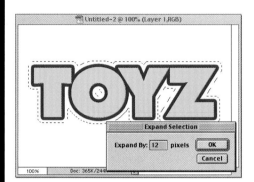

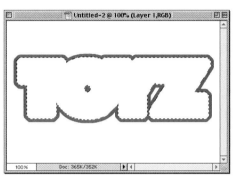

STEP FIVE: With your selection still in place, go under the Select menu, under Modify, and choose Expand. Enter 12 and click OK to expand your selection outward by 12 pixels, as shown above.

STEP SIX: Switch your foreground color to white by pressing the letter "d," then the letter "x." Press Option-Delete (PC: Alt-Backspace) to fill your selection with white. At the bottom of the Layers palette, click-and-hold on the little *f* icon to bring up the Layer Style list. Choose Stroke from this list to bring up the Layer Style Stroke dialog box.

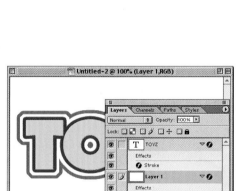

STEP SEVEN: From the Layer Style Stroke dialog box, choose 6 for Size. Click the color swatch and choose a red color for your stroke and click OK. Deselect by pressing Command-D (PC: Control-D). In the Layers palette, drag this red-stroked layer beneath your original Type layer (as shown above). Add a drop shadow to this layer by choosing Drop Shadow from the Layer Style pop-up menu at the bottom of the Layers palette (it's the little *f* icon). Increase the Distance to 15, Size to 10, and click OK.

STEP EIGHT: In the Layers palette, click on your original Type layer. Add an inner shadow to your type by choosing Inner Shadow from the Layer Style pop-up menu at the bottom of the Layers palette (it's the little *f* icon). Set the Distance to 6, the Choke to 15, and the Size to 10. Click OK to complete the effect.

Understanding Layer Effects (Styles)

Although most of the Layer Effects are often thought of as filter effects (such as glows, bevels, drop shadows, etc.), it's important to understand that you ARE NOT applying a filter. You are applying an effect to an entire layer. For example, let's say you have an image of a basketball on its own layer, and you apply the Drop Shadow Layer Effects to that layer. Once you've done that, anything else you do to that layer will also have the exact same drop shadow as the basketball. Paint a brush stroke? Boom, it has a drop shadow. Drag a square selection and fill it with a blur? Boom—another drop shadow. You have to remember they're called Layer Effects because they effect the entire layer.

Using Photoshop type for print work

At my live seminars, people often ask why I teach type effects when you can't really use type for print output. I always ask, "Who told you that?" and they usually say, "Somebody at my office." Rule # 1: Don't listen to anyone who says, "You can't." Rule # 2: Don't listen to anyone in your office. Rule #3: Don't listen to anyone in my office. Rule #4: (You get the idea).

Photoshop type can work great in print as long as you follow some simple rules:

(1) If you're going to rasterize your type, make sure you use a minimum resolution of 200 ppi for print work.

(2) Make sure that you don't use small rasterized type in Photoshop for print work. 12-point rasterized type is too small, and anything smaller is just about out of the question. 72-point, 100-point, 200-point—let 'er rip!

(3) If you're printing your image (with type) directly from Photoshop (or saving it as a PDF for print), you can use small sizes by leaving your type as vector. You do this by NOT rasterizing your type.

Mondo Cool Light Burst

A friend of mine showed me this effect a while back, and I was delighted—delighted because someone finally found a use for the Polar Coordinates filter. Besides that bonus, it's a pretty cool effect that simulates beams of light bursting, nah, exploding through your type.

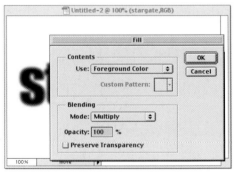

STEP ONE: Open a new RGB document. Set your foreground color to black by pressing the letter "d." Using the Type tool, set some very large type (72 points or higher). Rasterize your Type layer by going under the Layer menu, under Rasterize, and choosing Type. Hold the Command key (PC: Control key) and in the Layers palette click on your Type layer to put a selection around it. Go under the Select menu and choose Save Selection. Click OK in the dialog box.

STEP TWO: Deselect your type by pressing Command-D (PC: Control-D). Switch your foreground color to white by pressing the letter "x." Go under the Edit menu and choose Fill. In the Fill dialog box, change the mode to Multiply and click OK. Go under the Filter menu, under Blur, and choose Gaussian Blur. Enter 2.5 pixels and click OK.

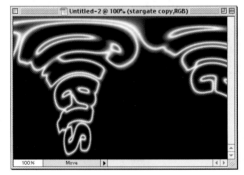

STEP THREE: Go under the Filter menu, under Stylize, and choose Solarize. Press Shift-Command-L (PC: Shift-Control-L) to run Auto Levels, brightening the image. Make a copy of your current layer by dragging it to the New Layer icon at the bottom of the Layers palette.

STEP FOUR: Next, go under the Filter menu, under Distort, and choose Polar Coordinates. In the Polar Coordinates dialog box, choose Polar to Rectangular and click OK. This makes your type look really, really bad, but don't let it dismay you—press on.

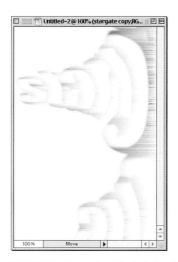

STEP FIVE: Go under the Image menu, under Rotate Canvas, and choose 90° CW. Invert your image by pressing Command-I (PC: Control-I). Go under the Filter menu, under Stylize, and choose Wind.

STEP SIX: When the Wind dialog box appears, choose Wind for Method and From the Right for Direction and click OK. Run this filter two more times by pressing Command-F (PC: Control-F) twice (for a total of three times).

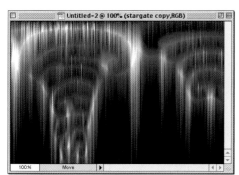

STEP SEVEN: Press Command-I (PC: Control-I) to Invert the image again. Press Shift-Command-L (PC: Shift-Control-L) to run Auto Levels again to brighten. Press Command-F (PC: Control-F) three times to run the Wind filter three more times. Go under the Image menu, under Rotate Canvas, and choose 90° CCW. Go under the Filter menu, under Distort, and choose Polar Coordinates.

STEP EIGHT: In the Polar Coordinates dialog box, choose Rectangular to Polar and click OK to create your light burst. Change the Layer blend mode from Normal to Screen to bring in your original type (it will still look a bit blurry at this stage).

CONTINUED

Quick filter tips:

• To change values in certain filter dialog boxes, use the Up/Down Arrow keys on your keyboard.

• To change the values in whole numbers or in increments of ten units at a time, hold the Shift key along with the Up/Down Arrow keys.

• If you want to reset the changes you made in the filter dialog, hold the Option key (PC: Alt key), and the Cancel button changes to a Reset button. Press it and you're back where you started.

• To return to a 100% preview, click on the zoom percentage in the filter dialog box (this works in most filter dialogs, but not all of them. Go figure).

Getting your last settings back

If you're working on a project in Photoshop, and you apply something like Levels or Curves and click OK, when you open the dialog box again, you start back at square one. For example, if you apply a custom curve, click OK, and go back to the Curves dialog box, all you'll find is the default straight curve. However, there is a trick for bringing back the last settings you used in a dialog—just add the Option key (PC: Alt key) when you press the keyboard shortcut. For example, to bring up Curves with the last curve setting you applied, press Option-Command-M (PC: Alt-Control-M) instead of just pressing Command-M (PC: Control-M), the regular keyboard shortcut.

STEP NINE: To add color, create a new blank layer, click on the Gradient tool, expand the Gradient Picker, choose the Violet, Orange gradient, and drag the Gradient tool through this layer. Change the blend mode to Color, and press Command-I (PC: Control-I) to invert the colors to green and blue.

STEP TEN: In the Layers palette, click on your Type layer copy (should be the layer below the one you're currently on). Go under the Filter menu, under Blur, and choose Radial Blur. In the dialog box, choose Zoom for Blur Method. Increase the Amount to 66 and click OK. Click on your original Type layer, go under the Select menu, and choose Load Selection. In the dialog box, choose Alpha 1 from the Channel pop-up and click OK. Press the letter "d" to set your foreground color to black, then press Option-Delete (PC: Alt-Backspace). Deselect by pressing Command-D (PC: Control-D) to complete the effect.

QUICK TIP
To jump instantly to a 100% view of your image, double-click on the Zoom tool. To have your image instantly "Fit on Screen," double-click on the Hand tool.

Carved in Stone

This is a classic Photoshop effect that gives the appearance that your text (or EPS artwork) has been chiseled into stone. This effect was always accomplished using a series of channel operations that made it a bit tedious. Here's how to use Photoshop's Layer Effects to cut it down to about 30 seconds.

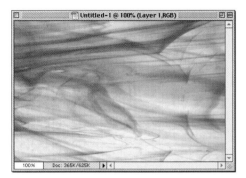

STEP ONE: Open a background image that would be suitable for a carved stone effect. Press the letter "t" to switch to the Type tool. Up in the Options Bar, click on the second button from the left (the Type Mask tool). Rather than creating type on a layer filled with your foreground color, this tool creates a selection in the shape of type.

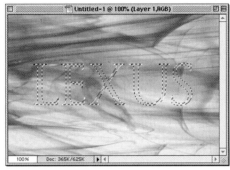

STEP TWO: With the Type Mask tool as your current tool, click and enter your type. Click on the check button in the Type Options Bar to accept your text edits. Your type will appear as a type selection (as shown above).

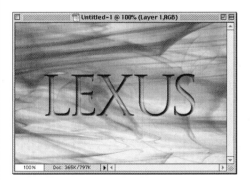

STEP THREE: Press Command-J (PC: Control-J) to put the image within your type selection onto its own layer. Then go under the Layer menu, under Layer Style, and choose Inner Shadow. When the Inner Shadow dialog box appears, increase the Opacity setting to 90% and click OK.

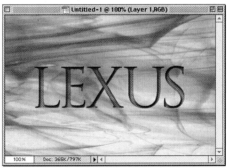

STEP FOUR: The final step is to darken the inside of the letters to help sell the effect that the type is carved into the background. To do this, press Command-L (PC: Control-L) to bring up the Levels dialog. Move the bottom right Output Levels slider to the left until you reach approximately 210, then click OK to complete the effect.

Removing Layer Effects in 6.0

If you've applied a Layer Effects to a layer and later decide you want to delete that effect, you can do it directly from the Layers palette. Just click on the named effect in the palette and drag it to the trash can icon at the bottom of the Layers palette.

If you just want to hide the effect from view (and not delete it entirely), click on the Eye icon next to the effect you want to hide. To reveal the effect again, click where the Eye icon used to be.

There's something about taking a dull, flat image and making it shiny and rounded that really appeals to

Heavy Metal
Metal and Chrome Effects

me. I think it's the "Inner Emboss" that lives deep inside us all (this is what happens when they make me write chapter intro's after 2:00 a.m.).

I really hadn't intended to write a chapter about chrome and metal effects, until someone looked at some early proofs of the book and said "Hey, you're really into this metal stuff aren't you?" It was at that moment that I realized "Hey, I'm really into this metal stuff." When I really took a good look at it, I saw that I had at least a chapter's worth of chrome and metal effects interspersed throughout the book. I thought to myself, "Hey, I could gather it together, creating what could possibly be the world's first all chrome and metal chapter. Hey, that would make this really special and unique. Then I could start to focus on why I keep injecting the word 'Hey' into all my inner thoughts." I'm not saying this stuff out loud, am I?

Try different curve settings for different metallic effects

The curve setting shown in Step Five will do a good job of producing metal, but this is one area where you can really experiment and have some fun. The curve shown in this example has just one hill, then it heads back up. For a more dynamic effect, try a curve with two or three hills. The more hills, the wilder it gets. If your curve starts introducing all sorts of weird colors, don't sweat it. When you're done with your curve, press Shift-Command-U (PC: Shift-Control-U) to take all the color out of your image, leaving just the shiny metal. The point is: There are no "right" curves; just move the points until something looks good to you.

Instant Chrome Effect

Here's one of the easiest and quickest ways to create a metallic chrome effect. Don't worry if you've never used curves before. Although they play a major role in this effect, you're only in curves for a few seconds and the step is simple.

STEP ONE: Open a new document, any size, in RGB mode. Click on the Type tool and create some text. Hold the Command key (PC: Control key) and click once on your Type layer in the Layers palette to put a selection around your text. Go under the Select menu and choose Save Selection. When the dialog appears, click OK. Press Command-D (PC: Control-D) to deselect. Now, delete your Type layer by dragging it into the trash can at the bottom of the Layers palette.

STEP TWO: Go to the Channels palette (under the Window menu, choose Show Channels) and click on Alpha 1. (If your channel looks different than the one above [it has black text on a white background] press Command-I (PC: Control-I) to invert it.) Next, go under the Filter menu, under Blur, and choose Gaussian Blur. Enter 1 pixel and click OK. (Note: The 1-pixel setting is for 72-ppi images. High-res images will require a 2- or 3-pixel blur. The more blur, the wider the bevel.)

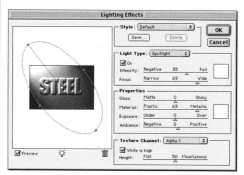

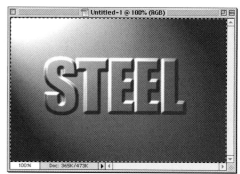

STEP THREE: Return to the Layers palette and click on the Background layer. Then go under the Filter menu, under Render, and choose Lighting Effects. When this dialog box appears, you only have to make one small change. At the bottom of the palette, where you choose the Texture Channel, choose Alpha 1 from the pop-up menu, then click OK.

STEP FOUR: Your background layer should now look like the image above. Press Command-A (PC: Control-A) to select the entire background layer.

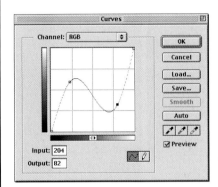

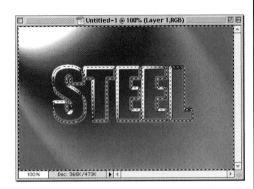

STEP FIVE: Press Shift-Command-J (PC: Shift-Control-J) to put this entire image on its own layer. Go under the Image menu, under Adjust, and choose Curves. Create a curve that looks like the one above by clicking on the lower left-hand side of the curve and dragging upward. Release the mouse button, then click on the right-hand side and drag downward. As you drag the second point downward, you'll see the chrome effect start to appear. When your curves look somewhat similar to the one shown above, click OK.

STEP SIX: Go under the Select menu and choose Load Selection. When the dialog box appears, make sure Alpha 1 is chosen under the Channel pop-up menu, then click OK. This reloads a selection around your type, but you'll notice it's too small to encompass the entire beveled type.

STEP SEVEN: Go under the Select menu, under Modify, and choose Expand. This is the only slightly tricky part: you've got to guess how many pixels we need to expand so that it selects all of the text. In this case we chose 3 pixels (if 3 isn't correct, choose Undo and try a higher or lower number). When the text is selected, press Shift-Command-I (PC: Shift-Control-I) to inverse and press Delete (PC: Backspace) to remove the background.

STEP EIGHT: Press Command-D (PC: Control-D) to deselect. Add a soft drop shadow by choosing Drop Shadow from the Layer Style pop-up menu at the bottom of the Layers palette (it's the one with the little *f* icon). That completes the metallic effect, but you can continue on to Steps Nine and Ten on the next page if you want to add a brushed metal background behind your type.

CONTINUED

The "make anything chrome" trick

If there is anything that you want to turn into chrome, there's just one trick you have to know (besides the curve shown at the left): You've got to bevel the object first. The chrome won't work on a non-beveled object. That's why we use the Lighting Effects filter on a blurred channel—it creates a beveled effect. The rest is simple enough—just draw a hill in the curves window.

So the next time you want to turn something into chrome, think first about how to bevel or emboss it, then think chrome. Tip: The Bevel and Emboss Inner Bevel Layer Effects will usually do the trick, but right after you apply it, you have to create a new blank layer, drag it below your beveled and embossed layer, click on your beveled layer, and choose Merge Down from the Layers palette's pop-down menu. If not, the chrome curve interacts with the live bevel effect and it looks … well, bad.

Tip #2: Alien Skin's Inner Bevel plug-in from their EyeCandy collection also works like a charm.

Fixing the edges of a Motion Blur background

In the last step of the effect at the right, I have you quickly create a brushed metal background using Noise and Motion Blur. The only drawback is the left and right edges of the background: you can see the Motion Blur streaks start to fall apart at the edges, and they look a bit cheesy and artificial. Here's a quick fix: Make a rectangular selection all the way around your image about 1/2" from the outer edge of your document (so you have a big rectangular selection taking up most of your image). Press Command-T (PC: Control-T) to bring up Free Transform. Grab the right center point and drag past the right edge of your document to stretch the good part of your blur to the right edge. Then grab the left center point and drag left past the left edge of the document to do the same. When your edges look good, press Return (PC: Enter).

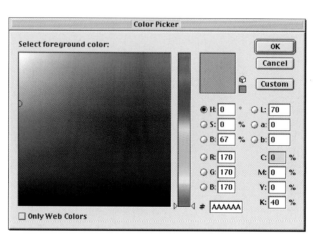

STEP NINE: Click on the Background layer, then click on the Foreground color swatch (at the bottom of the Toolbox) to bring up the Color Picker. In the CMYK portion of the box, change the C, M, and Y values to zero, and enter 40 for K. Click OK to change your foreground color to 40% gray.

STEP TEN: Press Option-Delete (PC: Alt-Backspace) to fill with 40% gray. Go to the Filter menu, under Noise, and choose Add Noise. Choose between 20 and 30 pixels of Gaussian, Monochromatic noise and click OK. Go under the Filter menu again, under Blur, and choose Motion Blur. Choose a distance between 20 and 30 pixels and set your angle to 30°. Click OK to complete the brushed metal-looking background.

QUICK TIP
If you click on the Foreground color swatch and your Color Picker doesn't look like the one shown here, you might have inadvertently switched your Color Picker. Press Command-K (PC: Control-K) to bring up Photoshop's General Preferences dialog. Under the Color Picker pop-up menu, make sure the chosen picker is "Adobe." (Note: in previous versions of Photoshop, the chosen picker was called "Photoshop.")

Arched Cutout Type

This effect combines gradients and Photoshop 6.0's Warp Text feature to create an effect that is very popular in athletic logos. We also used a combination of Layer Effects and, in particular, Photoshop 6.0's ability to apply a gradient as a stroke.

STEP ONE: Open an RGB document and create some type. Go under the Layer menu, under Layer Style, and choose Inner Shadow (or choose Inner Shadow from the Layer Style pop-up menu at the bottom of the Layers palette—it's the little *f* icon). We'll use the default settings, but don't click OK yet. Instead, in the list of Styles on the left side of the dialog, choose Stroke.

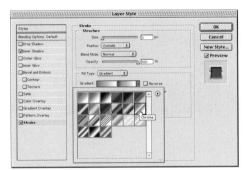

STEP TWO: When the Stroke dialog box appears, change the Fill Type to Gradient, then click the down-facing triangle next to the gradient sample to reveal the Gradient Picker. Choose the Chrome gradient. Don't click OK yet. Instead, in the list of Styles on the left side of the dialog, choose Drop Shadow. Increase the Opacity to 100% and click OK.

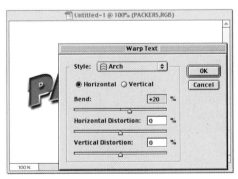

STEP THREE: Go under the Layer menu, under Type and choose Warp Text (shortcut: You can also click the Warp Text icon up in the Options Bar. It's on the right side of the bar; its icon has a letter T followed by three dots [T...] with an arched line below it). When the dialog box appears, choose Arch from the Style pop-up menu. Decrease the Bend amount to +20 and click OK.

STEP FOUR: After you click OK in the Warp Text dialog box, the effect is essentially complete. In the example above, I filled the background with 70% black just to enhance the effect. TIP: Another nice thing about this effect is that we never had to rasterize the type during this technique, which means the type is still totally editable. To edit it, just use the Type tool to highlight the text and then type in a new word.

How to find the Chrome gradient

When you have the Gradient tool, the Options Bar immediately displays the Gradient tool options. If you click on the down-facing triangle immediately to the right of the gradient sample of your currently selected gradient, a flyout Gradient Picker will appear with all the gradient presets you have loaded. Now, how do you know which one is the Chrome gradient? Well, if you have the Tool Tips preference turned on (it's on by default), just hold your cursor over any gradient swatch and it's name will appear. If you've turned off Tool Tips (frankly, they drive me crazy, except for finding gradients), then you can choose to view your gradients by name rather than by thumbnails. You do that by clicking on the right-facing triangle in the Gradient Picker to display a pop-up menu where you can choose Text Only to display the gradients by name. This makes finding the Chrome gradient a snap.

Gradient tips

• To switch to Photoshop's Gradient tools, press the letter "g."

• To bring up the Gradient Editor, switch to the Gradient tool, and in the Options Bar up top, click once on the gradient sample.

• To add a new Color Stop to your gradient, click anywhere below the Gradient Editor bar.

• To remove a Color Stop, click-and-drag downward.

• To edit the color of any Color Stop, double-click directly on the Color Stop itself.

• To change the opacity setting for the Gradient tool, press the 1–9 number keys on your keyboard (2=20%, 3=30%, etc.) while the Gradient tool is selected.

• To step through the blend modes in the Gradient's palette, press Shift-+.

• To delete a gradient, hold the Control key (PC: Right-click) and click-and-hold on the gradient you want to delete, then choose Delete Gradient from the pop-up list.

Star Wars Bevel

I've had a number of requests to show how the *Star Wars* logo was created. Don't feel bad if you don't happen to work for LucasArts—you can use this same technique for just about any large-sized text, not just the *Star Wars* logo.

STEP ONE: Create a new blank document in RGB mode. Create your type. In this case, I used the typeface Futura Extra Bold and drew some extra black squares where the letters bleed together. It's pretty crude, but you get the idea. (The official *Star Wars* typeface is available on the Web. Search for "Star Wars Font" and you'll find dozens of sites that have it available for free download). Rasterize your type by going under the Layer menu, under Rasterize, and choosing Type.

STEP TWO: Hold the Command key (PC: Control key), and in the Layers palette, click once on the Star Wars layer to put a selection around the type. Go under the Select menu, under Modify, and choose Expand. Enter 4 for the value and click OK. Next, create a new layer by clicking on the New Layer icon at the bottom of the Layers palette. Then press Option-Delete (PC: Alt-Backspace) to fill this selection with black. Press Command-D (PC: Control-D) to deselect.

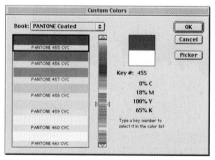

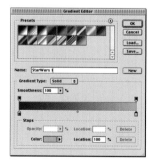

STEP THREE: We need to create two custom gradients for this effect. Click on the Gradient tool, and in the Options Bar up top, click once on the gradient sample to bring up the Gradient Editor. Double-click on the far left Color Stop (under the gradient bar), to bring up the Color Picker. Click the Custom button at the top right of the box to bring up the Pantone Color Picker. Type the number 455 and click OK to assign Pantone 455 (a dark brown color) to the left side of your gradient.

STEP FOUR: Now, double-click once on the right gradient Color Stop and click the Custom button again when the Color Picker appears. Type in 4525 to assign Pantone 4525 (a lighter brown) to the Color Stop on the right side of the gradient. In the Name field, name this gradient StarWars 1, then click the New button. This completes your first gradient, but don't click OK yet, because we have to build another gradient.

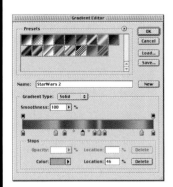

STEP FIVE: While still in the Gradient Editor, drag the right Color Stop (light brown) to the left until it's about ¼" from the left stop. You'll notice that the name of the gradient changes to Custom. Next, hold the Option key (PC: Alt key), click on the left stop (dark brown), and drag it to the right, passing over the light brown stop by about ⅛" (this creates a copy of the stop). Keep holding the Option key (PC: Alt key) and drag out light brown and dark brown Color Stops until your gradient looks approximately like the one shown above. Name this gradient StarWars 2 and click New. Click OK to exit the Gradient Editor.

STEP SIX: Hold the Command key (PC: Control key) and click once on Layer 1 in the Layers palette to put a selection around it. Press the letter "m" to switch to the Marquee tool. Hold the Option key (PC: Alt key) and draw a rectangular selection around the word "WARS" (this deselects the word, leaving "STAR" still selected). Press the letter "g" to switch back to the Gradient tool and draw a gradient from the top of the word "STAR" to the bottom. Instead of drawing perfectly straight, drag it at a slight angle. This creates the background bevel.

STEP SEVEN: Deselect by pressing Command-D (PC: Control-D). Next, we'll create the opposite selection of what we did earlier. Hold the Command key (PC: Control key) and in the Layers palette click once on Layer 1 to select its contents again. Press the letter "m" to switch to the Marquee tool. Hold the Option key (PC: Alt key) and draw a rectangular selection around the word "STAR" to deselect it.

STEP EIGHT: Switch back to the Gradient tool and drag (from top to bottom) through the word "WARS" at a slight angle. Deselect by pressing Command-D (PC: Control-D). Then go to the Layers palette and drag Layer 1 (the one with the gradients) down below your black Star Wars text to create what you see above. Click on Layer 1 and switch to the Gradient tool. In the Options Bar, choose the StarWars 1 gradient you created earlier.

CONTINUED

Want some cool metal gradients? You've already got 'em!

In the tutorial at the left, we're creating our own custom metallic gradients, but there are already a collection of cool preset metallic gradients just waiting for you to load. Luckily, loading them into your flyout Gradient Picker is a breeze. Here's how: First, switch to the Gradient tool. Then, in the Gradient tool Options Bar (up top), click on the downward-facing triangle right next to the gradient sample. This brings up the Gradient Picker. In the upper right side of this menu is a right-facing triangle, which is a pop-up menu. Click on it, and at the bottom of the menu, you'll see a list of gradient presets you can load just by choosing them from the menu.

To load the metallic gradients, choose the ones named "Metals" from the pop-up list, and Photoshop will ask you if you want to replace your current gradients with this set or append (add) them to your current set. It's that easy.

Changing your units of measurement

Another trick for quickly changing your unit of measure (say, from inches to pixels) is to open the Info palette and click on the little cross hairs in the lower left-hand corner of the palette. A pop-up list of measurement units will appear, and you can choose the one you want directly from there.

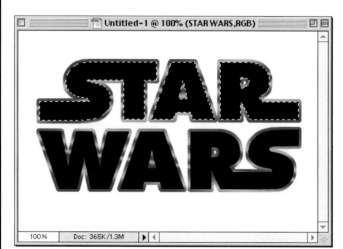

STEP NINE: You'll need to apply the StarWars 1 gradient to the word "STAR" and the word "WARS" separately (as we did in Steps Six and Seven). In the Layers palette, Command-click (PC: Control-click) on the Star Wars layer to select the letters. Hold the Option key (PC: Alt key) and use the Marquee tool to deselect the word "WARS." Choose your Star Wars layer and drag your gradient straight down (from top to bottom) just through the word "STAR." Deselect by pressing Command-D (PC: Control-D).

STEP TEN: Command-click (PC: Control-click) on the Star Wars layer (in the Layers palette) to select the letters. Hold the Option key (PC: Alt key) and use the Marquee tool to deselect the word "STAR." Press the letter "g" to switch to the Gradient tool and draw a gradient from the top of the word "WARS" to the bottom of the letters to complete the effect.

QUICK TIP

If you see banding when you print your gradient, go under the Filter menu, under Noise, and add 4 pixels of Monochromatic, Gaussian Noise. In most cases, when output at high resolution, the noise disappears and it hides the banding.

Chiseled Inner Bevel Type

Here's a type effect using just Photoshop's built-in filters to create an inner beveled chiseled look to your type. Effects like these were traditionally created using a complex series of channels, but this simple technique uses no channels at all. Note: Increase the values shown here for high-res, 300-ppi images.

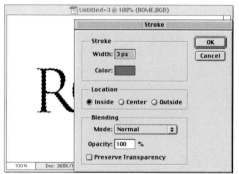

STEP ONE: Open a new 72-ppi document in RGB mode. Create your text in black (serif fonts, such as Goudy, Trajan, etc., set at large type sizes look best). Rasterize your type by going under the Layer menu, under Rasterize, and choosing Type. Click on the Foreground color to bring up the Color Picker and choose 50% gray as your foreground color (50% K).

STEP TWO: Hold the Command key (PC: Control key) and click once on your text layer's name in the Layers palette to put a selection around your text. Go under the Edit menu and choose Stroke. When the Stroke dialog box appears, use 3 pixels for the Width, choose Inside for Location, and click OK (don't deselect quite yet).

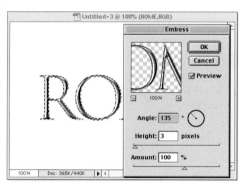

STEP THREE: Go under the Filter menu, under Stylize, and choose Emboss. For your Emboss settings, enter 135° for the Angle , 3 pixels for the Height , and 100 for Amount, then click OK. Press Command-D (PC: Control-D) to deselect. Press Command-U (PC: Control-U) to bring up the Hue/Saturation dialog box. Check the Colorize box in the bottom right-hand corner of the dialog box.

STEP FOUR: In the Hue/Saturation dialog box, slide the Hue slider to 38, Saturation to 70, and Lightness to -13, and click OK to give your text a gold hue. Go under the Filter menu, under Sharpen, and choose Unsharp Mask. When the dialog box appears, choose 125 for Amount, 1 for Radius, 10 for Threshold, and click OK to complete the effect. Of course, I'd probably add a drop shadow, but hey, that's just me. ;-)

High-powered chiseling

Photoshop 6.0 allows you to create a hard-edged chisel effect via the Bevel and Emboss Layer Effects by changing the Technique to Chisel Hard.

Another way to create a hard-edged chisel effect is to use Alien Skin's Inner Bevel plug-in from their EyeCandy 3.0 collection of Photoshop plug-in filters. For more information on their way-crazy cool plug-ins, visit them at www.alienskin.com.

Yeah, but how did he create the background?

After Doug created this cover effect, we showed how he created it (in the following issue of *Photoshop User*), and sure enough, after we did, we received e-mail asking, "OK, now how did he do the background?" Believe it or not, it was a stock photo background that was stretched a bit and had massive amounts of Unsharp Mask applied to make it look more metallic. The stock photo background was from PhotoDisc, a part of GettyOne (as are all the images in this book). They've got about a gazillion stock images on their Web site (www.gettyone.com) in both royalty-free and licensable images.

Doug's 5.5 *Photoshop User* Cover

Doug Gornick (Creative Director for *Photoshop User* magazine and all-around Photoshop brainiac) created this chrome effect for the cover of the magazine, and after it ran, I was deluged with questions on how he did it. Special thanks to Doug for letting me share his amazing technique.

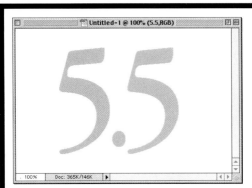

STEP ONE: Open a new document in RGB mode. Set 25% gray as your foreground color. Create your type (you'll need to use very large type for this effect, ideally 100-point or more). We used the typeface Garamond Condensed, but most serif fonts will work just fine.

STEP TWO: Rasterize this Type layer by going under the Layer menu, under Rasterize, and choosing Type. In the Layers palette, make a copy of your text layer by dragging it to the New Layer icon. Set your foreground color to 50% gray, and press Shift-Option-Delete (PC: Shift-Alt-Backspace) to fill this text layer with 50% gray. Press the letter "v" to switch to the Move tool.

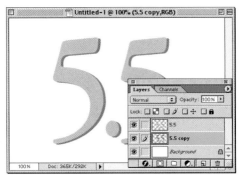

STEP THREE: Press the Right Arrow key on your keyboard five times then the Down Arrow key five times to nudge this darker gray layer down and to the right. In the Layers palette, drag this darker layer down directly below your lighter layer. In the Layers palette, click once on your top (lighter) layer, then press Command-E (PC: Control-E) to merge these two layers together.

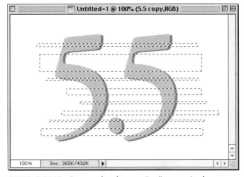

STEP FOUR: Press the letter "m" to switch to the Rectangular Marquee tool. Draw a thin rectangular selection across the top of your text, then hold the Shift key and add a series of thin rectangles with varying depths across your type (as shown above).

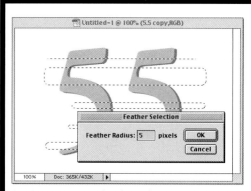

STEP FIVE: Go under the Select menu and choose Feather. Enter 5 pixels for low-res images or 20 pixels for 300-ppi, high-res images, and click OK.

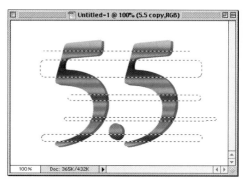

STEP SIX: Press Command-L (PC: Control-L) to bring up the Levels dialog box. Grab the bottom right Output slider, and drag it all the way over to the left until the readout shows 64, then click OK.

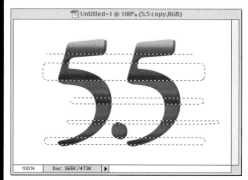

STEP SEVEN: Press the Down Arrow key on your keyboard eight times to move the selection downward. Then press Command-I (PC: Control-I) to invert the selection.

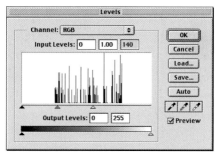

STEP EIGHT: Press Command-L (PC: Control-L) to bring up Levels again. Grab the TOP right *Input* slider, and drag it over to the left until the readout up top shows 140, then click OK. Deselect by pressing Command-D (PC: Control-D).

STEP NINE: Go under the Layer menu, under Layer Style, and Choose Bevel and Emboss. Increase the Depth to 500% and the Size to 8 (for high-res images, increase the Depth to 800% and the Size to 25).

STEP TEN: In the Layers palette, create a new layer. Drag this new layer just below your text layer, then click back on your text layer. Now press Command-E (PC: Control-E) to merge these two layers together. CONTINUED

Feathering trick

One of the downsides of the feathering feature is you can't see how much you're really feathering; it's pretty much a guess because there's no preview. Here's a cool trick that many people use to see a feathered edge effect before they apply it: First, make a selection (inside the edges of your image) and then press the letter "q" to enter Quick Mask mode (your selection will appear as a red box by default). Go under the Filter menu, under Blur, and choose Gaussian Blur. When you apply the blur, you'll see the edges become very soft. When the softness of the edges looks right, press the letter "q" again to return to normal mode and make your selection active. Go under the Select menu and choose Inverse to choose the background edges, rather than the inside of your selection, and press Delete (PC: Backspace) to softly feather the edges at the exact amount you saw in the Quick Mask preview.

If it's metal, sharpen the living heck out of it

First off, I had to say "heck," because there could be kids reading this book—and some of them might be really smart toddlers, so you can never be too careful. One thing that I've found (that *you* might find) helpful is that when you have a chrome or metallic image, you can apply the Unsharp Mask filter with very high Amount settings (like 300 to 500) and it looks just fine. In fact, sometimes I'll apply Unsharp Mask to chrome type three or four times in a row (with Amount settings around 100 to 150). Those hard edges just soak up the sharpening.

The main things you need to look out for are halos or weird unwanted colors which can start to creep into your edges. Otherwise, sharpen till the cows come home (if you don't have cows, just keep sharpening until someone yells, "Stop!" :)

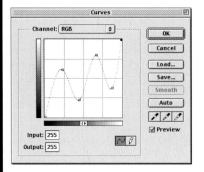

STEP ELEVEN: Press Command-M (PC: Control-M) to bring up the Curves dialog box. You'll see a straight line (the curve) at a 45° angle. Click once about 25% from the bottom left to add a point, and drag it upward (you're going to add four points to create the curve shown here). When your curve looks like the one above, click OK.

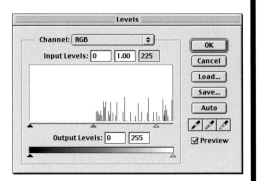

STEP TWELVE: Press Command-L to bring up the Levels dialog box. Grab the TOP right Input slider, and drag it over to the left until the readout up top shows 225 (this brightens the chrome), then click OK.

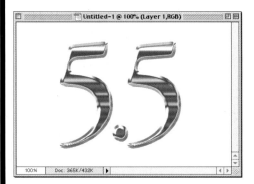

STEP THIRTEEN: Go under the Filter menu, under Sharpen, and choose Unsharp Mask. Drag the Amount all the way over to 500, put the Radius at 1, Threshold at 10, and click OK. (Note: For high-res images, you might apply this filter twice to really get the effect.)

STEP FOURTEEN: Go under the Layer menu, under Layer Style, and choose Drop Shadow. Increase the Size to 10, Distance to 10, and click OK to complete the effect. (Note: for high-res, 300-ppi or higher images, increase the Size to 45 and the Distance to 30.)

Reflective Chrome

NAPP member Mark Monciardini (www.designsbymark.com) came up with his own twist on this effect, which appeared in the *Photoshop 5.0/5.5 WOW! Book* (By Jack Davis/Linnea Dayton. Published by PeachPit Press). My thanks to Mark for letting me share his excellent Down and Dirty trick!

STEP ONE: Open a new document in RGB mode. Press the letter "d" to reset your foreground color to black. Select the Type tool and create some large type. Hold the Command key (PC: Control key), and in the Layers palette, click once on your Type layer to put a selection around your type. Go under the Select menu and choose Save Selection. When the dialog box appears, click OK. Delete your Type layer by dragging it to the trash can at the bottom of the Layers palette. Now you can press Command-D (PC: Control-D) to deselect.

STEP TWO: Go to the Channels palette, double-click on Alpha 1, name this new channel "Original," and click OK. Drag this channel to the New Channel icon to make a duplicate. Double-click on this duplicate channel, name it "Blurred," and click OK. Now, go under the Filter menu, under Blur, and choose Gaussian Blur. Enter 3.6 pixels and click OK (use a higher setting with larger or high-res images).

STEP THREE: Make a duplicate of the "Blurred" channel by dragging it to the New Channel icon. Double-click on it, name it "Trimmed," and click OK. On the Trimmed channel, hold down the Command key (PC: Control key) and click on the "Original" channel to select it. Go under the Select menu and choose Inverse. Press Option-Delete (PC: Alt-Backspace) to fill the selected area with black.

STEP FOUR: You'll need to save the "Trimmed" channel as a separate file on your hard drive. Click on the Trimmed channel, and from the Channel palette's pop-down menu, choose Duplicate Channel. When the dialog box appears, under Destination/Document choose New, and click OK. This channel will appear as a new document. Go under the File menu, choose Save As, and name this file "Map." Save this file in Photoshop (PSD) format. You can now close the "Map" document.

CONTINUED

Wrapping textures around objects

If you've ever wanted to wrap a texture around an object and have it hug every twist and turn like it was painted on, then take a good look at the effect on this and the following two pages. It uses the Distort Glass filter with a Displacement Map. The technique used in this effect is the same type of effect used to map a texture to an object.

Take a look at Step Eight on the next page. See how the type seems to push out from the photograph? Instead of type, that would be your object pushing out. You would then put your object on a layer beneath that photograph, go to the photo layer again, and change the mode to either Multiply or Overlay (depending on the photo). Then all you have to do is trim the excess photo away, leaving just your object. Take a good look at the step-by-step that follows; at some point, it'll hit you, and you'll go, "Oh, I get it."

Creating another document with the same exact specs as your current document

If you do much collaging of images, this tip will save you boatloads of time (meaning a cargo bay of cheap watches). To create a new document with the same size, resolution, and color mode as your current document, go under the File menu and choose New. While the New dialog box is on-screen, go under the Window menu. At the bottom of that menu, you'll see the name of your current document. Choose it, and Photoshop will automatically load its size, resolution, and color mode into your open "New" dialog box. All you have to do is click OK.

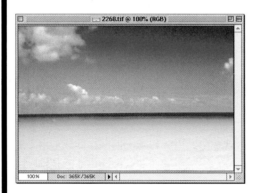

STEP FIVE: Back in your original document, in the Layers palette, click on the Background layer. Deselect by pressing Command-D (PC: Control-D). Now you'll need to find an image to use as a reflection map for the text. Pictures of sky and ocean or sky and land work best, so think "landscapes." Try to choose an image with detail as well (like trees, beach, weeds or rocks). In this example, we're using a beach shot.

STEP SIX: Open your "landscape" photo, then go under the Filter menu, under Blur, and choose Gaussian Blur. Enter 2.5 pixels, and click OK (use 6 for high-res images). Press the letter "v" to switch to the Move tool, then click-and-drag your landscape image into your main document.

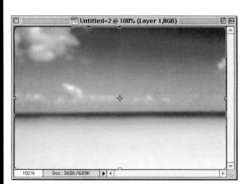

STEP SEVEN: The reflection map needs to cover the entire image. If it doesn't, press Command-T (PC: Control-T) to bring up Free Transform. Hold the Shift key, grab a corner, and drag till it fills the entire window. Press Command-A (PC: Control-A) to select all, then under the Image menu, choose Crop. Press Command-D (PC: Control-D) to deselect.

STEP EIGHT: Go under the Filter menu, under Distort, and choose Glass. Set the Distortion to 20 and the Smoothness to 9. Under the Texture pop-up menu, choose Load Texture. Browse to the "Map" file you saved earlier on your hard drive and open it. Click OK to apply the Glass filter.

STEP NINE: Go under the Select menu and choose Load Selection. From the Channel pop-up menu, choose "Original," and click OK. Inverse the selection by pressing Shift-Command-I (PC: Shift-Control-I). Press Delete on the keyboard (PC: Backspace) to remove the background surrounding your text. Deselect by pressing Command-D (PC: Control-D). Make a copy of your reflection map layer by dragging it to the New Layer icon at the bottom of the Layers palette.

STEP TEN: Next, change the layer blend mode from Normal to Color Dodge from the pop-down menu. Lower the Opacity of this layer to about 30%. This gives it a bright shine. Lastly, click on the original reflection map layer, go under the Layer menu, under Layer Style, and choose Drop Shadow. Click OK to add a drop shadow and to complete the effect.

QUICK TIP

When you're using the Crop tool, you can rotate your selected area before you crop by moving your cursor outside the bounding box that appears around your image where you dragged the Crop tool. You'll see that your cursor temporarily changes into a double-headed arrow, which enables you to freely rotate your object. When it's rotated just the way you like it, you have two choices: Double-click inside the bounding box or press Return (PC: Enter) to make the rotation permanent. If you're using the Crop tool and you decide that you don't want to crop the image after all, click once on the Crop tool icon in the Tool palette. A dialog box will appear giving you the option to Crop or Don't Crop.

If you're having trouble making the chrome look right…

Try a different image for your map. The image you choose makes ALL the difference in the world. I've seen this effect look stunning, and I've seen it fall completely flat, all based on the image chosen for the map. One of the things to look for is contrast. Look for blue skies with a reddish brown desert or green grass below. The effect is actually easy, you just follow along step-by-step; the tough part is finding the right image. Once you find it, save it for use on other projects (in fact, try to find two or three that work).

Adding glints to chrome

The type of effect shown at right is often accented with "glints" (little sparkles of light). Look in Chapter 7 for a step-by-step on how to add glints and how to create your own custom glints as well.

Airbrushed Chrome Gradient

This effect mimics the style of chrome gradients created by traditional airbrush artists. It uses one of Photoshop's built-in gradients, but we added a little twist that makes it look realistic (the Chrome gradient has a horizon line that is perfectly straight, and it looks too contrived using it "as is").

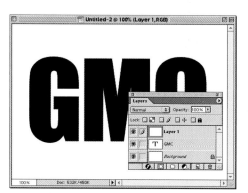

STEP ONE: Open a new RGB document at 72-ppi, and use the Type tool to create some type. Create a new blank layer by clicking once on the New Layer icon at the bottom of the Layers palette.

STEP TWO: Switch to the Rectangular Marquee tool by pressing the letter "m," and draw a rectangular selection slightly larger than your type.

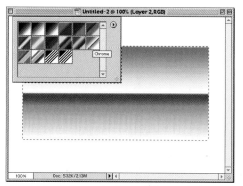

STEP THREE: Press the letter "g" to switch to the Gradient tool, and in the Options Bar up top, click on the down-facing triangle next to the gradient sample to reveal the flyout Gradient Picker. Choose the Chrome gradient (if you can't find it, choose Text Only in the Gradient Picker's pop-down menu). With the Gradient tool, drag from the top to the bottom of your selection to fill it with the Chrome gradient (blue should appear on top with brown at the bottom).

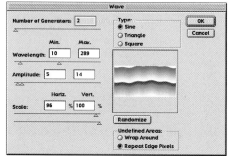

STEP FOUR: Go under the Filter menu, under Distort, and choose Wave (to help us make a slightly rolling horizon line). In the Wave dialog box, set the Type to Sine and lower the Number of Generators to 2. For Wavelength, choose 10 for Min. and 289 for Max. For Amplitude, choose 5 for Min. and 14 for Max. Leave the Horiz. and Vert. Scale set at 100% and then click OK. (Note: If you don't like what you're seeing in the preview window, click the Randomize button a few times.)

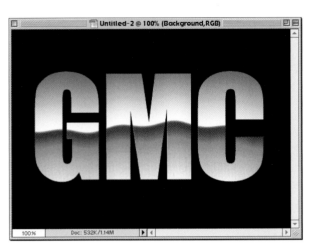

STEP FIVE: Deselect by pressing Command-D (PC: Control-D). To get your Chrome gradient inside your type, press Command-G (PC: Control-G). Press the letter "d," then in the Layers palette, click on the Background layer. Press Option-Delete (PC: Alt-Backspace) to fill the background with black.

STEP SIX: Click on the Type layer, then go under the Layer menu, under Layer Style, and choose Bevel and Emboss. In the Bevel and Emboss dialog box, under Shading, click the downward-facing triangle next to the Gloss Contour sample to reveal a flyout menu of preset contours. Click on the "Triple Ring" contour, turn on the Anti-Aliasing check box, and click OK. Lastly, create a new layer above your gradient layer, and add some white airbrush glints using the technique shown on page 118 in Chapter 7.

QUICK TIP

If you click-and-hold the Marquee tool, a flyout menu of additional tools will appear, including two tools that select single rows of pixels either horizontally or vertically.

Fill shortcuts

Here are some quick shortcuts that can be real timesavers for filling selections or layers. For example:

• To fill an entire layer with your foreground color, press Option-Delete (PC: Alt-Backspace).

• To fill just an object on a layer (not the entire layer), press Shift-Option-Delete (PC: Shift-Alt-Backspace).

• To fill with your background color, press Command-Delete (PC: Control-Backspace).

• To fill your layer with black, press the letter "d," then Option-Delete (PC: Alt-Backspace).

• To fill your layer with white, press the letter "d," then the letter "x," then press Option-Delete (PC: Alt-Back space).

Have you ever stopped to think about why so many people use Photoshop? Obviously, it's an amazing program with incredible depth, and that alone will draw people, but it's also a kind

Freeze Frame
Photographic Effects

of complex program. If you search on the Web for Photoshop instruction books, you'll be able to dig up over a hundred in short order. Usually, a complex program with incredible depth means only a handful of people have actually learned enough about it to use it. But in the case of Photoshop, millions around the world use it every day. And every day, people who have never used it before buy it, launch it, and use it—many without ever reading the manual. That's because Photoshop has an incredible advantage over most other graphics applications. You can start with something: a photo. Think about it. With a page-layout application, or Illustration program, you start with the scariest thing a fledgling designer can ever face—the blank page. But in Photoshop, you can start with a photo and build your creation from there. That's what this chapter is all about. (The melancholy music slowly fades).

Getting better results from the Eyedropper tool

There's one setting you should change immediately that will give you better results from your Eyedropper tool. Click on the Eyedropper, and in the Options Bar, change the Sample Size from Point Sample to 3 by 3 Average. This helps keep you from getting erroneous readings when using the Eyedropper, because when it's set to Point Sample, you get the reading from one single pixel, which might not be representative of the colors in the area where you're clicking. Set to 3 by 3 Average, it averages the color of the pixels surrounding the area that you clicked, which is considered by many to provide a much more usable reading when doing color correction.

Visual Color Change

If you have a color image, and there's something in that image that you wish was a different color, this is just about the quickest way to get there—that is if you're not real fussy about the color being a specific shade.

STEP ONE: Open a color image that contains an object or part of an object that you want to change the color of.

STEP TWO: Select the object you want to apply a quick color change to (in this example, we used the Lasso tool to select the woman's blouse).

STEP THREE: Go under the Image menu, under Adjust, and choose Hue/Saturation. When the Hue and Saturation dialog box appears, check the Colorize box in the lower right corner.

STEP FOUR: Now, simply grab the Hue slider (the top one) and drag it until your image has changed to a color you like (of course, make sure the Preview box is checked in this dialog box, or you'll be doing this blind). When it looks good, click OK.

Changing to a Specific Color

This is great technique when you have a product shot and the client is demanding that a particular object in the photo (like clothing) be a particular color. You could select the item and use Hue/Saturation to come up with a close match, but this method lets you choose the specific color you need, rather than a "close match."

STEP ONE: Open the image which contains an area that you want to change to a specific color (in this case, a shirt). Select the area using one of Photoshop's selection tools (in this example, I used the Magnetic Lasso tool).

STEP TWO: To help smooth the transition between colors, go under the Select menu and choose Feather. Enter a radius of 1 pixel and click OK. Press Shift-Command-U (PC: Shift-Control-U) to remove all color from your selected area (this is the Desaturate command).

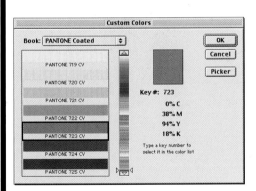

STEP THREE: Next, click once on the Foreground color swatch to bring up the Color Picker, select the exact color you'd like to place into your image (in our example, we clicked on the Custom button and chose Pantone 723), and click OK.

STEP FOUR: To complete the color change, go under the Edit menu and choose Fill. When the Fill dialog box appears, change the fill mode from Normal to Color and click OK.

Better-looking color-to-grayscale conversions

If you have a color image that you want to convert to a grayscale image, you can choose Grayscale from the Mode menu, but Photoshop just throws away the color, and you generally end up with a bland-looking grayscale image. Here's a tip for getting a better color-to-grayscale conversion: Rather than choosing Grayscale, go to the Channels palette and click on each individual color channel (the Red, Blue, and Green). These channels appear in grayscale mode by default, and more often than not, one of those channels (by itself) makes a pretty good-looking grayscale image. Keep that one, and drag the other two to the trash. Now, when you go under the Image menu, under Mode, and choose Grayscale (it doesn't have any color to throw away, you already did that), you wind up with a great-looking grayscale conversion.

Color correction for dummies

I know, I know, there should be a book with that title, but until one comes out, Photoshop has the next best thing. It's called Variations. You can find it under the Image menu, under Adjust, and what it does is display your original image and half a dozen different color variations of that image. All you have to do is decide which variation looks better than your original. It also shows you a lighter and darker version of your image, and if one or the other looks better than your original, pick it. Every time you click on one of these thumbnails, it updates your current pick. Your original is always displayed at the top of the dialog, along with your current pick right alongside, so you can easily compare the two. This is a very basic correction tool, and frankly, it's not the greatest, but if you have no color correction experience, this is the place to start. The best part is, when you open the dialog box, you'll realize that it's so easy, you really need no instructions to use it (even though I just gave them to you).

Tinting Images for Effect

This is handy when combining multiple images. Even though the subject might work in your collage, sometimes the colors clash with the other images that are already there. Using this simple technique, I can keep the subject, but put in the color that I need to match the rest of the collage.

STEP ONE: Open a color image you want to add to a collage you're creating.

STEP TWO: Remove all the color from the image by pressing Shift-Command-U (PC: Shift-Control-U), which instantly desaturates the entire image.

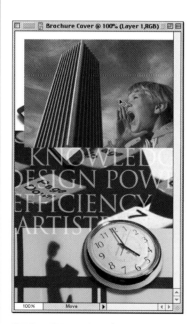

STEP THREE: Using the Move tool, drag this image into the collage document you're working on. Go under the Image menu, under Adjust, and choose Hue/Saturation.

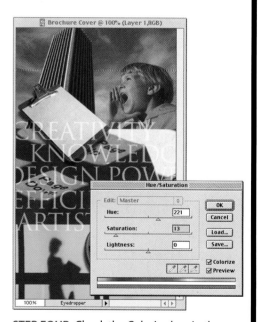

STEP FOUR: Check the Colorize box in the lower right-hand corner of the dialog box. Move the Hue slider to dial in a color tint that matches the rest of the collage. Lower the Saturation of the color if the tinting looks too intense or obvious.

Creating Gradients from Photos

This is a great trick for creating some really usable gradients because they're based on colors in real photographs. I use this trick whenever I need a photographic-looking studio background. I open a stock image of a product shot and sample the colors from right within the image, and it looks great!

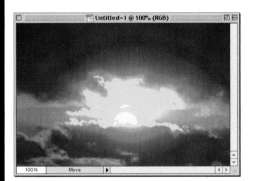

STEP ONE: Open a color image that contains colors (usually in the background) that you want to base your gradient on. This works great with product shot backgrounds, and it works particularly well if you use outdoor shots of nature, such as sunsets, ocean shots, landscapes, etc.

STEP TWO: Click on the Gradient tool, and in the Gradient Options Bar, click once on the gradient sample to bring up the Gradient Editor (shown above). Click once on the first Color Stop on the bottom left of the gradient bar (it looks like an upward facing triangle with a small box beneath it).

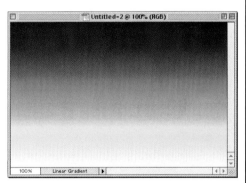

STEP THREE: Move your cursor outside the Gradient Editor, right over your image, and click on the first color you want in your gradient (my image is a sunset, so I clicked near the top). Your Color Stop now takes on this color. Add another Color Stop by clicking just to the right of your first stop, under the gradient bar. Again, move outside the Gradient Editor into your image and sample the next color down in your image.

STEP FOUR: Continue adding stops and sampling colors until your gradient has the same number of stops that your background image has colors (within reason, of course). Lastly, in the Name field, give your new gradient a name (I named mine Sunset Gradient) then click on the New button to add this new custom gradient to the Gradient Picker, where you can access it at any time.

How to get an undo, three days after you closed your document

You're probably already familiar with Photoshop's History feature, which by default, lets you undo your last 20 steps. Unfortunately, when you close Photoshop, those undos go away. But there is a way to undo color or tonal corrections days, weeks, or months later. Here's how: The next time you're going to apply a tonal change of some sort (using either Levels, Brightness/Contrast, Curves, Hue/Saturation, Color Balance, or a few others), don't just choose them from the menus. Instead, go to the bottom of the Layers palette and click on the New Fill or Adjustment Layer icon. It's the little circle that is half black and half white. A pop-up menu will appear and you can choose which tonal change (or fill) you want to apply. A special layer will appear in your Layers palette with the name of your tonal change (such as Color Balance). After you save your *layered* document, when you reopen it, the Color Balance layer will still be there. To edit your original Color balance adjustment, double-click on it. To undo your color balance change, drag the Color Balance layer into the trash.

Making precise-sized selections, method #1

If you know the exact size you want to make a selection, there are a couple of things you can do to get there. The quickest and easiest is to switch to the Rectangular Marquee tool, open the Info palette (shortcut: press F8), and as you start dragging your selection, glance in the bottom right-hand corner of the Info palette and you'll see a W (for Width) and an H (for Height) reading. As you drag, you'll see (in real time) the size of your selection, displayed in your current unit of measurement (inches, pixels or whatever you have it set to).

Ripped Edge Effect

This is a quick trick for creating a wavy, ripped edge border for your image. The wave part is created by using the Shear filter, and the ripping is courtesy of the Sprayed Strokes filter. The whole effect takes just seconds and can be used to add some visual interest to an otherwise flat image.

STEP ONE: Open the image you want to add the effect to. Press Command-A (PC: Control-A) to select the entire image, then press Shift-Command-J (PC: Shift-Control-J) to put the background image on its own layer. Draw a rectangular selection about 1" inside the edge of your image on all sides. Press the letter "q" to enter Quick Mask mode.

STEP TWO: Go under the Filter menu, under Brush Strokes, and choose Sprayed Strokes. For Stroke Length choose 15, for Spray Radius choose 17, and for Stroke Direction choose Vertical, then click OK. Choose Sprayed Strokes again, but this time enter 19 for the Stroke Length and 22 for the Spray Radius, and click OK.

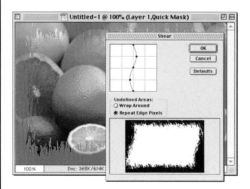

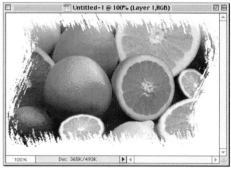

STEP THREE: Go under the Filter menu, under Distort, and choose Shear. On the center vertical grid line, click once on the 25% mark, once on the center mark, and once on the 75% mark. Grab the 25% mark and move it slightly to the left. Grab the 75% point and drag it slightly to the right (as shown above). Choose Repeat Edge Pixels, then click OK.

STEP FOUR: Press the letter "q" again to leave Quick Mask mode and enter Normal mode. Your jagged selection will appear on screen. Go under the Select menu, and choose Inverse. To complete the effect, press Delete (PC: Backspace), then deselect by pressing Command-D (PC: Control-D). You could also add a drop shadow to enhance the edges.

Classic Vignette Effect

This was one of the first effects that I ever learned in Photoshop, and it's still in wide use today. It creates a soft-edged effect, and you can use it any time you want to add softness to an image. It's also used to add a touch of elegance and can be found in print ads for golf courses, swanky hotels, and jewelry.

STEP ONE: Open the image you want to give the vignette effect. This is a photo of my son Jordan (a.k.a the coolest little guy in the whole wide world).

STEP TWO: Make a selection at least $^1/_4$" to $^1/_2$" inside the border of your image using either the Rectangular or Elliptical Marquee tool (press Shift-M to toggle back and forth between the two tools).

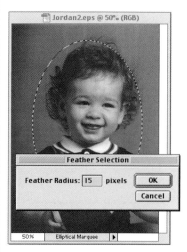

STEP THREE: Go under the Select menu and choose Feather. When the dialog box appears, you'll be prompted to enter a Feather Radius. The higher the number you enter, the softer your edges will be. In this example, I entered 8 pixels. Click OK.

STEP FOUR: Go under the Select menu, and choose Inverse. Press Delete (PC: Back-space) to remove the area from around your image. Press Command-D (PC: Control-D) to clearly view your soft-edged effect.

Precise-sized selections, method #2

Another way to make a selection in the exact size that you need is to click on the Rectangular Marquee tool and change the style in the Options Bar Style pop-up menu. By default, it's set to Normal, but if you choose Fixed Size, you can type in your desired size in the Width and Height fields just to the right of the pop-up menu in the Options Bar.

Now, when you click the Rectangular Marquee tool anywhere within your image, a selection in that fixed size (and only that size) will appear.

What to check if you can't save your file in the format you want

If you go to save your Photoshop document and you get a warning in the dialog saying that "Some of the document's data will not be saved using the chosen format," here's what to check for:

(1) Layers: If you have layers in your document, you can only save in Photoshop or TIFF format without losing data.

(2) Check for extra channels: If you have an extra channel (perhaps a saved selection), you cannot save in the EPS format without losing data. Go to the Channels palette, drag the channel to the trash, and then you can save as an EPS.

(3) You need a Background layer: If your only layer is named Layer 1 or Layer 0, Photoshop treats it as a layered document. You first have to go under the Layers palette's pop-down menu and choose Flatten Image.

(4) Check your color mode: There are some file formats that aren't available for certain color modes. For example, BMP doesn't show up as a choice when you're in CMYK mode.

Adding Objects Behind an Existing Image

Over the years, I've had question after question on how to add a person to an existing image so that it looks as if they were standing behind other people in that image. Here's a very flexible and visual way to do just that.

STEP ONE: Open the image you want to add another person (or object) to.

STEP TWO: Use the selection tool of your choice (Lasso tool, Pen tool, etc.) to select the area where you want the additional person to appear in your image.

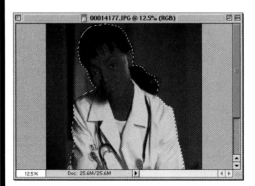

STEP THREE: Open the image file you want to add to your original photo. Use the selection tool of your choice to select the person (or object). Go under the Edit menu and choose Copy. Switch back to the main document. Go under the Edit menu and choose Paste Into. This will place your copied selection (in our example, a head shot of a person) into the selection in your main document.

STEP FOUR: Press the letter "v" to switch to the Move tool. You can now reposition your pasted person without them leaving the originally selected area, because when you use Paste Into, Photoshop automatically creates a Layer Mask for you. This gives you the flexibility to reposition your image as you like.

STEP FIVE: After you reposition the pasted image, chances are good that the size of it won't be correct (it'll either be too large, as in this case, or too small). Also, the contrast of your pasted image probably won't match the rest of the image either, so we'll have to adjust both.

STEP SIX: First, we'll adjust the size by pressing Command-T (PC: Control-T) to bring up Free Transform. Hold the Shift key, grab one of the top corner handles, and drag downward (or upward if your image is too small) to resize the person to match the others in the image. You can also reposition the image as you resize; just click-and-drag inside the Free Transform bounding box.

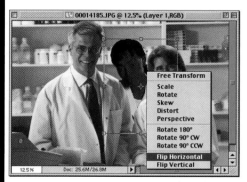

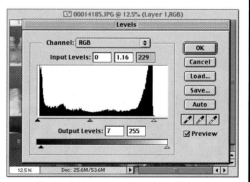

STEP SEVEN: You'll also notice in our particular image, the light appears on the opposite side of the woman's head than it does on the other subjects in the image. While your Free Transform box is still active, Control-click (PC: Right-click) within the bounding box to bring up a pop-up menu, then choose Flip Horizontal (reposition your image if necessary). Press Return (PC: Enter) to complete the change.

STEP EIGHT: Next, we have to deal with the contrast of the pasted image. In this example, she looks too saturated in comparison. A quick trick for matching contrast is to press Command-L (PC: Control-L) to bring up the Levels dialog. Grab the lower left Output slider and drag it to the right (as shown above) to lighten the overall contrast of your pasted image to match more closely. Click OK.

Resizing by the numbers

In the effect on the left, we resized the woman's head by bringing up Free Transform, holding the Shift key (to constrain its proportions), and dragging a corner handle. However, there's a much more precise way to resize objects on a layer, and this way lets you input a variety of measurement values to get the exact size you want. Here's how:

Press Command-T (PC: Control-T) to bring up the Free Transform function. Now, look up in the Options Bar and you'll see fields where you can increase/decrease the Width and Height. By default, these fields are set up to increase/ decrease by percentages (200%, 300%, and so on), so you can type in any percentage resize you'd like. However, you can also type in other measure-ment units. For example, if you wanted your image to be 3" x 3", in the Width field type "3 in" (for inches), and in the Height field type "3 in." If you want your resize to be in pixels, type "px" after your value (such as "468 px").

Getting around your image, one button at a time

There are a dozen or so keyboard shortcuts for zooming in and out of your image: switching to the Zoom tool, zooming to Fit on Screen, and a bunch more. But there are some lesser-known shortcuts that can be helpful when you're working on large, high-res images. These are mostly one-button wonders that are available to anyone with an extended keyboard (which is just about everybody not using a laptop). Here goes: To jump up one full screen in your image, press the Page Up key. To jump down one full screen, press the Page Down key. To move to the left one full screen, press Command-Page Up (PC: Control-Page Up). To move right one full screen, press Command-Page Down (PC: Control-Page Down). To jump to the upper-left corner of your image, press the Home key. To jump to the lower-right corner of your image, press the End key.

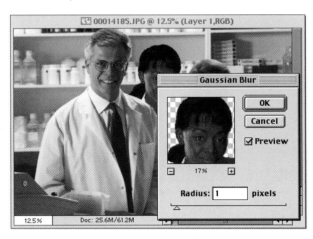

STEP NINE: The contrast is better, but the pasted image is too sharp and crisp in comparison. Add a slight blur by going under the Filter menu, under Blur, and choosing Gaussian Blur. Choose a very slight amount of blur around 1 or less (higher for high-res images).

QUICK TIP
To temporarily switch to the Zoom tool from the tool you're currently using, you can hold Command-Spacebar (PC: Control-Spacebar). When you release those keys, you instantly jump back to the last tool you used.

STEP TEN: Here's the final image. Notice the light source on the left side of the woman's face that we pasted in matches the man's light source to the left, and now the overall contrast and sharpness is a better match as well.

Depth of Field Effect

This effect imitates a shot taken with a camera up very close to the subject. This causes the area closest to the lens to be in very sharp focus, but the image immediately starts to go out of focus as the depth of field changes.

STEP ONE: Open the image you want to apply the effect to. Switch to Quick Mask mode by pressing the letter "q." Press the letter "d" to set your foreground color to black. Click on the Gradient tool, and in the Options Bar, make sure the gradient chosen is Foreground to Background.

STEP TWO: Using the Gradient tool, start at approximately the area that you want to be in focus and click-and-drag about 2" toward the area that you want out of focus. (In the example shown here, I started at the bottom right side of the wrench and dragged diagonally to the left). When you do this, a red-to-transparent gradient will appear across your image.

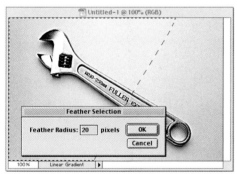

STEP THREE: The red portion of your gradient should appear over the area you want to remain in focus. Switch back to normal mode by pressing the letter "q" again. Go under the Select menu and choose Feather. Enter a value of 20 and click OK (use a higher number for high-res images). Don't deselect yet.

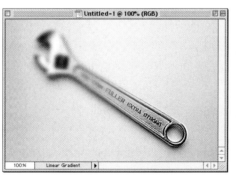

STEP FOUR: Go under the Filter menu, under Blur, and choose Gaussian Blur. As you drag the Radius slider to the right, you'll see your selected area start to blur. Choose the amount of blur that looks good to you and click OK. Deselect by pressing Command-D (PC: Control-D) to complete the effect.

Navigating with the Navigator palette

Yet another option you have for getting around your document is the Navigator palette. It's kind of a one-stop-shop for navigating your document. It shows you a little thumbnail version of your image in which you can drag a view box to display the part of the image you want to work on. To create your own view box (at the size you want), hold the Command key (PC: Control key) to change your cursor into a magnifying glass. Now, you can click-and-drag within the thumbnail preview window, and when you release the key, you have a new view box.

Other ways to navigate inside this palette include dragging the slider to zoom in and out, typing in the exact percentage of zoom you want, or clicking on the tiny mountain icons to zoom either in or out. I don't use the Navigator palette myself; I prefer to use just keyboard shortcuts, but I know some people who use the Navigator palette exclusively, and they seem to be perfectly nice and well-adjusted.

Layer Masks tips

The tutorial on the right uses my favorite layers' feature—Layer Masks. Here are a few tips for working with Layer Masks that you'll enjoy (OK, I don't know if you'll actually "enjoy" them, but they might come in handy).

• To delete your Layer Mask, drag just the Layer Mask thumbnail into the trash can at the bottom of the Layers palette.

• You can view the Layer Mask as a red rubylith. Hold Shift-Option (PC: Shift-Alt) and click on the Layer Mask thumbnail (if you don't already know what a rubylith is, then you probably won't care about this feature).

• You can disable the Layer Mask by holding the Shift key and clicking on the thumbnail.

• You can move the image independently of the mask by clicking directly on the Link icon between the layer thumbnail and the mask thumbnail.

Blending Images for Instant Collages

This is one of the fastest and most fun ways to blend (or collage) two images together. It uses Photoshop's Layer Mask command. This is so easy to do, yet so effective, that it opens up a whole new way of collaging multiple images for many people.

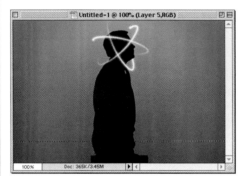

STEP ONE: Open a background image (either RGB or Grayscale). Press the letter "d" to set your foreground color to black.

STEP TWO: Open a second image that you want to use in your collage. Press the letter "v" to switch to the Move tool and drag this image on top of the background image in your original document. Make sure this dragged layer covers (or at least significantly overlaps) the background layer.

STEP THREE: Go to the Layers palette, and at the bottom of the palette, click on the Layer Mask icon (it's the second one from the left). The image doesn't change, but if you look in the Layers palette, you'll see another thumbnail icon added to the right of your top layer's thumbnail icon. This represents your Layer Mask.

STEP FOUR: Click on the Gradient tool, and in the Options Bar, click on the downward-facing triangle and the flyout Gradient Picker will appear. Make sure the selected gradient is Foreground to Background, then take the Gradient tool and drag it through the image on the top layer, stopping before you reach the edge of that image. You'll notice that the images blend together.

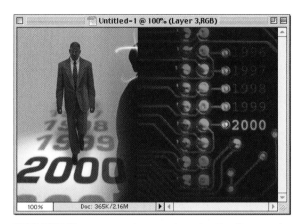

STEP FIVE: You can continue to drag the Gradient tool over and over again, until the blend looks just the way you want. If you see the edge of your image, you've dragged too close to the edge or past it. Try re-dragging the Gradient tool, stopping about 1" before the edge of your image.

STEP SIX: If you want more control over how your images blend, you can paint directly on the mask by pressing the letter "b" to switch to the Paintbrush tool, choosing a large, soft-edged brush, and painting. When you paint with black as your foreground color, the background image paints in. When you paint with white, the top image paints over the background. That's all there is to it.

QUICK TIP

If you want to actually see your Layer Mask (rather than seeing your image), hold the Option key (PC: Alt key) and click directly on the Layer Mask's thumbnail icon, and the mask will be displayed in your image window. You can continue to paint directly onto this mask, and any changes you make to this mask will be reflected in your image.

If you don't like your Layer Mask, start over

If you applied a Layer Mask to your image and you can't get it to look quite right, sometimes the best thing to do is just start over. There are a couple of ways to do this. You can click directly on the Layer Mask thumbnail and drag it into the trash can at the bottom of the Layers palette, but there's another way that might be quicker because you don't have to create a new mask in the Layers palette. Hold the Option key (PC: Alt key) and click on the Layer Mask icon (this displays the mask), then press Option-Delete (PC: Control-Backspace), which fills your Layer Mask with white; and basically, you're "reset" and ready to start over. Option-click (PC: Alt-click) on your Layer Mask thumbnail again, then drag a gradient through your image, or start painting directly on your image (of course, you're really painting on the mask).

Merging your visible layers in one shot

In the effect at the right, you wind up with three separate layers. If you merge these layers one-by-one, the effect might wind up changing or disappearing altogether, because, as you merge down, the order of your layers changes (as they are combined) and that changes the blending. Instead, there's a keyboard shortcut you can use that will get around this problem. It's Command-Shift-E (PC: Control-Shift-E). This is the keyboard shortcut for Merge Visible, and it takes all the currently visible layers and flattens them into one layer (it's like having a keyboard shortcut for Flatten Image).

Gen X Color Effect

This effect seemed to pop up just about everywhere in the late '90s, and it is still pretty popular today. It looks as if color has been poured on to your image, and it was made popular by some of the largest stock photo agencies. Here's how to give your own images that "Generation X" color effect.

STEP ONE: Open the RGB image you want to add the color effect to.

STEP TWO: Make a copy of the image layer by dragging it to the New Layer icon at the bottom of the Layers palette. Press Command-I (PC: Control-I) to invert the image.

STEP THREE: Go to the Layers palette and change the layer blend mode (for your inverted layer) from Normal to Difference.

STEP FOUR: Make a copy of your original background layer by dragging it to the New Layer icon at the bottom of the Layers palette. Drag this new layer to the top of your layer stack above the inverted layer. To complete the effect, change the layer blend mode from Normal to Luminosity.

Adding Motion without Adding Mayhem

If you've ever tried to add a sense of motion to an image using Photoshop's Motion Blur filter, you've probably already noticed that the effect is often too intense and tends to overwhelm the image. Here's how to apply a Motion Blur then selectively decide how much blur and where you want it to appear.

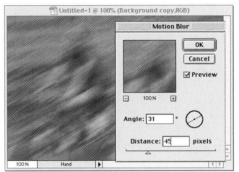

STEP ONE: Open the image that you want to apply a Motion Blur effect to. Make a copy of the Background layer by dragging it to the New Layer icon located at the bottom of the Layers palette.

STEP TWO: Go under the Filter menu, under Blur, and choose Motion Blur. Enter an Angle for your blur matching the direction of the object (in this case, it's around 30°). Choose between 40 and 50 pixels for your Distance. Click OK.

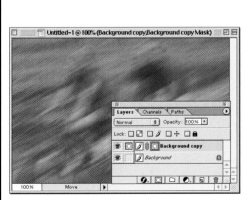

STEP THREE: Press the letter "d" on your keyboard to reset your foreground color to black (the default). Click on the Layer Mask icon at the bottom of the Layers palette (the first icon from the left). This will not affect your image, but it will add a second icon next to your Background copy layer in the Layers palette. Switch to the Paintbrush tool and make sure that your foreground color is still set to black.

STEP FOUR: Choose a large, soft brush, and paint over the areas where you DON'T want the Motion Blur effect to appear. (We painted over the cyclists' faces, over parts of the handlebars, wheels, and their legs). If the effect is too intense, lower the Background copy layer's opacity. The lower you go, the less effect is applied. Also, if you erased too much motion and need to add some back in, switch your foreground color to white and paint the motion back in.

Erasing back your original image

If you're working on an image and things start to look bad, you have a few choices. You can go under the File Menu and choose Revert, which reverts your image to how it looked when you opened the image. But what if you like some of the things you've done thus far and don't want to revert the whole image back to the original? What you can do is switch to the Eraser tool, hold the Option key (PC: Alt key), and start erasing over the areas that you don't want to keep. Usually, the Eraser tool erases your image, but when you hold the Option key (PC: Alt key), it erases back to how the image looked when you originally opened it. Kind of a revert in a brush. This is called the History Eraser, and it works much like the History Brush, but for some reason, many people seem to be more comfortable using the Eraser tool in this capacity rather than using the History Brush.

The express lane to backscreening

If you're not real fussy about the exact percentage of backscreening, there's a faster way to backscreen an image. Make your selection, and then press Command-L (PC: Control-L) to bring up the Levels dialog box. Drag the left bottom Output Slider to the right to instantly backscreen your selected area.

Backscreening Effect

This is a popular effect in print and multimedia, and it's used when the background image is very busy or very dark (or both) and you want to place ad type over your image that can easily be read. This effect is particularly popular in print advertising.

STEP ONE: Open a background image that you want to put type over.

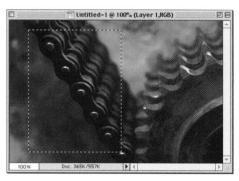

STEP TWO: Using the Rectangular Marquee tool, make a selection of the area where you want your type to appear.

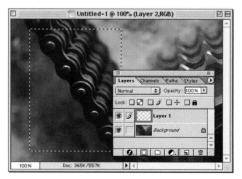

STEP THREE: While this area is still selected, create a new layer by clicking on the New Layer icon at the bottom of the Layers palette.

STEP FOUR: Press the letter "d," then the letter "x" to set your foreground color to white. Then fill your selection with white by pressing Option-Delete (PC: Alt-Backspace). Deselect by pressing Command-D (PC: Control-D).

STEP FIVE: Lower the opacity of this layer to create the amount of backscreen effect you'd like. A 20% screen is a very popular choice for backscreening, and to achieve a 20% screen, you'd lower the opacity to 80% on this layer. In the example above, I actually lowered the opacity to 60%. This lets a bit more of the background show through, but because the black text is so large, it's still very readable.

STEP SIX: To add more depth to your backscreen effect, you can add a drop shadow behind it. Just click on Layer 1 (the backscreened layer) in the Layers palette to make it active, click on the little *f* icon at the bottom of the Layers palette for a pop-up menu of Layer Effects, and choose Drop Shadow. Click OK in the Drop Shadow dialog to complete the effect.

QUICK TIP
When making a selection with the Rectangular Marquee tool, you have several buttons in the left-hand side of the Options Bar that control how the tool will interact with a selection that has already been made. Your choices are creating a new selection, adding to an existing selecting, subtracting from an existing selection, or making the selection from the area where selections intersect.

Backscreens aren't just white

Depending on the image, sometimes when you attempt a backscreen effect, a light backscreen won't work. If the image is already of a lighter nature, a light backscreen can get lost, so instead, try a dark backscreen. You can do this in the Levels dialog. Press Command-L (PC: Control-L) to bring up the Levels dialog box, and drag the right Output Levels slider to the left. This darkens your selected area. If you prefer to use Curves, you can add a light backscreen by dragging the bottom point of the curve straight upward. To add a dark backscreen, drag the top-right point straight downward.

A quick way to adjust tones between two dissimilar images

You can also use the technique at the right to colorize a grayscale image by converting your grayscale image to RGB mode. Sample (with the Eyedropper) a background area from a color image, then make a selection of a background area in the grayscale image. Use the technique at the right to add realistic tones to your grayscale image.

Matching Overall Tone

Here's a trick for adjusting the overall tone in one image to match another. By using the Color Sampler tool and curves, we can adjust the tones in one picture (below left) to more closely match the tones of another picture (the warmer image, below right).

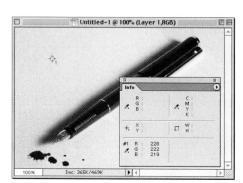

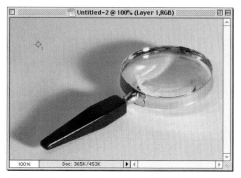

STEP ONE: Open an image that already has an overall tone that you're happy with (shown above). Press Shift-I to toggle to the Color Sampler tool and click once in the background area. The Info palette will appear, and the RGB values for the area under your Color Sampler will appear beside the #1 (in the bottom left-hand corner).

STEP TWO: Write down the RGB settings that appear beside #1 in the Info palette (in this example, they are R=228, G=222, B=219). Next, open an image that you want to change to match the overall tone of the image you opened in Step One. With the Color Sampler tool, click in the background area and a Color Sampler target will appear.

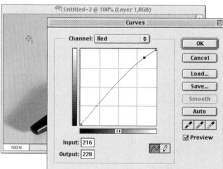

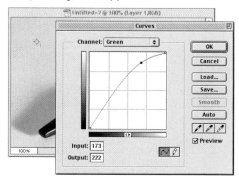

STEP THREE: Next, go under the Image menu, under Adjust, and choose Curves. From the Channel pop-up menu at the top, choose the Red channel. Hold the Command key (PC: Control key) and click once directly on the Color Sampler target in your image to add a point to your curve. Two fields (Input and Output) will appear at the bottom left-hand corner of the dialog. In the Output field, type in the Red (R) value you noted from your original image (in this case, 228).

STEP FOUR: Switch to the Green channel (from the pop-up menu), hold the Command key (PC: Control key), and click once directly on the color sampler target in your image. This will add a point to your curve. In the Output field, type in the Green (G) value you noted from your original image (in this case, it was 222).

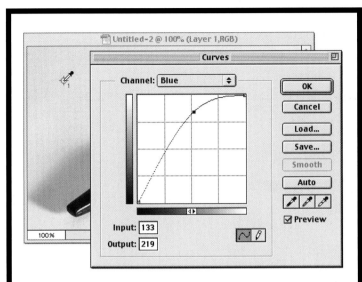

STEP FIVE: Switch to the Blue channel (from the pop-up menu), hold the Command key (PC: Control key) and click once directly on the Color Sampler target in your image. This will add a point to your curve. In the Output field, type in the Blue (G) value you noted from your original image (in this case, it was 219) to complete the tone correction.

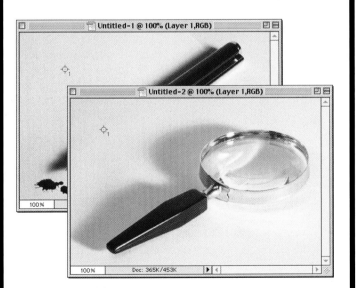

STEP SIX: There really isn't a Step Six, I just thought we'd spend some quality time together. While you're here, as you can see in the two examples above, the corrected image's overall tone (on top) now more closely matches the target image from Step One (below it). I'm glad we had this time together. Really.

QUICK TIP

In the technique shown here, we used one Color Sampler target. You can use up to four, and the Info palette will automatically expand to display all four settings. To remove a color sampler, hold the Option key (PC: Alt key) and your cursors changes into a pair of scissors. Click once directly on the color sampler to delete it.

Getting rid of blemishes and scratches on your image

If you have an image with blemishes, spots, or scratches (generally called "artifacts"), here's a little trick that will help get rid of them. Click on the Blur tool. In the Options Bar, lower the tool's Opacity setting to 20%, change the blend Mode to Lighten, and start painting over your scratches. In just a few strokes, you'll see your scratches start to disappear.

6

I knew there would be certain little tricks that really didn't fit under a particular category (at least within the categories in this book), so I created this "catch-all" chapter with some of my favorite projects and other misfit toys. I even included a couple of Web-optimization tricks that could've gone into the Web Effects

Dirty Deeds Done Dirt Cheap
Down & Dirty Little Tricks

chapter, except for the fact that they're not really effects, they're tricks, so they landed here.

Speaking of dirty tricks, here's one you can play on your Photoshop buddies: On the Photoshop CD-ROM, there's a plug-in called Filter Factory for creating your own custom plug-ins. It's a whole "Mr. Science" kind of math thing, and virtually nobody but Stephen Hawking is smart enough to understand it, but don't sweat it. Just put it in Photoshop's plug-ins folder and restart Photoshop. Then, from the Filter menu, choose Filter Factory. Don't mess with any of the scary looking sliders, just pick a funny name for your bogus plug-in (something like "Reformat Hard Drive" or "Initiate Chicken Sacrifice"), and then choose which filter submenu you want it to appear under. Save the plug-in, then sneak it into some unsuspecting co-worker's copy of Photoshop. The filter won't actually do anything, but it'll turn an otherwise boring day of prepress work into a momentarily funny yet ultimately boring day of prepress work.

Jumping right to the tool you want

Most of Photoshop's tools have a one-letter shortcut you can press to switch you to that tool. You don't really have to memorize them, because most of the shortcuts are the first letter of the tool. For example, the letter L switches you to the Lasso tool, P is for the Pen tool, E is for Eraser, T for the Type tool, G for Gradient, H for the Hand tool, and I for Eyedropper (I for Eyedropper? Hmmmm).

If the tool has two words in its name, the shortcut is often the first letter of the second word, like W for Magic Wand, B for Paintbrush (OK, Adobe makes that one word, but…ya know), S for Rubber Stamp, and M for the Rectangular Marquee tool. There are a few that make you think, like V for the Move tool (M was already taken) and K for the Slice (think knife). And some just don't add up, like A for the Path Component and Direction Selection tools and Y for the History Brush.

You can usually toggle between tools that have other tools nested behind them by adding the Shift key in front of their letter (for example, Shift-M to toggle Marquee tools).

Creating Slide Mounts

I saw this effect on the cover of a travel brochure that was designed to look as if they had taken color slides and casually tossed them on a background—it looked great! If you create your own slide mounts using Photoshop layers, you can change the image inside the slide in about 30 seconds. Here's how:

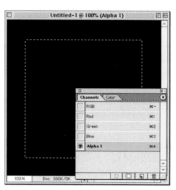

STEP ONE: Open a new document in RGB mode. Press "d," then "x" to make your foreground color white.

Go to the Channels palette and click the New Channel icon. When the new channel appears, press "m" to get the Marquee tool. Hold the Shift key and drag a square selection that is 75% as big as your document. Press Option-Delete (PC: Alt-Backspace) to fill this selection with white. Press Command-D (PC: Control-D) to deselect.

STEP TWO: Go under the Filter menu, under Blur, and choose Gaussian Blur. Enter 5 for Radius (for high-res images, use 8) and click OK. Go under the Image menu, under Adjust, and choose Threshold. When the dialog box appears, just click OK. This removes the blur and rounds your corners. Next, go to the Layers palette and click on the Background layer. Add a new layer by clicking on the New Layer icon, then go under the Select menu and choose Load Selection.

STEP THREE: When the dialog box appears, choose Alpha 1 from the Channels pop-up menu, then click OK. The rounded corner selection appears. Next, click the Foreground color swatch and choose a shade that is approximately 15% gray and click OK. Press Option-Delete (PC: Alt-Backspace) to fill your selection with 15% gray. Press Command-D (PC: Control-D) to deselect.

STEP FOUR: Press the letter "m" to get the Marquee tool again and draw a rectangle in the middle of your gray box (as shown above), then press the Delete key (PC: Backspace).

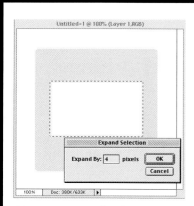

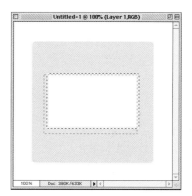

STEP FIVE: Go under the Select menu, under Modify, and choose Expand. When the dialog box appears, enter 4 pixels and click OK. Then press Command-L (PC: Control-L) to bring up the Levels dialog. Drag the bottom-left Output Levels triangle to the right to about 128 to lighten this border selection and click OK.

STEP SIX: Hold the Option key (PC: Alt key) and draw a rectangular selection that starts just outside and down from the top-left corner of your current selection, stopping just short of the right edge and extending down below the bottom of your slide opening (as shown above). This should leave an upside-down, L-shaped selection on just the right side of the border (shown in the next step).

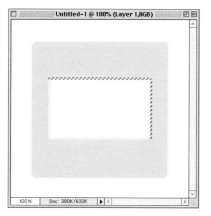

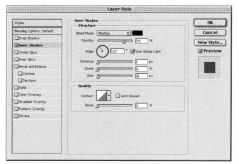

STEP SEVEN: Press Command-L (PC: Control-L) to return to Levels. This time, move the bottom right Output Levels slider to the left until you reach approximately 210 to darken this side of the border (and give the appearance of depth). Click OK and deselect by pressing Command-D (PC: Control-D). Enter the text (in all caps) "THIS SIDE TOWARD SCREEN" (on two lines) in Helvetica Condensed Bold (or a similar typeface). Use a small point size and similar leading, so your text will fit into the right border of the slide.

STEP EIGHT: When you've created your text, click on the Move tool, then press Command-T (PC: Control-T) to bring up Free Transform. Control-click (PC: Right-click) on your text and choose Rotate 90° CW from the pop-up menu, and then press Return (PC: Enter). Go under the Layer menu, under Layer Style, and choose Inner Shadow. Set your Distance to 1, Size to 4, and click OK to make the text look pressed into the slide. Repeat this step (Step Eight), but this time use the text PLASTIMOUNT + ® MADE IN USA (on two lines). Drag your two blocks of text into position (see the following image).

CONTINUED

Pasting Layer Effects to multiple layers

After you apply a Layer Effects to a particular layer, you can copy that effect, link as many layers as you want to your original layer, and make that same effect appear on every single linked layer with just one click. The feature is called "Paste Layer Style to Linked." To use it, hold the Control key (PC: right-click) and click on the layer that contains the effect you want to copy. When the pop-up menu appears, choose Copy Layer Style, then start linking the layers you want to affect by clicking in the center column next to them in the Layers palette. To apply your copied style to every linked layer, hold the Control key (PC: right-click), click on your current layer, and when the pop-up menu appears, choose Paste Layer Style to Linked, and you're done!

Changing Image Size? Let Photoshop do the math

In Photoshop's Image Size dialog box, there's a button that most people ignore. It's called Auto, and here's how it works: You tell Photoshop what line screen you need to output your file at and what level of quality you're looking for (Draft, Good, or Best), and it will do the math, calculating the proper resolution for you based on your choices.

Here's what it does: If you enter 133 line screen and choose Best quality, it doubles that figure and puts your resolution at 266. At Good quality, it gives you 1.5 times the line screen, and at Draft it gives you 72 ppi.

When using this feature, be careful to start with a 300-dpi scan or higher. If you start with a 72-dpi scan, and choose 133 line with Best quality, it'll jump you up to 266 ppi; but it doesn't warn you that your image will look so pixelated when printed that it will trash your whole project, because you can't add resolution that's not really there to begin with.

STEP NINE: Open the image you'd like to appear inside your slide opening. Press "v" to get the Move tool and drag this image into your slide document. In the Layers palette, drag this layer below your slide layer. Press Command-T (PC: Control-T) to bring up Free Transform. Hold the Shift key, then grab a corner point to scale your image to fit within the slide opening. Press Return (PC: Enter) when the image fits within the slide opening.

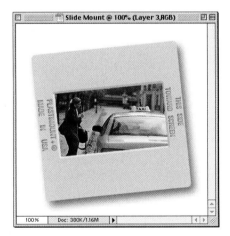

STEP TEN: In the Layers palette, click on the layer with the slide mount (Layer 1). Press Command-E (PC: Control-E) to merge Layer 1 with the image below it. Next, add a drop shadow by choosing Drop Shadow from the Layer Style pop-up menu (*f*) at the bottom of the Layers palette. Lastly, link your Type layers to your slide mount layer, press Command-T, drag your cursor outside the bounding box, and rotate it a bit so that it doesn't look so uniform.

QUICK TIP

If you make a selection, deselect it, then go on about your business and later realize that you forgot to save that selection, you can get your last selection back as long as you haven't made another selection. Just go under the Select menu and choose Reselect, and the last selection that you made reappears.

How to Straighten Any Image

If you have a scan that's crooked, you can get it perfectly straight in just seconds by using this simple trick, courtesy of Photoshop's Measuring tool (you knew they put it in there for a reason, didn't you?)

STEP ONE: Open a scan that needs to be straightened. Press Shift-I until the Measure tool appears in the Tool palette.

STEP TWO: With the Measure tool, drag across the top edge of your scan (if, for some reason, you don't have a top edge, drag it along something in the image—like a table or road—that you know should be perfectly straight).

STEP THREE: Go under the Image menu, under Rotate Canvas, and choose Arbitrary. When the dialog box appears, the proper amount of rotation to make your image perfectly straight is already entered into the dialog box for you. All you have to do is click OK.

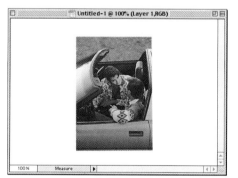

STEP FOUR: When you click OK, your image instantly straightens on screen. After it's straightened, you might have to crop it to size. Just draw a rectangular selection around your image area, then go under the Image menu and choose Crop.

Crop and rotate at the same time

If you have an image that needs to be straightened and cropped, you can do both at the same time using the Crop tool. To switch to the Crop tool, press the letter "c."

Drag out your cropping border where you want, and you can rotate it by simply moving your cursor outside the cropping border. You'll see your cursor change into a two-headed bent arrow, and you can rotate the entire cropping border to fit your image. When it's a snug fit, press the Return (or Enter) key and your image will be cropped and rotated at the same time. This method won't give you the precision of the method shown at left, but it is quick, down, and dirty.

Isn't there an easier way to curl that page corner?

Actually, there are two other ways, but they ain't free (I know, I know. They *aren't* free. Gees). First, In Kai's PowerTools 3.0, there is a Page Curl filter that does the technique taught on this page. That's great if you have KPT 3.0, if not, well … that's why I put it here in this book.

If you don't have KPT 3.0 still lying around, perhaps you have KPT 5.0. If you do, take a look on the install CD because it includes a free copy of the entire KPT 3.0 collection, including the KPT Page Curl filter, which did a great, simple, totally automated job of this popular effect.

There's also a relatively new plug-in (just for PCs) from AV Bros. called "Page Curl" that is a one-trick pony born to curl pages, and it does a pretty nice job of it.

Corner Page Curl

This effect is pretty popular in magazine ads and billboards. Several different methods can be used for creating this effect, and a number of plug-ins can be used, as well. The method we use here is fairly simple and uses only Photoshop's built-in features.

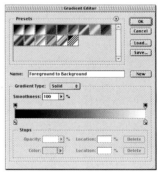

STEP ONE: Open an image in RGB mode. Press the letter "p" to switch to the Pen tool. Draw a path similar to the one shown above. In the Paths palette, double-click on the name Work Path. When the Save Path window appears, click OK, and the path will be saved as Path 1.

STEP TWO: We need to create a gradient for this effect. Click on the Gradient tool, then up in the Options Bar, click once on the gradient sample to bring up the Gradient Editor window (shown above).

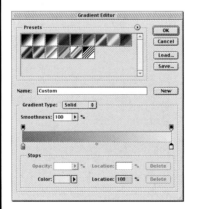

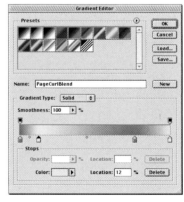

STEP THREE: In the Gradient Editor, double-click on the left Color Stop. When the Color Picker appears, highlight the K (black) field (in the lower right-hand corner) and lower the setting from 100% to 50% and click OK. Now, double-click on the right Color Stop, and this time choose 10% K (black) in the same field. Don't click OK quite yet.

STEP FOUR: Click once on the left Color Stop, then hold down the Option key (PC: Alt key) and click-and-drag it (making a duplicate) 1" from the right end of the Gradient Editor bar. Do the same for the right Color Stop, but drag it to the left about $^1/_4$" from the left end of the bar as shown above. Give your gradient a name, click New, then click OK.

STEP FIVE: In the Layers palette, click on the New Layer icon to create a new layer. Go to the Paths palette, hold the Command key (PC: Control key), and click on Path 1 to make the path an active selection.

STEP SIX: Press the letter "g" to switch to the Gradient tool. Draw a gradient from right to left in a slightly upward angle. It may take a few attempts to achieve the gradient shown above. Don't deselect yet.

STEP SEVEN: Create another new layer by clicking on the New Layer icon in the Layers palette. Press the letter "d" to set your foreground color to black. Click on the Gradient tool, and in the Options Bar, click on the down-facing triangle to reveal the flyout Gradient Picker. Choose the Foreground to Transparent Gradient (second from the top). Once again, using the Gradient tool, drag from right to left until you achieve an effect similar to the one above.

STEP EIGHT: Click on Layer 2 in the Layers palette, and drag it between Layer 1 and the Background layer. Press Command-T (PC: Control-T) to bring up Free Transform. Hold down Command-Shift (PC: Control-Shift), click on the top left adjustment point, then drag it to the top left corner of your image. Press Return (PC: Enter).

CONTINUED

How to view at just the right percentage

If you want to view your document at a specific percentage, you can jump right to that view by highlighting the view percentage (in the lower left-hand corner of your document window), typing in the exact percentage you want, and then pressing the Enter key.

Getting rid of on-screen jaggies

Have you ever noticed that sometimes when you're viewing your Photoshop document, some edges, or even type, can look jaggy? That happens when you view your document at sizes other than 100%, 50%, 25%, or 12.5%. For example, when you view your document at 66.67% (a common size when you zoom in and out), Photoshop's display can look jaggy. To see the clean, crisp look of your image, make sure you view it at 100% (or 50%, or 25%, or 12.5%). By the way: why does Adobe let these other sizes look jaggy? To speed things up. When you zoom out to 16.67% on a 100-MB image, do you really want to sit there while this tiny postage stamp of an image redraws at high-res? Didn't think so. That's why Adobe uses a low-res redraw on these zoomed-out images. Pretty smart, those Adobe folks.

STEP NINE: Press Command-D (PC: Control-D) to deselect. Under the Filter menu, under Blur, choose Gaussian Blur. Type in 5 pixels and click OK. In the Layers palette, click on Layer 2 and change the opacity to 65%. Hold the Command key (PC: Control key) and click on Layer 1 to select it.

STEP TEN: Press the letter "L" to switch to the Lasso tool. While holding down the Shift key, click-and-drag around the bottom right corner of your image so that it is added to the existing selection. It should look like the selection above.

STEP ELEVEN: Click on the Background layer in the Layers palette, and press Delete (PC: Backspace) to remove the part of the image behind the curled edge. Press the letter "g" to select the Gradient tool, then click-and-drag slightly down from left to right to create the shadow effect in the image above.

STEP TWELVE: Press the letter "t" to select the Type tool. Click to the right of the curl on your image, and type in your text. Press the letter "v" to switch to the Move tool. Adjust the text so that it's partially hidden behind the page curl to add more dimension to your image.

Bevel Any Object Instantly

Here's a way to bevel any object in about 45 seconds with just four quick steps, and you won't even break a sweat. The bevel created here is slightly different than a bevel created by the Layer Effects Bevel and Emboss, and although we're using text in this example, this technique works equally well with an object.

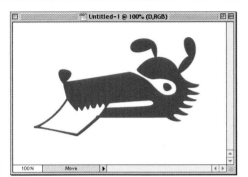

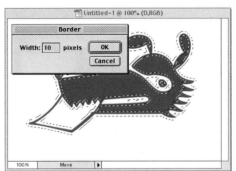

STEP ONE: Open a new RGB document. Pick a vivid color for your foreground color. Get the Type tool and create the text you'd like beveled (large type, 80 points or higher, works best) or import an image you want to bevel. In this case, we used the font Big Cheese, which has images as its characters. If you use text, go under the Layer menu, under Rasterize, and choose Type.

STEP TWO: Next, hold the Command key (PC: Control key) and click once on Layer 1 in the Layers palette to put a selection around your image. While it's still selected, go under the Select menu, under Modify, and choose Border. When the Border dialog appears, enter the number 10 and click OK. (Enter a higher number if you want a larger bevel.) Don't deselect yet.

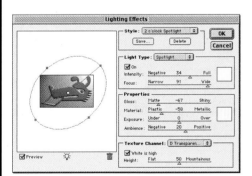

STEP THREE: Go under the Select Menu and choose Save Selection. When the Save Selection dialog box appears, press OK. Press Command-D (PC: Control-D) to deselect. Go under the Filter Menu, under Render, and choose Lighting Effects. From the Style pop-up menu at the top right of the Lighting Effects dialog box, choose 2 o'clock Spotlight. At the bottom right corner, change the Texture Channel to Transparency and click OK to complete the effect.

STEP FOUR: Add a soft drop shadow to help add more depth by clicking on the little *f* icon at the bottom of the Layers palette, choosing Drop Shadow from the pop-up menu, and clicking OK.

Changing values fast

When you open a dialog box, you can change the values of the current field without highlighting it—just use the Up/Down Arrow keys on your keyboard for a quick change of those values. Holding the Shift key while pressing the Up/Down Arrows will increase/decrease the value in larger increments. For example, in the Border Selection dialog box, when you press the Up/Down arrow keys, it moves the Radius value in increments of 1. However, if you hold the Shift key and press the Up/Down Arrow keys, it moves in increments of 10.

Jump to Overlay mode shortcut

In the TV Scan lines effect, after you create your scan lines and put them on their own layer, you have to change the blend mode to Overlay. I show you how to do that by choosing Overlay from the pop-up menu in the Layers palette, but actually, there's a way to change to Overlay mode without going to the Layers palette at all. Just use the keyboard shortcut Shift-Option-O (PC: Shift-Alt-O), and your active layer will switch to Overlay mode. Before you do this keyboard shortcut, make sure you have the Move tool selected (shortcut: Press the letter "v"). The reason is that if you have one of the Paint tools selected, you'll end up changing the blend mode for that tool instead, because just like layers, Paint tools have blend modes too, and they share the same keyboard shortcuts as well.

TV Scan Lines Effect

This technique came out of obscurity and has caught on in a big way. Now everybody's using it from TV to print ads, and it's very popular on the Web as well. It simulates the scan lines of a TV screen, and it gives your images a high-tech sort of feel.

STEP ONE: Open the image that you want to apply TV scan lines to (either RGB or Grayscale will work).

STEP TWO: Go to the New dialog box (under the File menu) and create a new document that is 1 pixel wide by 4 pixels high. Choose the same mode as your open image (for example, if you want to add scan lines to an RGB image, choose RGB).

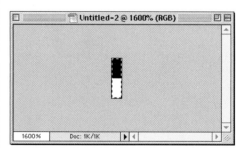

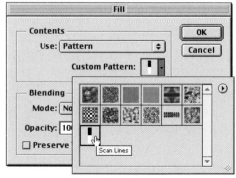

STEP THREE: Zoom in on this tiny document until it's easily seen (you might have to zoom in as much as 1200%). Set your foreground color to black, then take the Pencil tool and fill in the top half of your image with black (as shown above). Under the Select menu choose All, then go under the Edit menu and choose Define Pattern (this makes your black-and-white document a repeating pattern). A dialog box will appear where you can name your new pattern "Scan Lines."

STEP FOUR: Create a new layer in your original document (click on the New Layer icon at the bottom of the Layers palette). Under the Edit menu, choose Fill. In the Fill dialog box, choose Pattern from the Use pop-up menu, then click the downward-facing triangle next to the Custom Pattern sample to reveal the Custom Pattern Presets. At the end of the presets is the Scan Lines pattern you just saved. Click on it, then click OK to fill this layer with your black-and-white scan lines pattern.

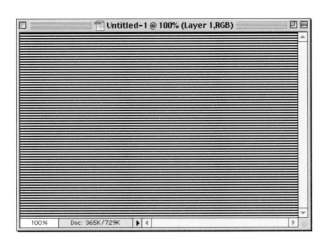

STEP FIVE: Your new layer is now filled with a black-and-white pattern (as shown above).

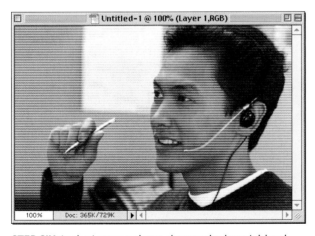

STEP SIX: In the Layers palette, change the layer's blend mode from Normal to Overlay. Lower the opacity so that the effect isn't too strong (in other words, adjust to taste) to complete the effect.

QUICK TIP

In Step Three, I mention that you might have to zoom in as much as 1200%. A quick trick for zooming in on your image is to press Command-+ (PC: Control-+). Each time you press this combination, Photoshop zooms in closer, so you just have to press it a few times and you're really zoomed in. To zoom back out, use the same modifier key, but instead of using the plus sign (for zooming in), use the minus sign.

Getting your image down to size

When you're dragging Photoshop layers between documents, have you noticed that if part of your layer extends outside the edge of your document window, Photoshop doesn't delete those areas? Yup, it's still there. For example, if you drag an image of a car over to a new document and position it so that only the front half is showing, the back half (even though you can't see it) is still there. If later you decide that you want to show the whole car, you can simply drag your car further into your image window and the parts hidden off screen will appear. That's good, right? Well, sometimes. Actually, it's only good if you think that, at some point, you might need those parts. Otherwise, you're eating up memory storing stuff that you don't need. Want to get rid of all that excess image data? Press Command-A (PC: Control-A) to Select All, then go under the Edit menu and choose Crop. Everything outside your image window gets cropped off, shrinking your file size in the process.

Automate this conversion

The process shown at the right is totally actionable (meaning you can write a Photoshop action that will do the entire conversion to Indexed, back to RGB, and back to Indexed color). I wrote this simple action right after I learned the trick, and our whole Web team uses it daily. To create your own action, open an RGB image, go to the Actions palette, choose New Action from the pop-down menu, name your action (I named mine "Index to RGB"), choose a Function key (F-key) to assign it to, then press the Record button. Follow the steps on the right, and when you are done, go to the Actions palette and click on the Stop button at the bottom of the palette (it's the first icon from the left) and you're done. Now, when you hit that F-key, you'll be putting the squeeze on your Web graphic file sizes.

Putting the Squeeze on GIF Images

This is a down and dirty little trick for squeezing more file size out of GIF images for the Web. The great thing about this trick is that, not only can you save up to 50% or more on file size, but all your colors are Web safe as well.

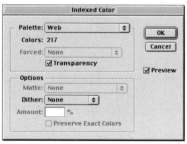

STEP ONE: Convert your RGB image to Indexed color by going under the Image menu, under Mode, and choosing Indexed Color. In our example in the Indexed Color dialog, Photoshop chose an Exact Palette using 31 colors. Change the Palette to Web, then click OK.

STEP TWO: When you choose the Web Palette, it uses a color table comprising the 217 colors which can be accurately displayed by Web browsers on both the Macintosh and Windows platforms.

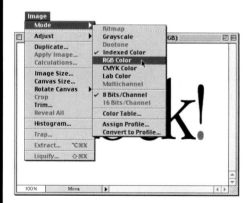

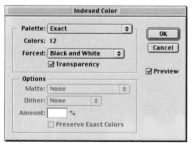

STEP THREE: Go under the Image menu, under Mode, and choose RGB Color again to convert your Web-safe image back into RGB mode. You won't see any changes or be prompted for any input—it just switches modes.

STEP FOUR: Go under the Image menu, under Mode, and choose Indexed Color again. You'll notice that the Palette has changed from Web to Exact. Now it only uses the exact number of Web-safe colors (in this case, just 12) that are needed to create this image, and this results in a significantly smaller Indexed Color image, because instead of using 31 colors, you're now using just 12.

Product Shot Backdrop Trick

This is a great trick for taking almost any textured background and transforming it into a studio backdrop for a portrait or product shot. Although the stock images in this book are from PhotoDisc (www.photodisc.com), this particular backdrop image is courtesy of Mark Hunt Backdrops (www.markhuntbackdrops.com).

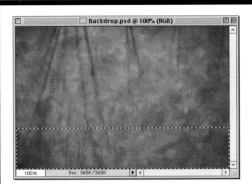

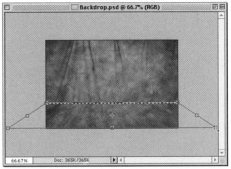

STEP ONE: Open a textured background image (it must have a texture for this technique to work). Press the letter "m" to switch to the Rectangular Marquee Tool, and select the bottom ¼ to ⅓ of your background (as shown above). Switch to the Zoom tool, hold the Option key (PC: Alt key), and click in your image to zoom out.

STEP TWO: Press Command-T (PC: Control-T) to bring up the Free Transform bounding box. Hold Shift-Option-Command (PC: Shift-Alt-Control), grab the lower right corner adjustment point, and drag outward to create a perspective effect (this creates your "floor"). Click Return (PC: Enter) to lock in your transformation.

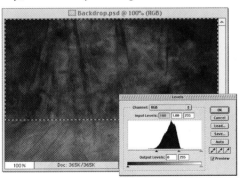

STEP THREE: Go under the Select menu and choose Inverse to change your selection to the top half of your background image. Go under the Select menu again and choose Feather. Enter 20 and click OK (Enter 50 for high-res images). Next, press Command-L (PC: Control-L) to bring up the Levels dialog. Drag the left shadow slider to the right to darken this upper half and to enhance the appearance of having depth. Deselect by pressing Command-D (PC: Control-D).

STEP FOUR: Open the image file that has an object you want to appear on your backdrop (I used a person sitting). Select the object and drag it into your backdrop document. Create a new layer and drag it below your object. In this example, I used the Elliptical Selection tool to drag a circle under the body, then I held the Shift key to add another circle under his feet. I then filled the circles with black, added a 3-pixel Gaussian Blur, and lowered the opacity to 70% to complete the effect.

Resizing multiple layers at one time

Here's a real timesaving tip that enables you to resize objects or text on multiple layers—all at the same time. Just link together the layers that you want to resize, then press Command-T (PC: Control-T) to bring up the Free Transform bounding box. Hold the Shift key (to constrain proportions), then grab any of the bounding box handles and drag. As you drag, all of the linked layers will resize at the same time.

How to switch to the Precise Cursor any time

When using Photoshop's Paint tools, your cursor displays the size of the brush you're using. But if you ever need a more precise cursor for really detailed work, you can temporarily switch to the "Precise Cursor," which looks like a cross hair. To do this, just press the Caps Lock key on your keyboard and your cursor (not just your Paint cursor, but any cursor) will switch to the cross hair cursor. To switch back, press the Caps Lock key again.

If you don't know about this Caps Lock trick, it can be quite confusing because you could be using the Type tool with the Caps Lock turned on to type some text in all caps, and when you switched to another tool, it would be the cross hair cursor, and you wouldn't know why. Freaky!

Adding Motion Step-By-Step

This is an old trick that we've used for years to make an object look like it's in motion. This is more often used for making an object look like it's coming out of another object, such as an arm moving from off the screen, an object coming out of a box, and so on.

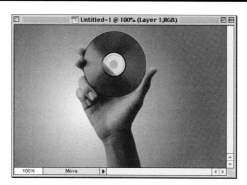

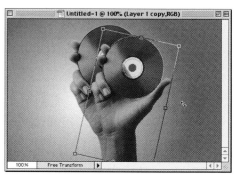

STEP ONE: Open the object that you want to give the effect of movement to, and put it on its own layer. Here we have an arm holding a CD-ROM with a gray-to-white gradient as the background. Make a copy of your object layer (in this case, the arm) by dragging it to the New Layer icon at the bottom of the Layers palette.

STEP TWO: Press Command-T (PC: Control-T) to bring up the Free Transform function. In the middle of the Free Transform bounding box is a center axis point. Drag it straight down until it touches the bottom center point. Move your cursor outside the bounding box and rotate your image to the right just a little. Now, hold the Shift key, grab a corner point, and drag inward to scale the image down a bit. Press Return (or Enter) to lock in your transformation.

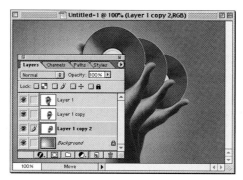

STEP THREE: Go to the Layers palette and drag this rotated layer behind your original arm layer. Now, make a copy of this rotated layer by dragging it to the New Layer icon at the bottom of the Layers palette. Repeat the same process you did in Step Two of bringing up Free Transform, dragging the center axis straight down, rotating the object, and making the object smaller.

STEP FOUR: Continue to repeat this process (rotating, making the copy smaller, etc.) until you have made three more copies, dragging each new layer behind the layer it was copied from. The objects in your image should resemble the image above.

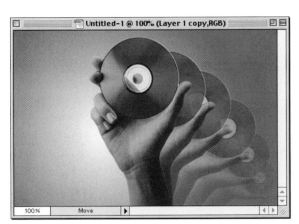

STEP FIVE: In the Layers palette, click on Layer 1 copy (should be the second layer from the top). Lower the opacity of this layer to 80%. Press Option-Left Bracket (PC: Alt-Left Bracket) to switch to the next layer below, then lower the opacity of this layer to 60%. Use that keyboard shortcut to continue moving down layer by layer, lowering the opacity by 20% each time. Make the last layer 10%.

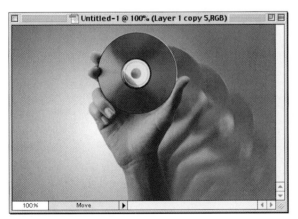

STEP SIX: In the Layers palette, click on Layer 1 copy again. Go under the Filter menu, under Blur, and choose Radial Blur. For Amount, use 8 pixels; for Blur Method, choose Spin; for Quality, choose Good; and click OK. Press Option-Left Bracket (PC: Alt-Left Bracket) to switch to the next layer below, then press Command-F (PC: Control-F) to run the same Radial Blur on this layer. Repeat this process for all the remaining layers to complete the effect.

QUICK TIP
In the adding motion example at left, we applied a Radial Blur to our layers to give the feeling of motion, but that particular filter doesn't work for every image. If the Radial Blur looks weird or out-of-place, try a Motion Blur instead. Just remember to move the angle of the blur in the direction your object should be moving.

You can still apply most transformations to editable Type layers

Many people don't realize that while you have an editable Type layer, you can still apply a number of transformations (such as Scale, Rotate, Skew, Flip Horizontal, and Flip Vertical), and your type will remain fully editable (meaning you can change the letters, tracking, leading, etc.). However, to apply Distort or Perspective transformations, you'll first have to Rasterize the Type layer first by going under the Layer menu, under Rasterize, and choosing Type.

Cropping tips

Here are some quick tips for getting the most out of Photoshop's Crop tool:

• To rotate the Cropping boundary, move your cursor outside the box and it will change to a two-headed arrow tool. Click-and-drag to rotate.

• To constrain your cropping to a perfect square, hold the Shift key as you drag the cropping box.

• If your cropping boundary snaps to the edge of your image window, hold the Control key (PC: Right-click), and you can resize the boundary without it snapping.

• To scale your cropping boundary from the center outward, hold the Option key (PC: Alt key) as you drag.

• To move the cropping boundary, click within the boundary and drag.

Instant Woodcut Effect

This is a quick effect that allows you to instantly transform a color RGB image into that drawn woodcut effect that's popping up everywhere. We see this effect on the Web quite often where a woodcut object is used as an icon, but the effect works just as well in print.

STEP ONE: Open the image that you want to turn into a woodcut, then double-click on the Background layer. When the dialog box appears, click OK and your Background layer will become a regular layer named Layer 0 (by default). Make a copy of this layer by dragging it to the New Layer icon at the bottom of the Layers palette.

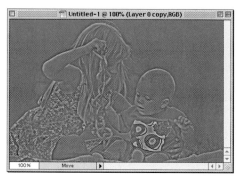

STEP TWO: Go under the Filter menu, under Other, and choose High Pass. Enter a value of 2.5 and click OK. Now, press Shift-Command-U (PC: Shift-Control-U) to desaturate your image (this removes all the color).

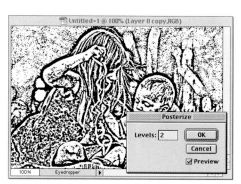

STEP THREE: Go under the Image menu, under Adjust, and choose Posterize. When the dialog box appears, enter a value of 2 and click OK.

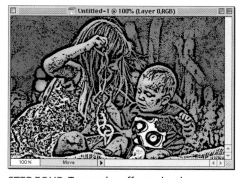

STEP FOUR: To see the effect take shape, change the layer blend mode (in the Layers palette pop-up menu) from Normal to Multiply. Next, in the Layers palette click on Layer 0 and lower the opacity of this layer to 60% to complete the effect. (You'll have to use your own judgement, but somewhere between 60% and 70% opacity usually looks about right.)

Quick Outer Glow Effect

This effect lets you instantly add a glow around an object or person. The effect works great on solid backgrounds, but it's equally effective on photographic backgrounds. I see this effect used everywhere, including print advertisements, media kits, brochures, billboards, posters and in Web design.

STEP ONE: Open a new document in RGB mode. Click on the Foreground color swatch to open the Color Picker. Choose your foreground color (in this example, I chose purple) and click OK. Press Option-Delete (PC: Alt-Backspace) to fill your background layer with purple.

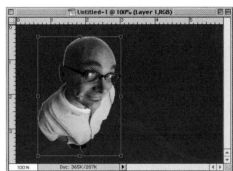

STEP TWO: Open an image of a person or object that you'd like to add a glow to. Drag the image into your background document. Press Command-T (PC: Control-T) to bring up Free Transform. Hold the Shift key and drag one of the corner adjustment points to scale (resize) the object proportionately to fit your background. Then press Return (PC: Enter).

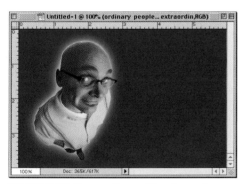

STEP THREE: Choose Outer Glow from the Layer Style pop-up menu at the bottom of the Layers palette (it's the little *f* icon). Click on the color swatch and change the color to white, then click OK. Now, change the Size to 30 pixels and click OK (feel free to experiment with the Size, Spread, and Opacity; there's no telling what kind of cool effects you'll come up with).

STEP FOUR: To add text, just press "t" to select the Type Tool, then type your message. Of course, the effect wouldn't be complete without adding a drop shadow to your Type layer. Choose Drop Shadow from the Layer Style pop-up menu at the bottom of the Layers palette (it's the little *f* icon). When the dialog box appears, click OK.

Where has the "Blur" Gone?

By now, you've probably noticed that Blur and Intensity have disappeared from some of the Layer Style dialog boxes (Inner Glow, Outer Glow, and Drop Shadow). But never fear; Adobe didn't remove these effects, they simply renamed them.

What used to control the amount of Blur is now controlled by Size, and what used to effect the Intensity is now called Spread.

These effects have also been enhanced. By changing the Spread (formerly Intensity), you can get a completely solid edge with just a small amount of blur (I'm sorry, Size). This is something that previously couldn't be accomplished in these dialog boxes.

The name change is a little weird, but hey, they could have changed the name to "Softening the edges of a predetermined selection in which the amount of said selection can be effected by the front-end user."

7

This chapter is actually much cooler than the name implies, it's just that I couldn't come up with a cooler sounding

Different Strokes
Paint & Brush Effects

name than Paint and Brush Effects, so don't hold that against the effects themselves— it's not their fault. I was afraid the name might scare some people away, because they might think "Oh, that's painting and working with brushes, and I can't paint, so I'll just skip over that and head on over to Advertising Effects." I don't think the Gary Coleman reference in the chapter head helped sell this chapter much either, but there's really some cool stuff in it, and you don't have to draw or paint anything. In fact, there's a trick in there for taking a photograph and making it look like you really can paint. It's called "The evil deceit trick." Not really, but I bet if it was, that's the first one you'd turn to. Yes you would. Oh come on, you act like I hardly know you.

Changing the mode of line art

If you open a line art scan (in Bitmap mode) in Photoshop, you'll have to convert it to a color mode before you can add color (that makes sense, right?). But Photoshop doesn't let you convert from Bitmap mode straight to RGB; you have to make an intermediate stop in Grayscale mode along the way. When you're in Bitmap mode, RGB mode is grayed out as a choice until you're in Grayscale mode. When you choose Grayscale (from the Mode menu), you are greeted with a dialog asking for Size Ratio. Leave the Size Ratio at 1 and click OK to convert your line art into Grayscale mode. Then, when you go under the Mode menu, RGB will be available as a mode choice.

Colorizing Line Art

Colorizing line art is really simple: start out by switching to RGB color mode, create selections inside your line art, and then colorize the selections on layers.

STEP ONE: Open your bitmap line art in Photoshop. The first step is to go under the Image menu, under Mode, and choose Grayscale. A dialog will appear for Size Ratio. Leave it set at 1 and click OK. Next, go under the Image menu again, under Mode, and choose RGB (after all, you have to be in a color mode to add color, right?).

STEP TWO: Press the letter "w" to switch to the Magic Wand tool. Click once in the white background area to select some of the white pixels in your image. Then go under the Select menu and choose Similar. Photoshop will then select all the other white pixels in your image.

STEP THREE: Go under the Select menu and choose Inverse to switch your selection from the background to the black lines of your line art image. Press Shift-Command-J (PC: Shift-Control-J) to put your selection on its own layer. Go under the Layer menu and choose Layer Properties. Rename this layer "Line Art" and click OK.

STEP FOUR: You should now have two layers—a white background layer and a Line Art layer which contains your image. Go to the Layers palette, switch to the Background layer, press Command-A (PC: Control-A) to select the entire background layer, and press Delete (PC: Backspace) to clear away any stray pixels that might have been missed when you moved the line art to its new layer.

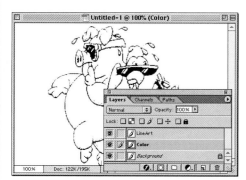

STEP FIVE: Deselect by pressing Command-D (PC: Control-D). We're now going to add our color on a separate layer, so create a new layer by clicking once on the New Layer icon at the bottom of the Layers palette. Go back to Layer Properties in the Layer menu and name this new layer "Color." From the bottom up, you should have the Background layer, the Color Layer, and the Line Art layer (as shown above).

STEP SIX: Next, choose a foreground color (in our example, we chose pink). In the Layers palette, click on the Line Art layer, then switch to the Magic Wand tool. Click once inside an area you want to colorize and the Magic Wand tool will select that area. In our example, we clicked in the main body of the pig. (Note: You can use any selection tool you'd like. If the Magic Wand doesn't work, try the Pen tool or the Lasso.)

STEP SEVEN: Click on the Color layer; you'll notice that your selection is still visible. Press Option-Delete (PC: Alt-Backspace) to fill your selection with the foreground color, then deselect by pressing Command-D (PC: Control-D). To colorize the rest of your line art image, repeat this process of (a) making a selection on the Line Art layer, (b) switching to the Color layer, and (c) filling your selection with your foreground color.

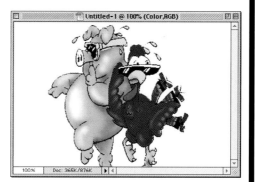

STEP EIGHT: The reason we keep the color on a separate layer is so we can keep the line art on a layer above it, giving the black lines strong definition. However, you may choose to hide (or even delete) the Line Art layer after you complete the colorization. The choice is yours.

Design tip

Filling your selections with a flat color can make your colorization look, well… flat. Instead, try filling your line art with a gradient that goes from a lighter color to a much darker shade of that same color. For example, set your foreground color to light pink and your background color to a very dark pink. Make your selection on the Line Art layer, click on the Color layer, switch to the Gradient tool by pressing the letter "g" (make sure your chosen gradient is Foreground to Background), then drag this gradient from left to right through your selection. This gives the illusion of a light source and adds interest to your image (as shown in the example at left). Note: Remember to drag your gradient in the same direction consistently so that your "shadows" will fall on the same side throughout your image (for example, always drag from left to right, top to bottom, and so on).

Paint tools have blend modes too

You're probably familiar with layer blend modes, where you change how a layer interacts with the layers beneath it. In Normal mode, it doesn't interact; it just covers whatever's beneath it. Well, Photoshop's paint tools have the same feature, and choosing any blend mode (other than Normal) allows your paint to interact with (be affected by) the colors in the image you paint on. These blend modes are accessed from the Options Bar when you have a paint tool selected.

Painting Away Color

This is a great way to put emphasis on a particular part of your image by using the Paintbrush tool to "paint away" colors, leaving the appearance of grayscale everywhere you paint, even though your image stays in RGB mode (if it didn't, you'd lose all the color).

STEP ONE: Open a color RGB image.

STEP TWO: Click on the Paintbrush tool and in the Options Bar, switch the Paintbrush blend Mode from Normal to Color.

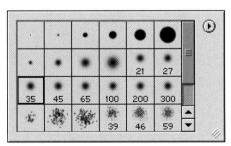

STEP THREE: In the Options Bar, choose a soft-edged, medium-sized brush from the Brushes flyout menu.

STEP FOUR: Start painting. As you paint, the color will disappear, leaving just grayscale in its wake.

Turning a Logo into a Brush

Tired of importing your client's logo into every little project you do for them? Well, here's a trick for turning their logo into a brush, so you can paint the logo (in black-and-white or grayscale) and choose it directly from the Brushes flyout menu in the Options Bar.

How to delete extra brushes

If you created a brush (or a number of brushes) that you don't want to appear in your Brushes flyout menu, all you have to do is hold the Command key (PC: Control key) and your cursor will change to an icon of a pair of scissors. Click once with the scissors on the brush that you want to delete and it's gone. If you decide that you want all of your new brushes deleted and that you want to return to the original factory default brushes, choose Reset Brushes from the Brushes flyout menu's pop-down menu.

STEP ONE: Open a new grayscale document. Open the document that contains your client's logo, then drag-and-drop the logo into the grayscale document. (Note: You can use a RGB document to create your brush, but the brush will be in grayscale.)

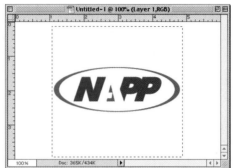

STEP TWO: Press the letter "m" to switch to the Rectangular Marquee tool, hold the Shift key, and draw a square selection around the logo.

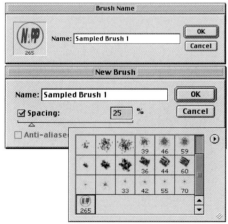

STEP THREE: Go under the Edit menu and choose Define Brush. Name your brush and click Ok. When the New Brush dialog pops up, just click OK. As soon as you do, that logo is added as a new brush (with a tiny thumbnail) at the bottom of your Brushes menu.

STEP FOUR: To use the brush, press the letter "b" to switch to the Paintbrush tool, then choose the new "logo" brush in the Brushes flyout menu. Click once for the logo to appear once. Click and drag for multiple logos.

Creating new brushes

You can create a new brush by choosing New Brush from the Brushes flyout menu's pop-down menu, but there's a quicker way—just click your cursor once in any open space within the Brushes palette and the New Brush dialog box will appear.

Adding Pre-made "Glints" to Your Image

If you want to add tiny sparkles (I call them "glints") to your image, it's easy because there's a custom glint brush already loaded on your hard drive. The only drawback of this pre-made glint is that it only works on low-res images, because the preset size of the glint isn't large enough to be seen well on high-res images.

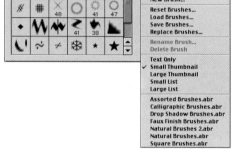

STEP ONE: Open a color RGB image. Set white as your foreground color by pressing the letter "d," then the letter "x." Press the letter "j" to switch to the Airbrush tool. In the Options Bar, lower the Pressure amount to 20% (the 50% default pressure setting seems a bit too high to give you enough control, so I lower it to 15% or 20%).

STEP TWO: In the Options Bar, click on the downward-facing triangle to make the Brushes flyout menu visible. In the flyout menu's pop-down menu, choose Assorted Brushes.abr. This loads an assortment of brushes that were predesigned by Adobe.

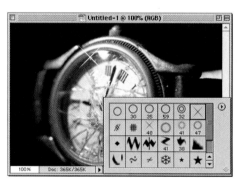

STEP THREE: Choose the large glint brush (the one that looks like an "x" selected in the Brushes flyout menu above), then click-and-hold for just a moment on a spot where you want to add a glint. The longer you hold the mouse button down, the more white paint the glint brush will spray out.

STEP FOUR: To give your glints a more realistic look, you can add a little glow to the center by switching to a medium-sized, soft-edged brush and clicking and holding for just a moment in the center of the glints you created earlier.

Creating Your Own Custom "Glint" Brush

The "glint" we loaded into Photoshop's Brushes flyout menu in the trick on the previous page only works on low-res images, so here's how to create your own custom glint that you can use on high-res (300-ppi and higher) images.

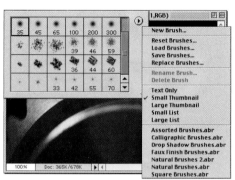

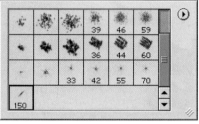

STEP ONE: Open a color RGB image that you want to apply glints to. Set white as your foreground color by pressing the letter "d," then pressing the letter "x." Click on one of Photoshop's paint tools. In the Options Bar, click on the downward-facing triangle to make the Brushes flyout menu visible. In the flyout menu's pop-down menu, choose New Brush.

STEP TWO: If you're creating this brush to use with high-res, 300-ppi images, make the diameter of your brush pretty large (probably at least 200 pixels). Set the Angle to 45° and the Roundness to 0 (zero), then click OK. This adds your new brush to the bottom of your Brushes menu.

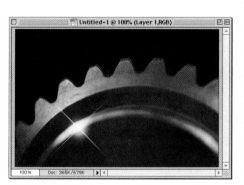

STEP THREE: Create another new brush using the same Diameter and Roundness, but this time set your Angle to -45° (minus 45 degrees). Click-and-hold this new brush for just a moment over an area where you want your glint to appear. Now, switch to the first glint brush you created earlier, and click-and-hold this brush on the center of the first glint you painted.

STEP FOUR: To give your glints a more realistic look, you can add a little glow to their center by switching to a large-sized, soft-edged brush (65 pixels should do), and clicking and holding for just a moment in the center of the glints you painted earlier.

Saving your brushes

Do you have to save any custom brushes you create? Any brush you create is automatically saved. The next time you launch Photoshop, that brush will automatically appear in the same position in your Brushes menu. However, if you reset your brushes to their factory defaults (by choosing Reset Brushes from the Brushes menu's pop-down menu), that brush will be gone forever. If that's a concern to you, make sure you save your new set of brushes by going under the Brushes flyout menu's pop-down menu and choosing Save Brushes. What I do is delete all the other brushes by holding the Command key (PC: Control key) and clicking once on them. Then, when I'm down to just the one brush I created, I choose Save Brushes from the Brushes Options Bar flyout menu and I name that brush with a name I'll remember (like Acme Co. logo), and I save it in the Brushes folder, inside the Preset folder, inside my Photoshop folder. Whew!

When to use Colorize

The only time you really need to check (turn on) the Colorize box in the Hue/Saturation dialog is when the image or selected area you're working on doesn't already contain color. Turning this check box on adds color to the image. If your image is already in color, and you want to change the color, you don't need to click Colorize, just move the Hue slider to pick a new color.

Colorizing Black & White Images (Method #1)

This is a technique for colorizing grayscale images and is great for getting that hand-tinted effect. This particular version uses Photoshop's Hue/Saturation command to add color to selected areas.

STEP ONE: Open a grayscale image that you want to colorize. In order to colorize a grayscale image, you have to be in a color mode, so go under the image menu, under Mode, and choose RGB to put your image into a color mode.

STEP TWO: Using one of Photoshop's selection tools, select the first area that you'd like to colorize (in this example, I used the Lasso tool to select an area).

STEP THREE: Go under the Image menu, under Adjust, and choose Hue/Saturation, or press Command-U (PC: Control-U). When the dialog box appears, check the Colorize box. Now you can move the Hue slider to choose the color you'd like. If the color seems too intense, lower the Saturation slider.

STEP FOUR: Continue this process of selecting areas, going to Hue/Saturation, checking the Colorize box, and moving the Hue slider to add color to your image.

Colorizing Black & White Images (Method #2)

This is an alternate method for colorizing grayscale images that uses the Paintbrush tool instead of making selections and using Hue/Saturation to bring in the color. Many people prefer this method because painting color feels more natural (as opposed to the other method of bringing it in with a slider).

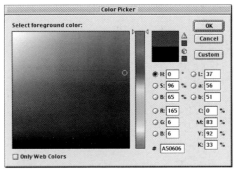

STEP ONE: Open a grayscale image that you want to colorize. In order to colorize a grayscale image, you have to be in a color mode, so go under the Image menu, under Mode, and choose RGB to put you image into a color mode.

STEP TWO: Set your foreground color to a color you want to paint in your image (in this example, I set my foreground color to red).

STEP THREE: Click on the Paintbrush tool to bring up its options in the Options Bar, and change the blend Mode to Color. Begin painting on your image. You'll notice that it doesn't paint over your image; it paints the color into your image, leaving the detail below the area in which you're painting.

STEP FOUR: Continue choosing colors and painting with the Paintbrush tool set to Color mode to complete colorizing the image.

Getting realistic colors

One trick that you can use to get more realistic colors for critical areas, like flesh tones, grass, hair, and sky, is to open a full-color image at the same time that you're trying to colorize your grayscale image. That way, when you're in the Color Picker, you can move your cursor outside the dialog to sample real colors right from the color image, and then return to your image and paint with those colors.

Accessing the Art History Brush

To get the Art History Brush, press Shift-Y. As you press Shift-Y, you'll see that in the Tool palette you're toggling between the History Brush (whose icon has an arrow in a semicircle around a paintbrush) and the Art History Brush (whose icon takes that arrow and makes it look, well… artsy).

Turning Photos into Paintings

Adobe introduced a feature back in version 5.5 called the Art History Brush that lets you turn photographs into paintings. It hasn't caught on in a big way, because if you just grab a brush and start painting, it looks nothing like a painting (nothing you could sell anyway). Here's how to make it work for you.

STEP ONE: Open the photograph that you want to give the appearance of a traditional painting style.

STEP TWO: Click-and-hold on the History Brush (in the Tool palette, it's the brush directly below the Paintbrush), and the Art History Brush will "fly out." Choose Art History Brush.

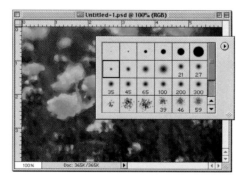

STEP THREE: In the Options Bar, click directly on the Art History Brush's icon (the first icon from the left) and in the pop-up menu, choose Reset Tool. From the Brushes flyout menu, choose the smallest soft-edged brush in the palette (if you're trying this on a high-res, 300-ppi image, you can use a slightly larger brush, but only slightly). Paint over the entire image.

STEP FOUR: If the background isn't very detailed, you can switch to the next larger brush to save time painting in the background. After you paint in the image, go under the Filter menu, under Artistic, and choose Dry Brush. Set your Brush Size to 2, Brush Detail to 8, Texture to 1, and click OK to add a dry brush effect to your image.

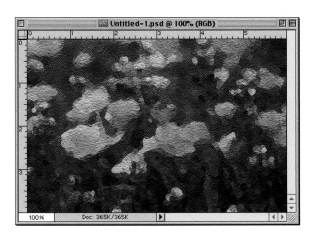

STEP FIVE: Go under the Filter menu, under Texture, and choose Texturizer. Choose Sandstone from the pop-up menu. Leave the scaling at 100%, Relief at 4, Direction at Top, and click OK.

STEP SIX: Switch back to the regular History Brush, and in the Options Bar, lower the opacity to 50%. Paint over the areas of the image that need some detail brought back in to complete the effect. (Note: The original photo will be painted back in as you paint, so be careful not to bring back too much detail, or it will start looking like a photograph again.)

QUICK TIP
You can change brush sizes without even having the Brushes flyout menu open. If you press the Left Bracket key, it decreases the size of the brush. If you press the Right Bracket key, it increases the size of the brush. If you hold either key down, it moves up or down very rapidly.

Another way to delete brushes

Another way to delete a brush is to Control-click (PC: Right-click) on it in the Brushes flyout menu and a contextual menu will pop up where you can choose Delete Brush from the menu.

If you're lucky enough to get to design advertising, Photoshop can really be a blast. One reason is

How to Succeed in Photoshop without Really Trying

Advertising Effects

the fact that Photoshop source material actually comes to you, 'most every day (accept Sundays, holidays, or if it's raining real hard). Your friendly U.S. Postal carrier delivers direct mail pieces, catalogs, and magazines laden with Photoshop effects right to your door. You never run out of new ideas, because you're blasted with Photoshop techniques in ads thousands of times a day. Billboards, TV ads, newspaper ads—it's Photoshop heaven. Think about it—you get to play around in Photoshop all day, then you get to send someone a bill for your time. It's almost like a scam. I used to design advertising myself, and I can tell you, it's like stealing. A drop shadow here, a glow effect there, and it's raining Ben Franklins. Here are some ideas to help them sprinkle on you. (Cha-ching!)

Saving selections for later use

If you have a selection that you think you can use later in the same project, you can save and store that selection until you need it. Here's how: While your selection is active, go under the Select menu and choose Save Selection. When the dialog box appears, just click OK. Your selection is now saved. If you want to get that selection back on screen at any time, go under the Select menu, but this time choose Load Selection. When the dialog box appears, chose your saved selection (named Alpha 1) from the pop-up menu, and click OK. Your saved selection will then appear within your image.

Creating 3D Packaging

You can use Photoshop's built-in tools to turn a flat image into an object with depth (such as product packaging or a video box). We'll be adding perspective to the image using Photoshop's transformation tool, but you'll also add shading and highlights to help "sell" the effect that your image has depth.

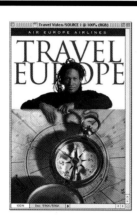

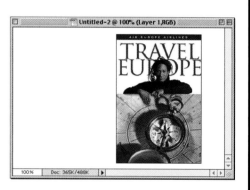

STEP ONE: Open the image that you want to use as the cover of your product box. Press Command-A (PC: Control-A) to select the entire image, then press Shift-Command-J (PC: Shift-Control-J) to put your cover shot on its own layer. Go under the Layer menu, choose Layer Properties, and rename this layer "Front."

STEP TWO: Go under the Image menu and choose Canvas Size. Enter a value that is a few inches longer and a few inches wider than your current image. This gives some needed work area around the image (as shown above). Press the letter "v" to choose the Move tool, and drag your layer named Front to the right side of the screen.

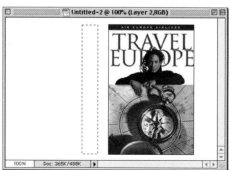

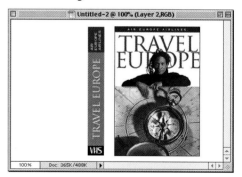

STEP THREE: To build the spine, create a new layer by clicking on the New Layer icon at the bottom of the Layers palette. Go under the Layer menu, choose Layer Properties, and name this new layer "Spine." Using the Marquee tool, draw a rectangular selection to the left of your box front. Choose a foreground color that will complement the colors in your box front.

STEP FOUR: Fill this selection by pressing Option-Delete (PC: Alt-Delete). I recommend adding some text to the spine to help sell the 3-dimensional effect, so use the Type tool to create your type, then go under the Layer menu, under Rasterize, and choose Type. Press Command-E (PC: Control-E) to merge this text layer with the Spine layer beneath it.

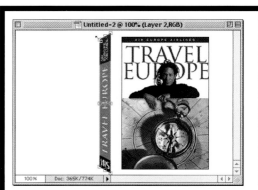

STEP FIVE: On the Spine layer, press Command-T (PC: Control-T) to bring up Free Transform. Hold Shift-Option-Command (PC: Shift-Alt-Control), then click-and-drag the top right handle of the bounding box straight upward about 1/2" above the box front (you'll see the spine stretch as you do this). Keep holding the same keys and grab the lower-left handle and drag it upward about the same amount. Release the keys, grab the left middle handle, and drag inward about the same amount to remove the distortion caused by the stretching. Press Return (PC: Enter) when it looks like the spine shown above.

STEP SIX: Switch to the Front layer. Press Command-T (PC: Control-T) again and do the same perspective transformations to the box front: Hold Shift-Option-Command (PC: Shift-Alt-Control), but this time, we're going to grab the upper-left handle and drag straight upward until it matches the height of the spine. Keep holding the same keys, grab the lower-right handle, and drag upward about the same amount. Release the keys and grab the middle handle on the right side and drag inward about 1". Press Return (PC: Enter) when it looks like the image shown above.

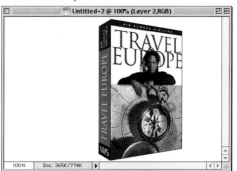

STEP SEVEN: Switch to the Spine layer. Press the letter "v" to get the Move tool and drag the spine to the right until it touches the left edge of the box. Press Command-L (PC: Control-L) to bring up Levels. Move the right bottom Output Levels slider to the left a bit to darken the spine (as shown above), then click OK. Next, switch to the Front layer and press the letter "j" to get the Airbrush tool. In the Options Bar, lower the pressure to 20%.

STEP EIGHT: Choose a small, hard-edged brush, and switch your foreground color to white. Hold the Shift key and click at the top corner between the box front and the spine and drag down the edge to the bottom to add a highlight to the front edge. Switch to the Background layer. Change the foreground color to black by pressing the letter "d" and choose a very large, soft brush. You still have the Airbrush tool, so paint a soft drop shadow below the box with one smooth stroke. That's it!

Getting rid of the checkerboard pattern

This should really be called "How to get rid of that annoying checkerboard pattern." I'm talking about the gray-and-white pattern that appears behind transparent layers to let you know which parts of the layer are transparent. In most cases, you don't need this pattern, because you already have something that lets you see what's transparent on a layer—they're called your eyes. Because of that, I constantly have people asking me how to turn it off, so I thought I'd better include this information PC: You go under the Edit menu, under Preferences, and choose Transparency & Gamut. Under Transparency Settings, choose None for Grid Size, click OK, and the pattern will be gone.

Turning part of a path into a selection

After you have part of a path selected using the Direct Selection tool, you can turn it into a selection by going to the Paths palette and choosing Make Selection from the palette's pop-down menu. The advantage of using this method is that you can add feathering, (among other options) in the Make Selection dialog box. The disadvantage is that, if you don't want feathering or some of the other path's options, you waste time in a dialog box you don't need.

Another method is to click on the Loads Path as a Selection icon at the bottom of the Paths palette. It's the third icon from the left that looks like a circle of dots. Be careful, though, because if you used the Make Selection dialog previously and added feathering, that amount of feathering that you used will be added when you click on the icon at the bottom of the palette. To avoid this, go back to the Make Selection dialog and change the feathering to 0 (zero).

Giving Depth to an Adobe Illustrator EPS Logo

Photoshop is often used to enhance Adobe Illustrator artwork. In this effect, I've imported the logo for the National Association of Photoshop Professionals (designed by Felix Nelson) into Photoshop. Here's how Felix added shadows, depth, and reflections using Photoshop's own filters and tools.

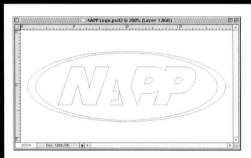

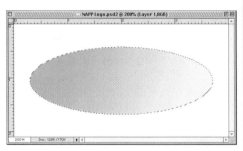

STEP ONE: If you want to follow along using the NAPP logo, you can download the EPS file from www.downanddirtytricks.com. Once you've done that, go to the Paths palette and click on Path 1 to view the paths imported from Adobe Illustrator. Press Shift-A to switch to the Direct Selection tool (the hollow arrow). Click once on the inner oval to select it, then load it as a selection by clicking on the Loads Path as a Selection icon (third icon from the left) at the bottom of the Paths palette.

STEP TWO: In the Paths palette, click in the gray area below Path 1 to deselect your path. In the Layers palette, create a new blank layer. Click on the Foreground color swatch, click the Custom button, and select Pantone 5575. Click on the Background color swatch, and make 6% black your background color. Click on the Gradient tool. In the Options Bar, make sure the selected gradient is Foreground to Background. Drag the Gradient tool from the upper-left side of the oval to the lower right.

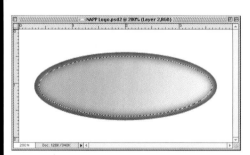

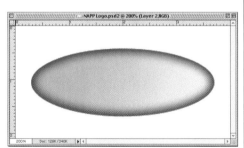

STEP THREE: Create another new layer by clicking on the New Layer icon at the bottom of the Layers palette. Click on the Foreground color swatch and select Pantone 5545. Press Option-Delete (PC: Alt-Backspace) to fill your oval with green. Go under the Select menu, under Modify, and choose Contract. Type in 5 pixels and click OK. Go to the Select menu and choose Feather. Type in 5 pixels, press OK, then press Delete (PC: Backspace).

STEP FOUR: Deselect by pressing Command-D (PC: Control-D), then press Command-E (PC: Control-E) to merge the two layers. Hold the Command key (PC: Control key), and in the Layers palette, click once on Layer 1 to select the oval. Go under the Select menu, under Modify, and choose Contract. When the dialog box appears, type in 5 pixels and press OK. Press Command-J (PC: Control-J) to copy your selection onto its own layer.

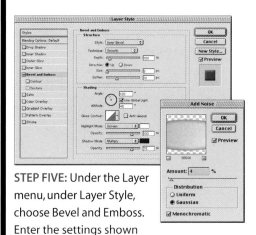

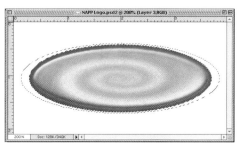

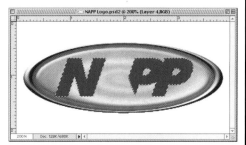

STEP FIVE: Under the Layer menu, under Layer Style, choose Bevel and Emboss. Enter the settings shown above and press OK. Hold the Command key (PC: Control key), and in the Layers palette, click on Layer 1 to put a selection around the oval. Go to the Filter menu, under Noise, and choose Add Noise. Enter the settings shown above and press OK. Go under the Filter menu, under Distort, and choose Twirl. Enter 999 for Angle and click OK.

STEP SIX: Create a new layer by clicking on the New Layer icon at the bottom of the Layers palette. Go to the Paths Palette and click on Path 1. Press Shift-A to switch to the Direct Selection tool. Holding the Shift key, click on both the inner and outer ovals of Path 1. Convert these paths into a selection by clicking on the Loads Path as a Selection icon at the bottom of the Paths palette. In the Paths palette, click just below Path 1 to deselect the path (but your selection will remain active).

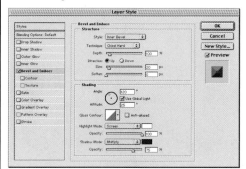

STEP SEVEN: Set your foreground color to 40% black, then press Option-Delete (PC: Alt-Backspace) to fill your selection with 40% black. Go under the Layer menu, under Layer Style, and choose Bevel and Emboss. Enter the settings shown above and click OK. Press the letter "d" to reset your foreground color to black. Go under the Edit menu and choose Stroke. Enter 1 for pixel width, Center for Location, 50% for Opacity, and press OK.

STEP EIGHT: Create a new layer. Set the foreground color to Pantone 2665 and the background color to Pantone 392. Go to the Paths palette and click on Path 1. Using the Direct Selection tool, click on the letter N in the oval, then hold the Shift key and click on both P's (include the inside of the P's). Turn them into a selection by clicking on the Loads Path as a Selection icon at the bottom of the Paths palette. Press Option-Delete (PC: Alt-Backspace) to fill these letters with the color Pantone 2665.

Quick access to the Direct Selection tool

When you're using the Pen tool, you adjust points and paths using the Direct Selection tool (which looks like a white hollow arrow). You can temporarily switch to this tool any time you're working with the Pen tool by holding the Command key (PC: Control key), and your current Pen tool will become the Direct Selection arrow. When you're done, release the Command key (PC: Control key), and you'll jump back to the last Pen tool you were using.

Rotating through the Pens

In Photoshop 6.0, you can only toggle between two of the Pen tools found in the Tool palette: the regular Pen tool and the Freeform Pen tool. To toggle between these two, press Shift-P.

However, when a path is selected, you can actually access other pens that don't even have keyboard shortcuts. For example, if you have an active path, and you move the Pen tool over a line segment—look at your cursor—it changes to the Add Anchor Point tool. Then, move the Pen tool over an anchor point and it changes into the Delete Anchor Point tool.

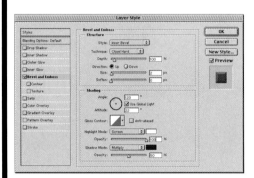

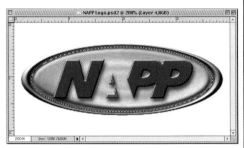

STEP NINE: Using the Direct Selection tool, click on the partial A from Path 1. Click the Loads Path as a Selection icon at the bottom of the Paths palette to turn it into a selection. Press the letter "x," and then press Option-Delete (PC: Alt-Backspace) to fill the A with Pantone 392. Deselect the path by clicking in the gray area of the Paths palette, then deselect your selection by pressing Command-D (PC: Control-D). Go under the Layer menu, under Layer Style, and choose Bevel and Emboss. Enter the settings shown above and click OK.

STEP TEN: Go under the Layer menu, under Layer Style, and choose Drop Shadow. Lower the opacity to 50% and click OK. Hold the Command key (PC: Control key) and in the Layers palette, click on Layer 1 to put a selection around the oval. Go under the Select menu, under Modify, and choose Contract. When the dialog box appears, type in 2 pixels, and press OK. For the next step, you'll need the Polygonal Lasso tool. Click-and-hold on the Lasso icon in the Toolbox to get the flyout menu for the Polygonal Lasso.

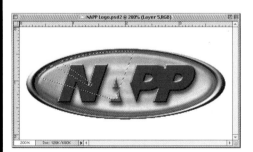

STEP ELEVEN: Using the Polygonal Lasso tool, hold down the Option key (PC: Alt key) to modify the oval selection, deleting areas of the oval until your selection looks something like the capture above. Press the letter "d," then "x" to set the foreground color to white. Click on the Gradient tool, and in the Options Bar, click on the down-facing arrow to display the Gradient Picker and choose Foreground to Transparent as the current gradient.

STEP TWELVE: Create a new layer by clicking on the New Layer icon. Drag the Gradient tool from the upper left to the lower right of the selection. Deselect by pressing Command-D (PC: Control-D). Press the letter "e" for the Eraser tool. Choose a very large, soft-edged brush. Erase a little bit just on the right side of your reflection to soften the edges. Finally, in the Layers palette, lower the opacity to 90% to complete the effect.

SI Pop-up Effect

This effect is inspired by *Sports Illustrated* magazine. It's a technique for focusing attention on one object in a background image. Basically, you select an object from the background, put that object on its own layer, lighten the background layer, and drop shadow the object to add depth and focus.

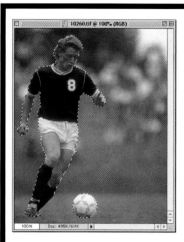

STEP ONE: Open a background image that has an element in it that you want to stand out. In this example, I wanted the soccer player to stand out, so I used the Magnetic Lasso tool to draw a selection around him.

STEP TWO: Press Command-J (PC: Control-J) to take your selection and copy it onto its own layer. Return to the Background layer by clicking once on it in the Layers palette.

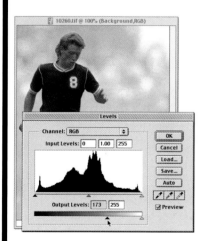

STEP THREE: Press Command-L (PC: Control-L) to bring up the Levels dialog box. When it appears, drag the lower left Output Levels triangle to the right to lighten the background. Drag to at least 140; move further to lighten even more. Click OK.

STEP FOUR: To help the object stand off the background, add a drop shadow. First, click on Layer 1 in the Layers palette, then go under the Layers menu, under Layer Style, and choose Drop Shadow. Click OK to complete the effect.

Jump to the Background layer

To jump instantly to the Background layer in your Layers palette, press Shift-Option-Left Bracket (PC: Shift-Alt-Left Bracket). To jump to the top layer in your layers stack, press Shift-Option-Right Bracket (PC: Shift-Alt-Right Bracket).

You can also jump to the Background layer from within your image itself when your using the Move tool by holding the Command key (PC: Control key) and clicking on any part of the Background layer in your image.

Quick Mask preferences

When you enter Quick Mask mode, as in the project shown at the right (by making a selection and pressing the letter "q"), the color red can display what's either masked or what's selected. By default, the color red shows the masked area. For some odd reason, I prefer having red show what's selected, so if what you see on your screen in Quick Mask is the opposite of what's shown in this effect while in Quick Mask mode, all you have to do is change a simple preference setting. To find the Quick Mask preferences, double-click on the Quick Mask icon (located in the Tool palette, directly below the Foreground and Background color swatches).

Backlit Backgrounds

I originally saw this effect used in a print ad displayed in the *Absolut Book*, which chronicles the history and artwork of the brilliant Absolut Vodka advertising campaign. It's a two-part effect: building the studio background and adding effects to your product shot to make it look like a studio shot.

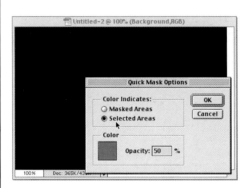

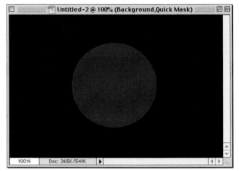

STEP ONE: Open a new document in RGB mode, and fill the background with black by pressing the letter "d" then Option-Delete (PC: Alt-Backspace). Double-click on the Quick Mask icon (right below the Foreground color swatch) to bring up its options and to enter Quick Mask mode. In the dialog, choose Selected Areas for Color Indicates. Click OK.

STEP TWO: Draw a circle in the center of the image using the Elliptical Marquee tool. Fill this circular selection by pressing Option-Delete (PC: Alt-Backspace). Your selection will appear in red to indicate your selected area.

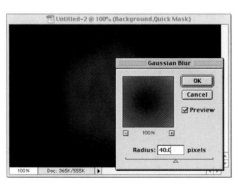

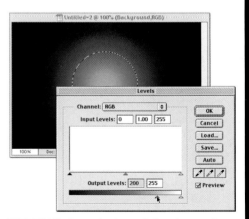

STEP THREE: Next, deselect by pressing Command-D (PC: Control-D). Go under the Filter menu, under Blur, and choose Gaussian Blur. Enter a high value (like 30 or 40) and click OK.

STEP FOUR: Press the letter "q" again to exit Quick Mask mode. Go under the Image menu, under Adjust, and choose Levels. When the dialog box appears, drag the lower left Output Levels triangle to the right to around 200, and a soft spotlight effect will appear on your black background. Click OK. Press Command-D (PC: Control-D) to deselect.

CONTINUED

Nudging layers

You can nudge layers around pixel-by-pixel by switching to the Move tool (press the letter "v") then using the Arrow keys on your keyboard to nudge (slowly move) your layer either up, down, left or right.

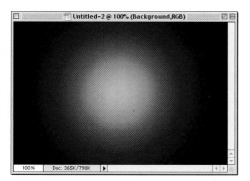

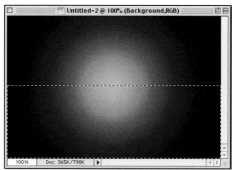

STEP FIVE: Press Command-U (PC: Control-U) for Hue/Saturation. Check the Colorize box in the lower right-hand corner. Move the Hue slider to the right until the edges of your spotlight become green (around 115). You can also lower the Saturation slider if your glow color looks a bit too intense.

STEP SIX: Switch to the Rectangular Marquee tool by pressing Shift-M. Use this tool to select the bottom half of your background (as shown above).

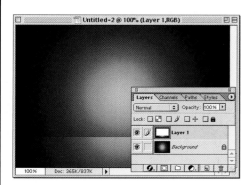

STEP SEVEN: Press Command-J (PC: Control-J) to put a copy of your selection up on its own layer. Press the letter "v" to switch to the Move tool and drag this new layer straight down until about only half of it is visible (as shown above).

STEP EIGHT: Open your object image (in this case, a trophy cup), press the letter "v" to switch to the Move tool, then drag this object onto your spotlight document. Position it in the middle of your bottommost spotlight. Next, make a copy of your object layer by dragging it to the New Layer icon.

Escape that dialog box!

Almost anytime you're in a dialog box in Photoshop and want to get out of there fast, you can press the Escape key, and the box will disappear with no changes made (the same as pressing the Cancel button in the dialog box).

STEP NINE: Press Command-T (PC: Control-T) to bring up Free Transform. Hold the Control key (PC: Right-click) then click-and-hold inside the Free Transform bounding box to bring up a contextual menu. Choose Rotate 180°. Control-click (PC: Right-click) again, but this time choose Flip Horizontal, then press Return (or Enter).

STEP TEN: With the Move tool, drag this copy of your object down just below the original object to where they're just overlapping (as shown above). Lower the opacity of the copy to around 40%, then in the Layers palette, drag this copy layer down below Layer 2 (your original object layer). Bring up the Levels dialog box again by pressing Command-L (PC: Control-L).

STEP ELEVEN: This time, drag the lower-right Output Levels slider to the left until you reach around 100 (or less) to darken the reflection, and click OK.

STEP TWELVE: Go under the Filter menu, under Blur, and choose Motion Blur. Enter an Angle of -90° and a Distance of 20. Click OK to complete the effect.

Magnifying Glass Trick

It's amazing how many times I've seen this particular Photoshop effect in ads lately. In this effect, we select and enlarge part of the background, copy it into memory, and then paste it into the circle of a magnifying glass. This makes it look like the magnifying glass is really magnifying what's beneath it.

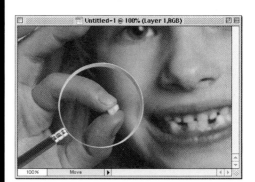

STEP ONE: Open your background image. Open an image of a magnifying glass, and using the Move tool, drag the magnifying glass into your background image (it will appear on its own layer). Position the magnifying glass over the part of the image you want to magnify.

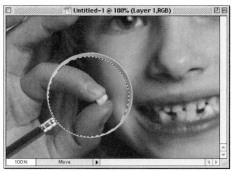

STEP TWO: Press the letter "w" to switch to the Magic Wand tool. Click once inside the round glass area to select it. In the Layers palette, click on the Background layer, then press Command-J (PC: Control-J) to put your selection on its own layer. Press Command-T (PC: Control-T) to bring up the Free Transform function.

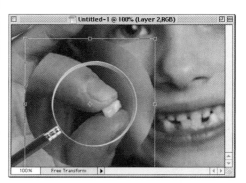

STEP THREE: When the bounding box appears, hold the Shift key, click on a corner, and drag outward until it gives you the amount of magnification you want. You can reposition the image as you like by clicking and dragging within the bounding box. When it looks right, press Return (PC: Enter). Hold the Command key (PC: Control key), and in the Layers palette, click on Layer 2 to select it. Then press Command-X (PC: Control-X) to cut your selection and save it into memory.

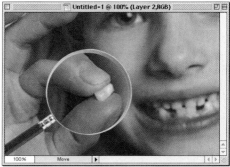

STEP FOUR: Delete your current layer by dragging it to the trash can at the bottom of the Layers palette. Click on Layer 1. Switch to the Magic Wand tool by pressing the letter "w." Click once inside the round glass area of your magnifying glass to select that area. Go under the Edit menu and choose Paste Into. Your enlarged image will now appear within your magnifying glass. You can switch to the Move tool (by pressing the letter "v") to reposition this enlarged piece to complete the effect.

Quickly setting the Magic Wand tolerance

When you use the Magic Wand tool, the amount that it selects is determined by the Tolerance setting in the Magic Wand's Options Bar. The higher the number, the more pixels out it selects. Here's a tip for quickly changing the Tolerance setting: Press the letter "w" to switch to the Magic Wand, then press the Return key (PC: Enter key). This highlights the Tolerance field so that you can type in your desired amount. This is a very fast way to change the Tolerance setting. The whole thing takes about two seconds.

Duplicating is faster than copying and pasting

I use the Option-Command-drag (PC: Alt-Control-drag) to make copies of objects because it's so much faster than copying and pasting. Try it for yourself: select an object, go under the Edit menu, and choose Copy, then choose Paste (or use the keyboard shortcuts for Copy and Paste). Now, select an object and use the Option-Command-drag (PC: Alt-Control-drag) method and you'll notice that your copy appears immediately. No delay whatsoever; it happens in real time. Another benefit is that if you have something saved in your clipboard memory, using the drag-copy method leaves that clipboard intact.

Building a Video Wall

This is how to take one monitor (or TV screen) and create an entire video wall. You start by taking a screen, duplicating and stacking it, and pasting one single huge image into a selection of each TV screen. Then you give the wall a sense of size by using Free Transform's Perspective effect and adding a reference image.

STEP ONE: Open a new document and fill the background with black by pressing the letter "d," and then Option-Delete (PC: Alt-Backspace). Open an image of a TV or computer monitor (in this case, we used a monitor from PhotoDisc's Object Series #15) and drag that image into your new document. Then, in the Layers palette, go to the Background layer and click on the Eye icon in the first column to hide your black background.

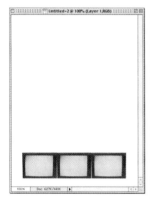

STEP TWO: Hold the Command key (PC: Control key), and in the Layers palette, click on Layer 1 (your monitor layer) to select the monitor. Next, hold Shift-Option-Command (PC: Shift-Alt-Control) and drag to your right to create a copy of your monitor. Drag it until the left edge of your monitor touches the right edge of the original monitor. Release the mouse button. While holding the same keys, repeat the drag to create a third image. Deselect by pressing Command-D (PC: Control-D).

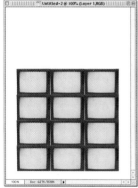

STEP THREE: Hold the Command key (PC: Control key), and in the Layers palette, click on Layer 1 (your monitor layer) to put a selection around the three monitors. Hold Shift-Option-Command (PC: Shift-Alt-Control) and drag upward to create a copy of your monitors. Repeat this process until you have a stack of monitors four rows high, resembling a video wall. Deselect by pressing Command-D (PC: Control-D).

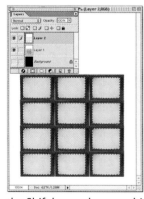

STEP FOUR: Press "w" to switch to the Magic Wand tool. Click once inside one of the monitor screens. Hold the Shift key and continue clicking until you've selected the entire screen. Continue to hold the Shift key and repeat this process until every screen is selected in your entire video wall. (We used the Magic wand, but you can use any selection tool you're comfortable with.) When all the screens are selected, press Shift-Command-J (PC: Shift-Control-J) to put them on their own layer.

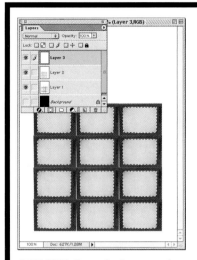

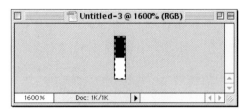

STEP FIVE: Go to the Layers palette and Command-click (PC: Control-click) on your screens layer to select the layer. Then, while it's selected, click on the New Layer icon at the bottom of the Layers palette to create a new layer. Next, go under the File menu and choose New to create a new document.

STEP SIX: When the new document dialog box appears, create a document that is 1 pixel wide by 4 pixels high in RGB mode. Make it the same resolution as your video wall document. Press Shift-B to switch to the Pencil tool. Press the letter "d" to set black as your foreground color, and draw in the top two pixels with black (as shown above.) Then press Command-A (PC: Control-A) to select all. Go under the Edit Menu and choose Define Pattern.

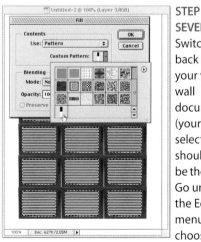

STEP SEVEN: Switch back to your video wall document (your selection should still be there). Go under the Edit menu and choose Fill. When the dialog box appears, choose Pattern for Contents, click on the down-facing arrow next to the pattern sample, choose the pattern you created, and click OK. This fills the selection with white and black lines. In the Layers palette, change the blend mode of this layer from Normal to Overlay. Merge this layer with the layer below it by pressing Command-E (PC: Control-E). Don't deselect yet.

STEP EIGHT: Next, open the image you want to paste into your video wall, then select the entire image by pressing Command-A (PC: Control-A). Press Command-C (PC: Control-C) to copy this image into memory. Switch back to your video wall image. In the Layers palette, click on Layer 1 (the video wall layer). Go under the Edit menu and choose Paste Into to put this image into your video wall. Click on the Eye icon next to Layer 2 in the Layers palette to hide the layer. Switch to the Move tool to position your image inside the wall. CONTINUED

Defining patterns

In previous versions of Photoshop, you could only define one pattern at a time. When you created a new pattern, the old pattern would disappear, never to be found again. Photoshop 6.0 comes with a number of preset patterns that you can use time and time again. You can also define your own patterns and add them to the Pattern Picker so that you can go back and use them whenever you want. Just go under the Edit menu, choose Define Pattern, name your pattern, and click OK to add your new pattern to the bottom of the Pattern Picker in the Fill dialog.

Speeding up Photoshop by merging layers

Photoshop is a slave to file size. The larger the size of your file, generally speaking, the slower Photoshop goes (especially if you're short on RAM). Every time you add a layer, it significantly adds to the overall file size of your image. That's why it's sometimes a good idea to merge together layers that you don't think you'll need to adjust later on.

For example, if you have ten layers of type, you can save a lot of file size by rendering each of the Type layers and merging them into one layer by clicking on the top text layer and pressing Command-E (PC: Control-E) to Merge down. This takes the layer you're on and merges it with the layer directly beneath it. When you do this, your file size shrinks, and in many cases, Photoshop goes faster. Be careful when merging layers with Layer Effects applied, though, because they have blend modes assigned by default, and merging them can change or hide those effects.

STEP NINE: Click on your top layer (the screens layer with scan lines). Make it visible again by clicking where the Eye icon used to be. Change the layer blend mode of this merged layer to either Soft Light, Overlay, or Screen (whichever looks best—try all three). Your Background layer should still be hidden, so go to the Layers palette, and in the palette's pop-down menu choose Merge Visible.

STEP TEN: Lastly, press Command-T (PC: Control-T), then Control-click (PC: Right-click) inside the video wall to bring up a contextual Free Transform menu. Choose Perspective, then drag the top left handle inward (to the right) and then drag the bottom left handle outward (to the left) to add a perspective effect to your wall. Click Return (PC: Enter) to complete the transformation. In the Layers palette, make your black background visible again by clicking where the Eye icon used to be. You can also change the black background to a gradient and add text and other images as shown above.

QUICK TIP
You can align objects on different layers by linking them together (click once in the center column beside each layer you want to link), going under the Layer menu, under Align Linked, and choosing how you want your layers aligned from the menu.

Rusted Metal Type Texture Effect

This technique makes use of one of Photoshop's own preset Actions for the background, then we pop-up and chisel some type out of that background with a combination of Layer Effects. In particular, we use the Bevel and Emboss Hard Chisel option introduced in Photoshop 6.0 to create the nice chiseled effect on the type.

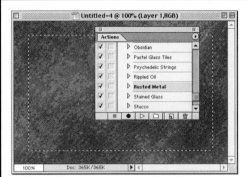

STEP ONE: Open a new document (RGB mode) and run the Rusted Metal action (to learn how, see the sidebar at right). Use the Rectangular Marquee tool to draw a rectangle about 1/2" inside your image border (as shown above). Press Command-J (PC: Control-J) to put this selected area on its own layer. Choose Bevel and Emboss from the Layer Style pop-up menu at the bottom of the Layers palette.

STEP TWO: Change the Direction to Down, Depth to 200, and Size to 10. Change the Highlight Mode to Multiply, click the color swatch, and change it to black. Use the Type tool to create your type. Hold the Command key (PC: Control key) and click on your Type layer to put a selection around it. Drag the Type layer to the trash. Click on the rusted metal layer (Layer 1). Press Command-J to make a rusted metal copy layer of your text.

STEP THREE: Make this new layer (Layer 3) your topmost layer. Choose Bevel and Emboss from the Layer Style pop-up menu. Change the Technique to Chisel Hard, set the Depth to 200, and the Size to 35. Then, in the list of Layer Styles on the left side of the dialog, check the Drop Shadow box and click OK. Press Command-L (PC: Control-L) to bring up Levels, and drag the right (highlight) Input slider to 190. Click OK to brighten your type.

STEP FOUR: Click on your rusted metal layer (Layer 1) and use the Elliptical Marquee tool to draw a circular selection (for your bolt). Press Command-J to put your bolt on its own layer, then make it the topmost layer. Choose Bevel and Emboss from the Layer Style pop-up. For Style choose Pillow Emboss and click OK. Then hold Shift-Option-Command (PC: Shift-Alt-Control), click on your bolt, and drag to create copies (as shown above). That's it!

Loading Action Sets

In the technique at left, you'll have to load a set of actions. In previous versions of Photoshop, you had to do more digging than a archaeologist to load a set of actions (they were buried deep within your drive, nested inside folder after folder). Not so in Photoshop 6; now they're just one click away. Here's how to load the Texture actions used in the technique at left: From the Window menu, choose Show Actions to bring up the Actions palette. From the palette's pop-down menu, choose Textures.atn. They'll appear as a folder in your Actions palette. Click the right-facing triangle beside the folder's name to show the contents of the folder. Scroll down to Rusted Metal and click on it. Then click the Play button (it's the right-facing triangle at the bottom of the Actions palette) and it will automatically create a new layer with a rusted metal background. Pretty sweet! While you're there, you might as well check out some of the other backgrounds. Some are pretty decent. Others are... well, let's just say they rhyme with "fame."

I'd be lying if I told you how much I love creating Photoshop textures. I'm just not really into it. I know, I know,

Baby Got Back
Texture and Background Effects

some people just love it—they love the whole "starting with nothing and coming up with something" scene, and I'm cool with that—it's just not for me. For me, a Photoshop texture has to be really useful, and it has to look different from a stock photo texture, or I could just use a stock photo texture, right?

Over the years, I've run across hundreds of different texture effects, but only a handful of them were so cool that I actually enjoyed making them, or were so useful that I had to memorize them because I knew I'd be using them regularly. I put that handful into this chapter. If you have any really great texture effects, don't send them to me. I'd only sell them to get money to buy RAM. It's sad, but if it's any consolation, I am seeking help.

Using the Clouds filter

The Clouds filter renders a random cloud pattern based on your current foreground color. The clouds generated by the Clouds filter are usually pretty light in density, so if you want darker clouds, instead of choosing the Clouds filter, choose the Difference Clouds filter.

Instant Marble Texture

Here's a technique that enables you to quickly create a marble texture, using Photoshop's built-in filters. In this tutorial, we're applying the marble texture to text, but you can add this effect to an object or even use it as a background.

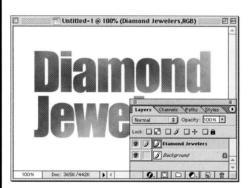

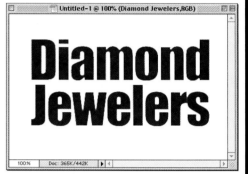

STEP ONE: Start by creating some type. Go under the Layer menu, under Rasterize, and choose Type to convert your Type layer into an image layer. Press the "/" key to turn Lock Transparent Pixels on for this layer, then go under the Filter menu, under Render, and choose Difference Clouds.

STEP TWO: Go under the Filter menu, under Stylize, and choose Find Edges. Next, press Command-I (PC: Control-I) to invert the image (your type will turn almost black).

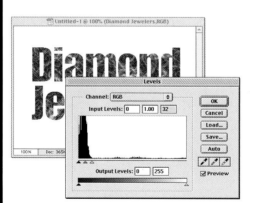

STEP THREE: To bring out the marble effect, go under the Image menu, under Adjust, and choose Levels. In the Input Levels area (under the graph), drag all three sliders so that they're positioned close together under the highest part of the graph (as shown above), and click OK . To add color to your marble, go under the Image menu, under Adjust, and choose Hue/Saturation.

STEP FOUR: Check the Colorize box in the lower right-hand corner. Move the Hue slider to the settings shown above, then click OK. Hold the Command key (PC: Control key) and click once on the layer's name in the Layers palette to select your type. Then go under the Select menu, under Modify, and choose Contract. Enter 2 pixels and click OK.

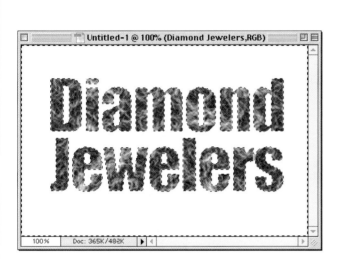

STEP FIVE: Inverse your selection by pressing Shift-Command-I (PC: Shift-Control-I) and then press Delete. Deselect by pressing Command-D (PC: Control-D). This removes the small white border from your type that was created when you used the Find Edges filter.

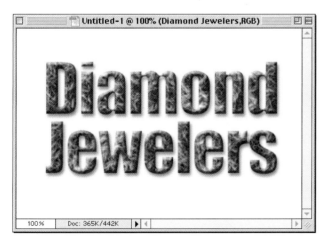

STEP SIX: Add a soft drop shadow by choosing Drop Shadow from the Layer Style pop-up menu at the bottom of the Layers palette (it's the little *f* icon). When the dialog box appears, click on the name Bevel and Emboss in the list of Layer Styles on the left side of the dialog. Set the Depth to 300 to give your type the beveled effect you see above and click OK. Tip: For a more chiseled effect, set the Bevel's Technique to Hard Chisel, the Depth to 100, and the Size to 100.

QUICK TIP

When you make a selection with one of Photoshop's selection tools, you can put a copy of that selection on its own layer by pressing Command-J (PC: Control-J). If you want to remove the selected object from the layer it's on and put it on its own layer, press Shift-Command-J (PC: Shift-Control-J).

Layer Effects and Global Light

When you use the Layer Effects Drop Shadow to apply a shadow to a layer, Photoshop notes the angle of that shadow, and it makes every shadow on every layer go in that exact same angle. This feature is called Global Light, and by tying all your light sources together, you can adjust the position of this Global Light source on any layer, and all the other shadows will automatically follow suit.

This comes in handy if you create a file with multiple Layer Effects and your client decides to change the angle of the sun (hey, it happens). Rather than going to every individual layer and changing the angle of every drop shadow, you can just go under the Layer menu, under Layer Style, and choose Global Light. When you change the angle here, all the other layers will change at the same time. You can also do the same thing by simply changing the angle of any shadow on any layer. If you want to have one layer with a shadow going a different direction, just uncheck the Use Global Light check box in the Drop Shadow dialog box.

Extract tool shortcut

If you have one of those incredibly hard-to-mask images, like someone with hair blowing in the wind or the delicate petals of a flower, there's a command in Photoshop that often works wonders. It's called the Extract command. It appears toward the bottom of the Image menu and the keyboard shortcut is Option-Command-X (PC: Alt-Control-X). When you choose Extract, it opens your image in a whole new window with its own interface and tools. You use the Highlighter tool (like a magic marker) and draw a border around the object that you want to remove from its background. Then you click the Paint Bucket tool inside this border to tell Photoshop, "This is what I want to keep," then you click the Preview button to see what happens. One of the secrets to getting Extract to work its miracle is this: Use a very small brush for well-defined areas and a very large brush for less-defined areas (like windblown hair). Now here's the tip: Press-and-*hold* the Left or Right Bracket keys to quickly zoom your brush size in or out 1 pixel at a time.

Quick Textured Backgrounds

This effect is ideal for just about anything from brochure covers to background templates for slide presentations. The effect is based on generating a simple background, using Render Clouds, adding texture with the Texturizer filter, and finally, adding depth with the Lighting Effects filter.

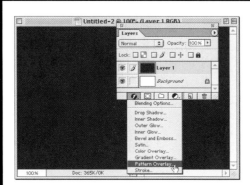

STEP ONE: Open a new RGB document. Add a new layer by clicking on the New Layer icon at the bottom of the Layers palette. Press "d" to set your foreground color to black, and fill your layer with black by pressing Option-Delete (PC: Alt-Backspace). Choose Pattern Overlay from the Layer Style pop-up menu at the bottom of the Layers palette (it's the little *f* icon).

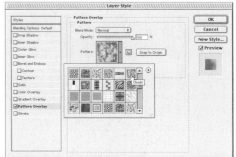

STEP TWO: In the Pattern Overlay dialog box, click the downward-facing triangle to reveal the Pattern Picker. Choose the Clouds pattern and increase the Scale to 400%. Then, in the list of Layer Styles on the left side of the dialog, click on Color Overlay. Change the color to a dark green, change the Mode to Screen, lower the Opacity to 50%, and then click OK. In the Layers palette, choose Flatten Image from the palette's pop-down menu.

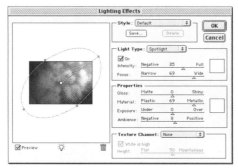

STEP THREE: Go under the Filter menu, under Texture, and choose Texturizer. Set the Texture to Sandstone, Scaling to 100%, Relief to 4, Light Dir. to Top, and click OK. Under the Filter menu, under Render, choose Lighting Effects. Use the Default settings, but move the light source so that it comes from the top right by dragging the end point of the preview oval's radius handle to the desired corner.

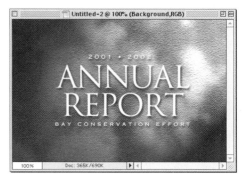

STEP FOUR: You can now place objects or text on your background. You might also want to add a soft drop shadow to your text to enhance the effect.

Instant Water Texture

OK, I've already told you before that I'm not a big fan of Photoshop textures, so if I'm sharing one in my book, it's got to be pretty slick. This one is, and I've already used it a couple of times in projects and it looks great.

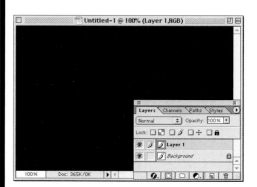

STEP ONE: Open a new document in RGB mode. Create a new blank layer by clicking on the New Layer icon at the bottom of the Layers palette. Press the letter "d" to make black your foreground color, then fill this layer with black by pressing Option-Delete (PC: Alt-Backspace).

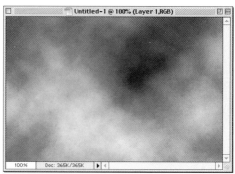

STEP TWO: Go under the Filter menu, under Render, and choose Difference Clouds.

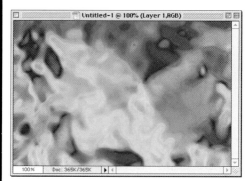

STEP THREE: Go under the Filter menu, under Sketch, and choose Chrome. In the Chrome dialog box, set the Detail to 4, the Smoothness to 7, then click OK. You can use this as your water texture. For a more "liquidy" effect, press Command-F (PC: Control-F) to run this same filter again (with the same settings). It's your call. I'd run it, and if you don't like the results, undo it.

STEP FOUR: Go under the Image menu, under Adjust, and choose Hue/Saturation. When the dialog box appears, check the Colorize box, then move the Hue slider to around 220 and the Saturation to around 50, then click OK (you're shooting for pool-water blue, so adjust it to suit your monitor). There you have it.

Filling with color

In the example at the left, we're using Hue/Saturation to colorize the water background at the end. Another way to colorize the image is to choose the foreground color that you'd like, go under the Edit menu, and choose Fill. In the Fill dialog box, change the Blend Mode from Normal to Color and click OK. It will pour on the color, but it will leave all the detail in the image.

Now, in Photoshop 6.0, you can also use the Color Overlay Layer Effects to overlay any color that you want to add to your current layer. Just choose it from the Layer Effects pop-up menu at the bottom of the Layers palette (it's the little *f* icon). This Color Overlay will cover any textures or detail on the layer, so you might need to change the Blend Mode to Multiply, Overlay, or Screen. You may also need to lower the opacity.

Levels tip

If you need to lighten or darken the overall image, the Output Levels sliders at the bottom of the Levels dialog box can help. Dragging the left slider to the right will lighten the overall image. Dragging the right Output Levels slider to the left will darken the overall image. Because this change is so global (effecting the entire image across the board), it is generally used for special effects rather than for image correction, in which case, you would use the Input Sliders up at the top instead.

Instant Cloud Backgrounds

If you ever used Photoshop's Clouds filter, you probably already found that it's great for creating a lot of different textures and effects. But unfortunately, creating realistic clouds ain't one of them. Here's a trick that uses Clouds with Color Range to create an effect that actually looks like. . . well, clouds.

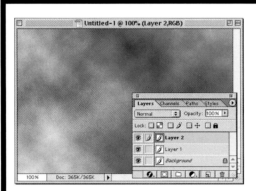

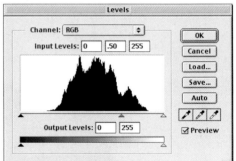

STEP ONE: Open a new document at least 5" x 5" in RGB mode. In the Layers palette, click on the New Layer icon twice (creating two new layers). Press the letter "d" (to reset your foreground and background colors to their defaults), then go under the Filter menu, under Render, and choose Clouds.

STEP TWO: Press Command-L (PC: Control-L) to bring up the Levels dialog. When the dialog box appears, press the Tab key once, type the number 0.5, and click OK. In the Layers palette, click on Layer 1. Then click on your Foreground color swatch to bring up the Color Picker. When it appears, click on the Custom button and type the number 2727 to choose Pantone 2727. Click OK.

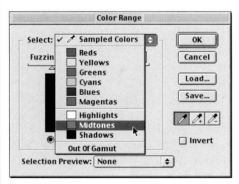

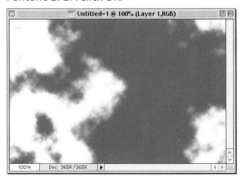

STEP THREE: Press Option-Delete (PC: Alt-Backspace) to fill Layer 1 with blue (you won't see this change except in the Layers palette thumbnail). Next, go to the Layers palette and click on Layer 2. Go under the Select menu and choose Color Range. When the dialog box appears, you will see at the top a pop-up menu asking you what to Select. Sampled Colors is chosen by default. Change it to Midtones and click OK. Don't deselect yet.

STEP FOUR: In the Layers palette, click on Layer 1. Press the letter "x" to make white your foreground color, then press Option-Delete (PC: Alt-Backspace) to fill the selected areas with white (you won't see the effect on screen quite yet). Now deselect by pressing Command-D (PC: Control-D). To see the final clouds effect, go to the Layers palette and drag Layer 2 into the trash.

Embossed Background Type

I saw this effect used recently in a television ad campaign for mutual fund manager T. Rowe Price. The effect was used on their name as their TV spot closed with a splash screen featuring their logo that was transparently embossed on a textured background. Here's how it was done.

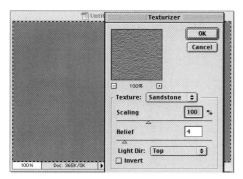

STEP ONE: Open a new document in RGB mode and choose a new foreground color (we chose Pantone 569). Fill your document with this new color by pressing Option-Delete (PC: Alt-Backspace). Next, go under the Filter menu, under Texture, and choose Texturizer. From the Texture pop-up menu in the dialog box, choose Sandstone and click OK.

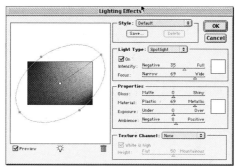

STEP TWO: Go under the Filter menu, under Render, and choose Lighting Effects. When the dialog box appears, make sure your light source is coming from the upper right-hand corner. If not, just grab the end of the oval's radius handle (in the preview window) and drag it around to the other side. When it looks like the preview above, click OK.

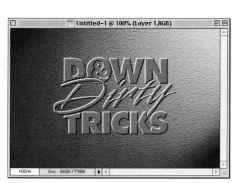

STEP THREE: Scan in the logo you want to use (in our case, we scanned the black-and-white logo in RGB mode, selected it, then dragged it into our document, as shown above). Next, go under the Filter menu, under Stylize, and choose Emboss. When the Emboss dialog box appears, use either the default settings or increase the Height setting to give the logo a more pronounced effect (we used a height of 3 in the example shown above).

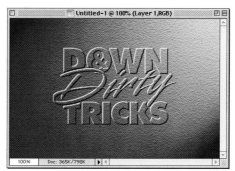

STEP FOUR: To complete the effect, go to the Layers palette and change the Layer mode (for the layer the logo is on) from Normal to Hard Light. This creates the transparent effect (as shown above).

Rounding the edges of your type

After you complete the effect shown at the left, you can add some roundness to your letters by clicking on the Lock Transparent Pixels check box in the Layers palette, going under the Filter menu, under Blur, and choosing Gaussian blur. A 1-pixel blur will add a slight bit of roundness to your letters. Increase the amount for light, fluffy-looking letters. The type won't get really blurry because you have locked the transparent pixels—the edges remain sharp and the blur only affects the inside of the letters.

Why we choose monochromatic noise

Every time we use the Noise filter (which is often in this book, particularly in this chapter), we also check the Monochromatic box at the bottom of the Add Noise dialog. The reason is that without Monochromatic being turned on, you get noise that, is composed of little red, green, and blue dots, and that can get in the way of colorization that will often take place later on in the tutorial.

Instant Wood Texture

I'm not a big fan of textures in general (OK, OK, I know you're tired of hearing me say that) but this particular one is so cool that I wanted to include it in this book. Even if you don't need a wood texture every day, this is a fun and interesting effect to run through.

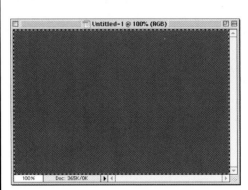

STEP ONE: Open a new document in RGB mode. Choose a dark brown (I chose the Pantone color 1405). Fill your document with Pantone 1405 brown by pressing Option-Delete (PC: Alt-backspace).

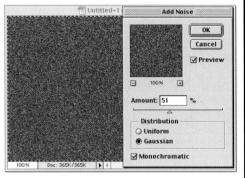

STEP TWO: Go under the Filter menu, under Noise, and choose Add Noise. When the dialog box appears, enter 51 for Amount, choose Gaussian for Distribution, check the Monochromatic box to turn it on, and then click OK.

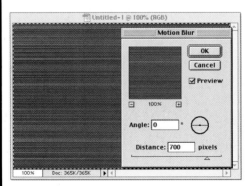

STEP THREE: Go under the Filter menu, under Blur, and choose Motion blur. In the Motion Blur dialog box, set your Angle to 0 (zero), your Distance to 700, and then click OK.

STEP FOUR: Go under the Filter menu, under Noise, and choose Add Noise. When the dialog box appears, lower the Amount to 10 and click OK.

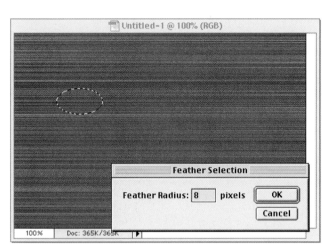

QUICK TIP
There's a keyboard shortcut to bring up the Feather dialog box. It's Option-Command-D (PC: Alt-Control-D).

STEP FIVE: We'll add a knot to make it look more realistic. Press Shift-M until the Elliptical (round) Marquee tool appears in the Tool palette. Use this tool to make a small oval selection on one portion of your wood background. Then go under the Select menu and choose Feather. When the dialog box appears, enter 8 for Feather Radius and click OK.

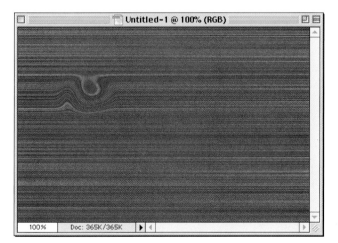

STEP SIX: Go under the Filter menu, under Distort and choose Wave. You can use the default settings (which work just fine), or you can experiment with the sliders until your selection looks more like a knot. You'll need to sharpen your selection to match the wood texture that surrounds it. So go under the Filter menu, under Sharpen, and choose Sharpen Edges. Deselect to complete the effect.

Why feathering is so important

Feathering effects the edge of your selection, and one of the main reasons to use it is to smooth the transition between your selection and the area surrounding it. In the example at the left, feathering the selection makes the transition smoother between the area with the applied Wave filter and the wood background. Without the feathering applied, there would be a harsh, obvious edge where the knot ends and the wood background begins.

This is a popular technique in photo retouching, where it is used to smooth the transition in areas that have been copied and pasted to hide defects or unwanted elements in the image.

Transparent gradients

In most cases, we're either using a Foreground to Background gradient, using one of the preset color gradients, or creating our own custom gradient; but one of the most useful (and coolest) gradients is the Foreground to Transparent gradient. When you set the Gradient tool to this gradient style and drag the gradient in your document, it goes from your foreground color to transparent (just what it sounds like it would do).

Instant Brushed Metal

You might as well learn this quick method for creating brushed metal, because you're gonna need it. It's a basic texture for creating hi-tech elements, and it saves you from searching for a brushed metal stock image.

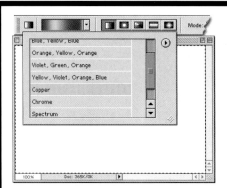
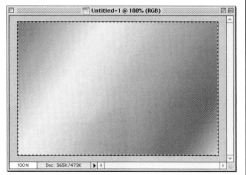

STEP ONE: Open a new document in RGB mode. Click on the Gradient tool and, in the Options Bar, click on the downward-facing triangle next to the Gradient sample and a flyout menu of preset gradients will appear (the Gradient Picker). Choose Copper as your gradient (we switched the view to Text Only from the pop-up menu to view the gradients by name).

STEP TWO: Using the Gradient tool, drag a gradient from the upper left-hand corner down to the bottom right-hand corner of your document.

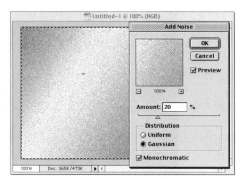
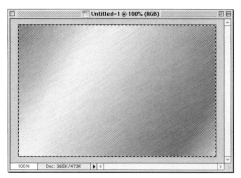

STEP THREE: Go under the Image menu, under Adjust, and choose Desaturate to remove the copper color. Go under the Filter menu, under Noise, and choose Add Noise. Enter between 20 and 30 for Amount, choose the Gaussian and Monochromatic options, and then click OK.

STEP FOUR: Go under the Filter menu, under Blur, and choose Motion Blur. When the dialog box appears, set your Angle to 29°, choose between 20 and 30 for Distance, and then click OK to complete the texture.

Instant Star Field

You never know when you'll need a quick star field. For example, you're sitting at your desk, the phone rings —it's NASA with a huge government-funded project. What's the first question they ask? That's right—can you create a star field from scratch? Why? Because it's almost time for them to fake a Mars landing. (Kidding). Maybe.

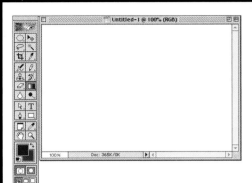

STEP ONE: Open a new document (RGB mode) at 72 ppi. Press the letter "d" to set your foreground color to black. Then click on the Background color swatch and choose a dark blue for your background color (I chose Pantone 280 by clicking on the Custom button within Photoshop's Color Picker).

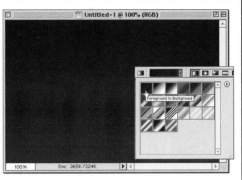

STEP TWO: Press the letter "g" to switch to the Gradient tool, and drag a Foreground to Background gradient (see sidebar for more info) through your image. Drag from top to bottom, with black on the top and blue on the bottom (shown above).

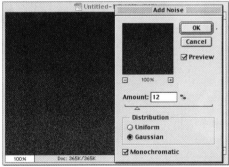

STEP THREE: Click on the New Layer icon to add a new layer, and fill it with black by pressing Option-Delete (PC: Alt-Backspace). Go under the Filter menu, under Noise, and choose Add Noise. Enter 12 for Amount (use 30 for high-res images), choose the Gaussian and Monochromatic options, and click OK. Next, Go under the Filter menu again, under Blur, and choose Gaussian Blur. For Radius, choose 1, then click OK (this blur makes some of the stars have a different size and brightness). Go under the Image menu, under Adjust, and choose Threshold.

STEP FOUR: When the dialog appears, drag the slider slowly to the left and stars will soon begin to appear; drag further for more stars. Next, go under the Image menu and choose Image Size. Enter 300 ppi and click OK. Then go to the Image Size dialog box again, but this time enter 72 ppi and click OK (this softens your stars nicely). Go under the Filter menu, under Render, and choose Lens Flare. Click OK. Lastly, change the blend mode of this layer from Normal to Screen to complete the effect.

Finding the right gradient

When you have the Gradient tool, you can access the built-in preset gradients (and your own custom gradients) from the Gradient Picker. This is found in the Options Bar by clicking on the downward-facing triangle just to the right of the Gradient sample (which shows your currently selected gradient). When you click on this triangle, it reveals the Gradient Picker. By default, the Foreground to Background gradient is the first swatch on the top row in the Gradient Picker. It's a smart thumbnail, because it changes to display your currently selected foreground and background colors.

CHAPTER

10

Dammit, Jim, I'm a Doctor, not a Pixel Jockey!

Interface Design

When I tell people I included a chapter on interface design, they always ask me what an interface is. I tell them it's the face inside their face. They never get that joke. I'm not sure I get that joke. In fact, I'm not sure it's a joke at all because it's missing a critical component of all jokes—the funny part. Anyway, interfaces are everywhere. From the remote control for your TV, to the interface for your car CD-player. These hi-tech interfaces are popping up everywhere, and they're especially popular on the Web, where they're most often used as navigation devices for sites. Sometimes they comprise the entire home page themselves. They're also a key component of multimedia CD-ROM authoring, touch screen kiosks, skins for MP3 players, and if you've ever looked at another person, pointed forward and said, "Engage" or "Make it so, Number One," then you'll just enjoy the sheer sci-fi aspect of creating your own interfaces, wires, tubes, and other hi-tech gear. Best of all, when you're done with this chapter, you'll be able to boldly go where … ah, forget it.

Indented buttons

To add an indented button to your interface, start by clicking on the New Layer icon at the bottom of the Layers palette to add a new layer above your interface. Draw a circular selection, fill it with a color, then add the Layer Effects Bevel and Emboss, but for Style, choose Pillow Emboss. This makes your new button appear indented into the interface.

Designing Your Core Interface

This technique is in wide use on the Web, and once you learn the secret, you can quickly create your own custom interfaces, navigation bars, and, if you like, even use your interface as an entire home page. Although this technique is being shown here in a Web context, it works equally well at high-res for print.

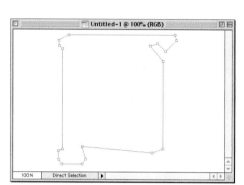

STEP ONE: Open a new document in RGB mode, then go to the Layers palette and create a new layer by clicking on the New Layer icon. Press the letter "p" to switch to the Pen tool. Create the outside shape of your interface using straight lines and angles (no curves). When you get back to your original starting point, click on it once to complete your path.

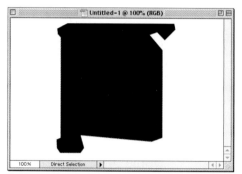

STEP TWO: Press Command-Return (PC: Control-Enter) to turn your path into a selection. Press the letter "d" to set black as your foreground color, then press Option-Delete (PC: Alt-Backspace) to fill your selection with black. Deselect by pressing Command-D (PC: Control-D).

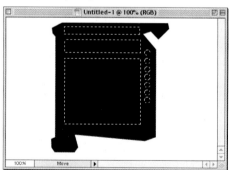

STEP THREE: Press the letter "m" to switch to the Marquee tool, and select the inside areas of your interface. These are the areas you will fill with photos, buttons, and so on. After you make your first selection, hold the Shift key to add additional selections.

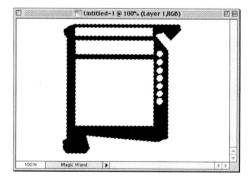

STEP FOUR: After all your selections are in place, press the Delete key (PC: Backspace). This creates the base of your interface. Hold the Command key (PC: Control key) and click once on Layer 1 to select the rest of the image. Go under the Select menu and choose Save Selection. When the dialog appears, click OK. Press Command-D (PC: Control-D) to deselect.

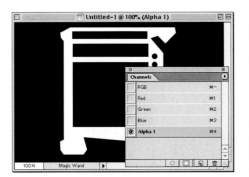

STEP FIVE: Now that you saved your selection, delete your interface layer by dragging it to the trash can at the bottom of the Layers palette. Next, go to the Channels palette and click on Alpha 1 (your saved interface channel).

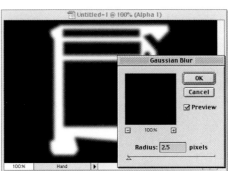

STEP SIX: To round the corners of your interface, go under the Filter menu, under Blur, and choose Gaussian Blur. We're going to apply a blur to Alpha 1. The more blur you apply, the rounder the corners will appear in your final interface. In this example, I applied a 2.5-pixel blur to this low-res image. For high-res (300-ppi) images, apply a 5-pixel blur or more.

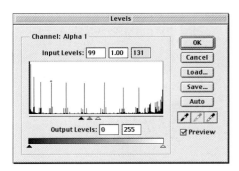

STEP SEVEN: To remove the blurriness and make your round corners appear smooth, press Command-L (PC: Control-L) to bring up Levels. When the dialog box appears, slide the far left and far right Input Levels sliders toward the middle (as shown above). As you drag them, you'll notice the blurriness disappear and the corners start to smooth. Drag them until they are about $^1/_8$" from each other, and click OK.

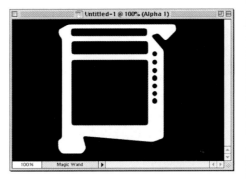

STEP EIGHT: Your interface should now have smoothly rounded corners (as shown above). Return to the Layers palette and click on the Background layer.

CONTINUED

Automated interfaces

When it comes to creating interfaces, the real fun is experimenting with different designs for your interface (it's not doing all those steps—if you can imagine that). You can focus on the fun part by writing your own Action that creates an instant interface. Just open the Actions palette, choose New Action from the pop-down menu, name your Action "Instant Interface," and click Record. Immediately go to the bottom of the Actions palette and click the Stop button, because you really don't want to start recording yet. First, do Steps One, Two, and Three (in the tutorial on the opposite page), then press the Record button (on the bottom of the Actions palette) immediately after you finish Step Three (creating the inside of your interface). In the future, you'll only have to do the first three steps (the fun part), and then run the action for your instant interface.

White is high?

In Step Nine of the effect on the right, we have you turn off the White is high check box. What this check box does is determine how your highlight is affected by the lighting; turning it on or off determines whether your interface will appear to pop up from the background (which is what we're looking for) or look sunken into the background. This changes, depending on where your light source is coming from (upper-right corner, lower-left corner, etc.) Click it on/off once or twice, then move the light source to another angle and try it again, and you'll see what I mean.

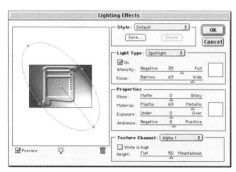

STEP NINE: Go under the Filter menu, under Render, and choose Lighting Effects. At the bottom of the dialog, under the Texture Channel pop-up, choose Alpha 1 from the pop-up menu and uncheck the check box for White is high (it's on by default, so turn it off). Click OK. Go under the Select menu and choose Load Selection.

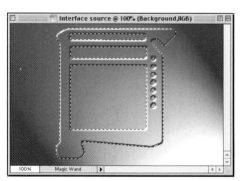

STEP TEN: When the dialog box appears, make sure Alpha 1 is chosen in the pop-up menu, and click OK to load the original interface selection onto your background (as shown here). Don't deselect yet.

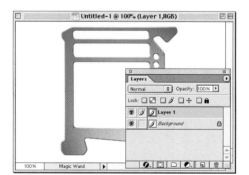

STEP ELEVEN: Press Shift-Command-J (PC: Shift-Control-J) to lift your interface off the Background layer and up onto its own layer. In the Layers palette click on the Background layer. Press Command-A (PC: Control-A) to Select All and then press Delete (PC: Backspace) to erase the background, leaving just your slightly beveled interface visible. Press Command-D (PC: Control-D) to deselect and then click back on your interface layer.

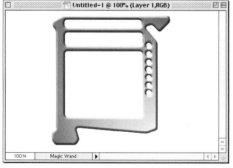

STEP TWELVE: To enhance the beveled effect, go under the Layer menu, under Layer Style, and choose Bevel and Emboss. When the dialog box appears, increase the Depth to 200% (use 400% for high-res images), the Size to 6 (use 10 for high-res images), and then click OK.

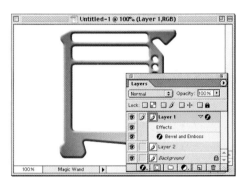

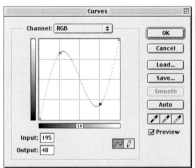

STEP THIRTEEN: At this point, we want to leave the bevel applied to our interface, but we want to remove the active Layer Effect to keep it from affecting other elements we add to this layer. To do that, click on the New Layer icon. Drag this new layer directly below your interface layer. Click back on your interface layer, then press Command-E (PC: Control-E) to merge your interface layer with the blank layer beneath it. This leaves the bevel on your interface, but removes the Layer Effect from your layer.

STEP FOURTEEN: Now it's time to add color/texture. You can add a texture to your interface by using a technique shown later in this chapter. For the interface I created in the opening of this chapter, I added a simple curve setting (shown above) to give it a shiny metallic look. Press Command-M (PC: Control-M) to bring up the Curves dialog box. Click once on the lower side of the curve (around the first square) and drag upward. Add another point near the upper right side and drag downward, then click OK.

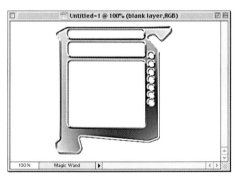

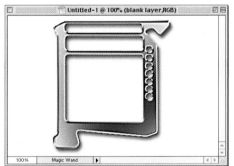

STEP FIFTEEN: Any time I create a metallic texture, I apply an Unsharp Mask to enhance the shine. Go under the Filter menu, under Sharpen, and choose Unsharp Mask. In the dialog, enter 150 for Amount, 2 for Radius, 5 for Threshold, and click OK.

STEP SIXTEEN: Lastly, to create a little more depth, add a drop shadow by choosing Drop Shadow from the Layer Style pop-up menu at the bottom of the Layers palette (it's the little *f* icon), then click OK to complete the core of your interface. The other projects in this chapter will show you how to add some of the more common elements to your interface to give it more of a sci-fi look.

Why we run the Lighting Effects filter on the Background layer

In the technique shown at the left, we apply the Lighting Effects filter to the Background layer rather than a new blank layer. If you try to apply the Lighting Effects filter to a blank layer, you'll get an error message that reads, "Could not complete the Lighting Effects command because the selected area is empty." It's right, ya know—a new layer is just an empty, transparent layer. However, the Background layer is actually filled with white, so you can apply the filter there. That's why we run it on the Background layer, load our original selection, and then put that up on its own layer.

Creating a custom metal gradient

To create a custom metal gradient that you can use anytime you want, follow these steps:

(1) Click on the Gradient tool to bring up its options in the Options Bar (which appears up top, just below your menu bar). To bring up the Gradient Editor, click once on the gradient sample in the Options Bar.

(2) The long black bar in the Gradient Editor is used to create custom gradients. Double-click the upward-facing triangle (called a "Color Stop") below the bar on the far left side to bring up Photoshop's Color Picker. In the bottom right, you'll see input boxes for CMYK values. Enter 0 for Cyan, 0 for Magenta, 0 for Yellow, and 65 for K (black). Click OK. Next, double-click the Color Stop on the far right side, and when the Color Picker appears, again enter 0, 0, 0, 65 for the CMYK values (just like the first time). Click OK.

(3) To add another color to our gradient, click once right below the now gray bar and a new Color Stop

continued on facing page

Transparent Interface Pop-up

There are numerous ways to create hi-tech, metallic-looking interfaces, but most are too time-consuming and complicated. The one I'm sharing here is quick and easy to recreate. The whole concept is based on dragging a gradient in one direction, shrinking the selection, and dragging another gradient in the opposite direction.

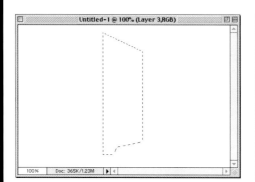

STEP ONE: Open an RGB document. Create a new layer by clicking once on the New Layer icon at the bottom of the Layers palette. Use the Pen tool or Lasso tool to draw the shape you'd like to turn into a pop-up interface. If you use the Pen tool, turn your path into a selection by pressing Command-Return (PC: Control-Enter).

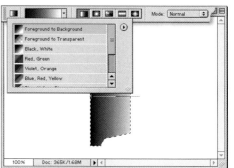

STEP TWO: Press the letter "d" to set your foreground color to black. Press the letter "g" to switch to the Gradient tool, and up in the Options Bar, click the downward-facing triangle to reveal the flyout Gradient Picker. Make sure the gradient style is set to Foreground to Background. Take the Gradient tool and drag a gradient from the left of your selection to 1/4" past the right of your selection. Don't deselect yet.

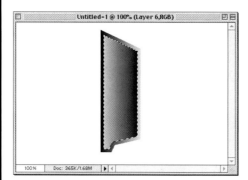

STEP THREE: Go under the Select menu, under Modify, and choose Contract. Enter 6 and press OK (this will shrink your selection by six pixels—feel free to vary this amount). With the Gradient tool, drag a gradient from the right 1/4" past the left edge of your selection (the opposite direction in which you dragged a moment ago).

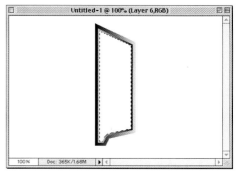

STEP FOUR: Go under the Select menu, under Modify, and choose Contract. This time, enter half of the number you used before (we used six pixels earlier, so this time we used three pixels.) Again, this shrinks the selection. Next, hit Delete (PC: Back-space), but don't deselect yet. This creates the outside metallic outline for your pop-up interface.

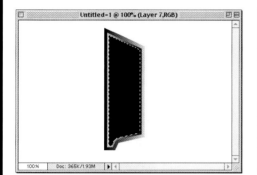

STEP FIVE: Create a new layer by clicking on the New Layer icon at the bottom of the Layers palette. Your selection should still be active, so press Option-Delete (PC: Alt-Backspace) to fill your selection with black.

STEP SIX: In the Layers palette, drag this black-filled layer under your interface outline layer. Lower the opacity of this black layer to 60%.

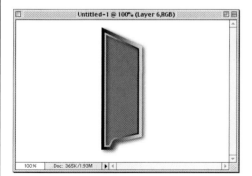

STEP SEVEN: Click on your pop-up outline layer again, and add a drop shadow by choosing Drop Shadow from the Layer Style pop-up menu at the bottom of the Layers palette (it's the little ƒ icon). Click OK.

STEP EIGHT: Drag your pop-up interface onto a background image. In this image, we dragged our pop-up interface just off the left edge. Add your text (in white) over the 60% black area to complete the effect.

continued from facing page

triangle will appear. In the Location field, type in 50%. Double-click on the new Color Stop to bring up the Color Picker again. Enter 0, 0, 0, 20 for the CMYK values (which creates 20% black). You now have a gradient that goes from 65% black to 20% black then back to 65% black. Click OK— you've created a custom metal gradient.

Making quick, round buttons

Round radio buttons are probably the most common quickie-button for the Web. You start by making a small circular selection, switching to the Radial Gradient tool by pressing the letter "g," and then in the Options Bar, choosing the second gradient tool from the left.

Drag a radial gradient through your selection. The tip to get this to work properly is that you have to set white as your foreground color, so press the letter "d" then the letter "x." Drag your Radial Gradient, and you'll get a quick round-looking button with a tiny white highlight. You can colorize your button by pressing Command-U (PC: Control-U) to bring up Hue/ Saturation, checking the Colorize box, and sliding the Hue slider to your desired color.

Creating Consoles with the Airbrush

Here's another interface technique that focuses mostly on using the Airbrush tool instead of using a complicated collection of channels. What's great about this technique is that after you learn it, you'll find dozens of other ways to incorporate it into other areas of your Photoshop work.

STEP ONE: Create a new document in RGB mode. Using the Pen tool, draw the shape that you'd like for your navigation panel. Create a new layer by clicking on the New Layer icon at the bottom of the Layers palette.

STEP TWO: Press Command- Return (PC: Control-Enter) to turn your path into a selection. Set your foreground color to 50% gray, then press Option- Delete (PC: Alt- Backspace) to fill the image with your gray foreground color.

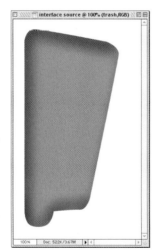

STEP THREE: Press the letter "d" to make your fore- ground color black. Press the letter "j" to switch to the Airbrush tool, and up in its Options Bar, lower the pressure setting to 20%. Choose a soft-edged, medium-sized brush from the brushes flyout menu. Use the Airbrush tool to paint a ¹/₄" to ¹/₂" black border inside your gray interface shape on just three sides. On the remaining fourth side, draw a smaller black stroke along the edge just to give it some definition.

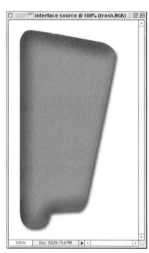

STEP FOUR: Deselect by pressing Command-D (PC: Control- D). If you're going to put this interface over a white background, you can add a drop shadow by choosing Drop Shadow from the Layer Style pop-up menu at the bottom of the Layers palette (it's the little *f* icon). Increase the size to 7, then click OK.

STEP FIVE: Press the letter "x" to switch your foreground color to white, choose the next smaller soft-edged brush (from the brushes flyout menu), then paint a straight line down the left side, close to the black line you painted earlier. After this straight line, follow the contours of the black lines at the top and bottom of the interface with another white Airbrush stroke.

STEP SIX: Press the letter "d" to set your foreground color to black, then use the Type tool to create your text. Put plenty of leading between the lines. After the text is in place, lower the opacity to at least 70% to make the text blend into the background image.

Quick access to Photoshop preferences

If you find yourself making a lot of little changes to Photoshop's preferences settings, you can save a lot of time by pressing Command-K (PC: Control-K) to bring up the General Preferences dialog box, but there is one additional shortcut that will really speed things up for you. After you press Command-K (PC: Control-K), press Command-2 (PC: Control-2) to jump directly to the Saving Files preference, Command-3 (PC: Control-3) to jump directly to Displays & Cursors, and so on.

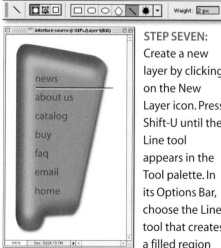

STEP SEVEN: Create a new layer by clicking on the New Layer icon. Press Shift-U until the Line tool appears in the Tool palette. In its Options Bar, choose the Line tool that creates a filled region (it's the last button in the group of three buttons on the left of the Options Bar), and set the Weight to 2 pixels. Draw a black horizontal line between the first two lines of text. To give the line an indented look, press the letter "x" to make white your foreground color, then draw another line directly under your black line (this line should actually touch, but not cover, the black line).

STEP EIGHT: In the Layers palette, Command-click (PC: Control-click) on the layer's name to put a selection around both the black and white lines. Switch to the Move tool. Hold Shift-Option-Command (PC: Shift-Alt-Control), click directly on the lines, and drag copies down between each line of text (as shown above). To trim the excess lines, make your interface layer active, Command-click (PC: Control-click) on the interface layer to load it as a selection. Press Shift-Command-I (PC: Shift-Control-I) to inverse the selection, and press Delete (PC: Backspace).

CONTINUED

Rotating selections

In the last step of the tutorial on this page, I took a notch out of my navigation panel and put a gray bar inside that notch (for effect). To do this, draw a tall thin selection, go under the Select menu, and choose Transform Selection. This brings up the familiar Free Transform bounding box. Move outside the bounding box and rotate the selection (just the selection, not any element of the image) to match the angle of the right side of your interface. You can click inside the bounding box at any time to reposition it, and you can move outside again to rotate. When you get it into position, press Return (PC: Enter) to lock in the transformation. In the Layers palette, click on the Interface layer (with the selection still active) and press Delete (PC: Backspace).

With the selection still active, create a new blank layer, make 80% black your foreground color, then press Option-Delete (PC: Alt-Backspace) to fill. Go under the Layer menu, under Layer Style, and chose Drop Shadow. Move this layer below your interface layer and nudge it to the left.

STEP NINE: Deselect by pressing Command-D (PC: Control-D). Create a new layer by clicking on the New Layer icon. Switch to the Elliptical Marquee tool and draw a small circle to the left of the first text entry. Fill it with a color of your choice and deselect by pressing Command-D (PC: Control-D). Go under the Layers menu, under Layer Style, and choose Bevel and Emboss. Under Style, choose Pillow Emboss from the pop-up menu. Click OK and your button becomes indented into your interface.

STEP TEN: In the Layers palette, Command-click (PC: Control-click) on the layer's name to select your indented button. Hold the Shift-Option-Command keys (PC: Shift-Alt-Control) and drag copies of your indented button down beside each line of text, as shown above. You can also draw a larger circular selection in the bottom-left corner. Switch your foreground color to black (press the letter "d"), then press Option-Delete (PC: Alt-Backspace) to fill your circular selection with black (it's automatically indented for you).

STEP ELEVEN: Click on the layer containing your main interface (probably named Layer 1). Switch back to the Airbrush tool, press "x" to set your foreground color to white, and choose a small, hard-edged brush. In the upper left-hand corner, paint a little arc in white (go in one direction, and then paint back over it). Then go to the opposite corner (lower right) and draw the same type of arc—make this arc about 50% of the size of your first arc to add highlights that make the interface look shiny.

STEP TWELVE: For the final touches shown here, you can colorize your interface by pressing Command-U (PC: Control-U) to bring up the Hue/Saturation dialog box. Click the Colorize button and move the Hue slider to select a new color. I added a "notch" in the interface shown above. To learn how I notched it, read the sidebar on the left of this page, called "Rotating Selections." I did one other thing: I thought my type was too large, so I lowered the size by four points.

Round-Cornered Boxes

Although Photoshop now has the Rounded Rectangle shape tool, this is another one of those "must-know" techniques if you're going to be creating interfaces. Luckily, it's pretty darn easy.

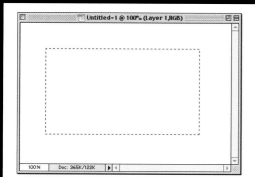

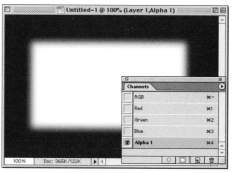

STEP ONE: Open a new document in RGB mode. Press the letter "d" to set your foreground color to black. Get the Rectangular Marquee tool by pressing the letter "m," then draw a selection approximately the size that you want your final round-cornered box.

STEP TWO: Go under the Select menu and choose Save Selection. When the dialog box appears, click OK. Deselect by pressing Command-D (PC: Control-D). Go to the Channels palette (found under the Window menu) and click on Alpha 1 (which is the selection you just saved). Go under the Filter menu, under Blur, and choose Gaussian Blur. Blur the channel until it has the roundness you want in your corners (as shown above).

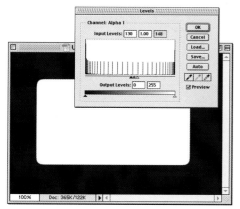

STEP THREE: To remove the blurriness, go under the Image menu, under Adjust, and choose Levels. When the Levels dialog appears, drag the end Input Levels sliders toward the middle until they almost touch (but don't let them). As you drag inward, you'll see the blurriness go away, and your corners will smooth out.

STEP FOUR: Go to the Layers palette and click on your Background layer. Create a new layer by clicking on the New Layer icon at the bottom of the Layers palette. Go under the Select menu and choose Load Selection. In the Load Selection dialog box, choose Alpha 1, then click OK. A selection will appear on your layer. To fill it with black, press Option-delete (PC: Alt-Backspace) to complete the effect.

Cleaning up line art scans using this technique

You can actually use part of the technique shown on this page to clean up jaggy line art scans. Here's how: Open your jaggy line art scan and convert it to Grayscale or RGB mode (if it's not already in that mode). Now, jump over to Step Two (to the left of this sidebar) and pick up where it says "Go under the Filter menu" about $2/3$ of the way through the step. Continue through Step Three, then stop. When you do, your line art scan will be smooth and the jaggies will be gone! (Yea! Yippie!). Note: This technique works on artwork, but not on text, because the smoothing of type does too much damage to the fine lines of type.

Tubes tip

The tubes (pipes, whatever) that you're creating in the adjacent tutorial seem to look better if you put two or three of them close together (almost touching) and then add them to your interface. You can group them like mufflers on a dragster (if you can picture that in your mind), and they look pretty cool. Especially if your interface looks like a dragster (kidding).

Adding Pipes/Tubes to Your Interface

Believe it or not, I get more requests for how to create tubes (and wires) than just about any other interface technique. These tubes look pretty odd at large sizes, but when you shrink them down, they look great.

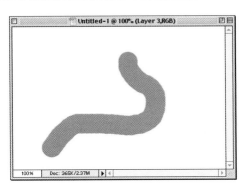

STEP ONE: Create a new document, then create a new blank layer. Set your foreground color to 50% gray. Get the Paintbrush tool and choose a large, hard-edged brush (I created a 40-pixel brush by choosing New Brush from the brushes flyout menu's pop-down menu). Use this brush to draw the shape for your tube.

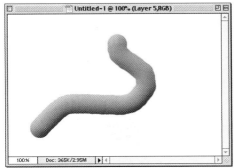

STEP TWO: Go under the Layer menu, under Layer Style, and choose Bevel and Emboss. Set the Depth to 300, Size to 10, Softness to 16, and then click OK.

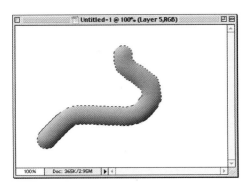

STEP THREE: Command-click (PC: Control-click) on the layer's name in the Layers palette to put a selection around it. While it is selected, create a new layer by clicking once on the New Layer icon at the bottom of the Layers palette. Don't deselect yet.

STEP FOUR: Press the letter "d" to reset your foreground color to black. Press Shift-U until the Line tool appears in the Tool palette. Draw 1- or 2-pixel lines that follow the contour of the tube (as shown above). Don't deselect yet.

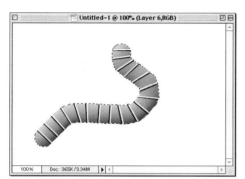

STEP FIVE: Press the letter "x" to make white your foreground color. Now you're going to draw another set of lines (in white) next to the black lines that you just drew. Your white lines should touch (but not cover) the black lines—there should be no space between the two lines. This makes your lines look indented into the tube. Don't deselect.

STEP SIX: Press the letter "d" to make black your foreground color. Press the letter "j" to switch to the Airbrush tool, and paint along the left side of your selected tube to make the left edge darker (as shown above). Then lightly touch the Airbrush to the right side in a few random places to make the tube look a bit weathered. Deselect by pressing Command-D (PC: Control-D).

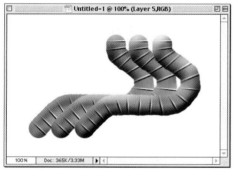

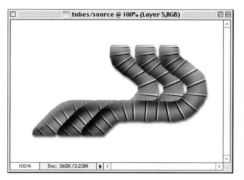

STEP SEVEN: Press Command-E (PC: Control-E) to merge your layer of lines with your tube layer. Press the letter "v" to switch to the Move tool. Hold Shift-Option-Command (PC: Shift-Alt-Control), click on your tube, drag a copy, and position it next to your original. Click-and-drag a third copy (as shown above). Click on the Eye icon next to the Background layer to hide it. Under the Layers palette's pop-up menu, choose Merge visible. Add a drop shadow from the Layer Style pop-up menu at the bottom of the Layers palette (it's the little *f* icon).

STEP EIGHT: The tubes still have rounded ends. At this point, I will usually draw a rectangular selection around the ends and hit Delete (PC: Backspace) as shown above. In the interface that appears earlier in this chapter, I left the round ends intact, added a blank layer beneath the tube layer, drew three circles, and filled them with gray. I then added a Bevel and Emboss Layer Effect with the Style set to Pillow Emboss to make them look attached to the interface.

Deleting layers the fast way

If you want to delete a number of layers from your Layers palette, you can trash those puppies really fast by using this trick. Rather than dragging them one by one all the way down to the trash can at the bottom of the Layers palette, click on the first layer you want to delete, then Option-click (PC: Alt-click) on the trash can icon. If the layers that you want to delete are all in a row, just keep Option-clicking (PC: Alt-clicking) on the trash can. If you need to move down through your layers to get to a layer that you want to delete, press Option-Left Bracket (PC: Alt-Left Bracket) till you get to that layer, and then Option-click (PC: Alt-click) on the trash can icon again. You can get pretty quick at deleting those unwanted layers by using this technique.

Cool trick for eliminating backgrounds

In Step Two of the tutorial at the right, we created a path and stroked it with the Paintbrush tool to add a brush stroke along that path. You can use that same technique to help you remove an object from its background. Just draw a loose path (with the Pen tool) around the object you want to remove from its background (don't let it touch the edge of the object, just get close). Then follow Step Two in the tutorial at the right, but instead of choosing the Paintbrush tool, choose the Background Eraser tool, then click OK. You'll be amazed, because it traces around the edge of your image, erasing all the way around, in about two seconds. Plus, it's fun to watch. Note: Make sure you choose a hard-edged brush for your Background Eraser tool before you try this trick.

Creating Wires/Cables

What would an interface be without some wires and cables that house critical electrical components of the interface? (OK, that's a stretch, but they do add a sci-fi look to your interface that's hard to beat.)

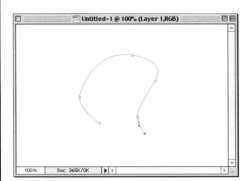

STEP ONE: Open a new document in RGB mode (72 ppi). Create a new layer by clicking on the New layer icon at the bottom of the Layers palette. Using the Pen tool, draw the path you'd like your wire to follow. Click, hold, and drag to create curves in your path. Pick a new foreground color (like a dark green).

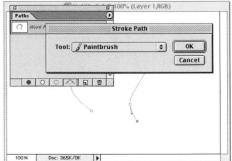

STEP TWO: Switch to the Paintbrush tool and choose a small, hard-edged brush. Go to the Paths palette, and in the pop-down menu, choose Stroke Path. Choose Paintbrush from the Tool pop-up menu, and click OK. In the Paths palette, drag your Work Path into the trash can at the bottom of the Paths palette to delete it (you don't need it anymore).

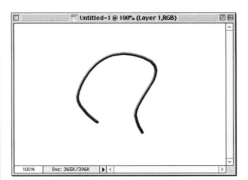

STEP THREE: Go under the Layer menu, under Layer Style, and choose Bevel and Emboss, then click OK to complete your first wire. Make a copy of this layer. Press Command-T (PC: Control-T) to bring up Free Transform, and slightly rotate your wire. Choose a new foreground color and press Shift-Option-Delete (PC: Shift-Alt-Backspace) to add your new color to your wire copy.

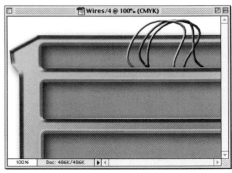

STEP FOUR: Create a third wire by copying your wire layer, choosing a new color, and colorizing it. Click on the Eye icon next to the Background layer to hide it, then choose Merge Visible from the Layers palette's pop-up menu. Drag this new layer into your interface and use Free Transform to scale it. Make a rectangular selection on the bottom of the wires and press Delete (PC: Backspace) to trim excess wire.

Inset Lines

This is used for adding little inset lines, or indentations, into your interface. This effect is so easy that the hardest part is getting your Rectangular Marquee tool selection down to just two pixels high. Luckily, a quick trick with the Info palette makes this an absolute breeze.

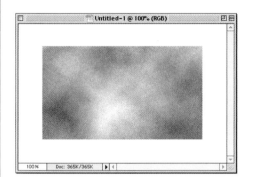

STEP ONE: I created a simple texture as a background for this example. If you want to do the same, start by making a selection using the Rectangular Marquee tool. Go under the Filter menu, under Render, and choose Clouds. Then go under the Filter menu, under Noise, and choose Add Noise. Use 12 pixels for Amount, select Gaussian and Monochromatic, and then click OK.

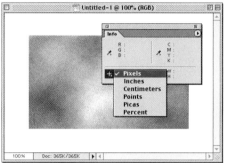

STEP TWO: Open the Info palette, and at the left bottom side of the palette, switch the measurement unit to pixels by clicking directly on the cross hair icon and choosing Pixels from the pop-up menu.

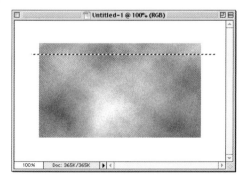

STEP THREE: With the Rectangular Marquee tool, make a selection that is 2-pixels high by just a little longer than your textured background. You can make it exactly 2 pixels by looking in the Info palette. At the bottom right, it will now show how many pixels wide (and high) your selection is as your draw it.

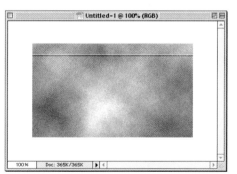

STEP FOUR: Press Command-L (PC: Control-L) to bring up Levels. Press the Tab key once to move to the middle Input Levels field, type the number 2, and click OK. Press the Down Arrow key on your keyboard twice to move your selection down 2 pixels. Then bring up Levels again, press the Tab key once, but this time enter .4 (point 4) and click OK. Deselect to complete the effect.

Bringing up the Info palette

Adobe assigned a few F-keys to bring up certain palettes, and they're already preassigned when you install Photoshop. To bring up the Info palette (used in Step Two of the tutorial on the left), press F8 and it pops up.

Creating one layer with the contents of all your layers

There's a little trick that you can use that takes the layer you're on and converts it into a new layer that is a flattened version of all your layers. It doesn't actually flatten your layers; it gives you one single layer that looks like what your image would look like if you flattened it at that point. To do this, start by creating a new blank layer, then hold the Option key (PC: Alt key), go under the Layers palette's pop-down menu, and choose Merge Visible. A new "merged contents" layer will now appear in your palette. Why would you need this? I have no earthly idea, but hey, you might need it one day, and now you know. However, you'll never remember which page this tip was on, and it'll take you hours to go through every tip and find out, so maybe you're better off just forgetting this tip now, while you're still sane.

Combining Objects to Form the Base of Your Interface

What really makes a great interface is starting with a great shape for your core. When you're ready to start creating more advanced shapes, you can combine common shapes (like ovals, squares, and rectangles) to form more interesting (OK, weird-looking) interfaces that look . . . well, weird (yet strangely cool).

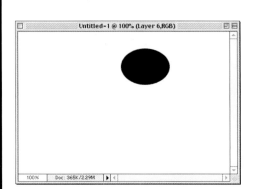

STEP ONE: Start by creating a new layer by clicking on the New Layer icon at the bottom of the Layers palette. Set your foreground to black by pressing the letter "d," then (using the Elliptical Marquee tool), draw a simple oval selection and fill it with black by pressing Option-Delete (PC: Alt-Backspace).

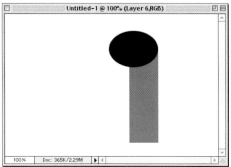

STEP TWO: Create another blank layer, then press Shift-M to switch to the Rectangular Marquee tool. Drag a vertical rectangular selection, line it up so that it touches the edge of your oval, then fill with black by pressing Option-Delete (PC: Alt-Backspace). Lower the opacity of this layer to 60%.

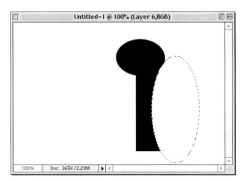

STEP THREE: Press Shift-M to toggle back to the Elliptical Marquee Tool, and draw an oval selection that digs into your rectangle, starting at the bottom of your top oval. Press Delete (PC: Backspace) to remove the excess rectangle, and then raise your opacity for this layer back to 100%. Deselect by pressing Command-D (PC: Control-D).

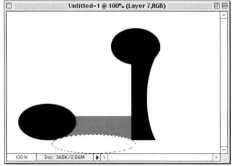

STEP FOUR: Create a new layer, draw an oval selection to the left of your structure, and fill it with black. Create another new layer, draw a rectangular selection between the two structures, fill it with black, and lower the opacity to 60% (to see what you're doing). Draw another oval selection that digs into your new rectangle and press Delete (PC: Backspace) to remove the excess rectangle.

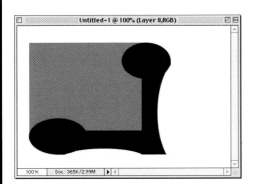

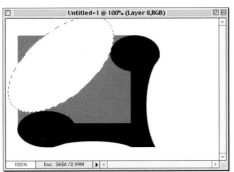

STEP FIVE: Raise the opacity back to 100%. Create a new layer, draw a large square rectangle that goes from the top of your top oval to the left edge of your left oval, and fill it with black. Lower the opacity to 60% so that you can see the structure below it. Draw a large oval in the middle of your image. Go under the Select menu and choose Transform Selection. This brings up transformation handles just like Free Transform.

STEP SIX: Move your pointer outside the bounding box and rotate your oval into position, touching the edges of your two black ovals. Press Delete (PC: Backspace) to remove the excess rectangle. Use the Eraser tool to clean up any stray pieces of your rectangle. Raise the opacity back up to 100%.

Shortcuts for aligning type

When you're working with Type in Photoshop, you can change the alignment of your type (flush left, centered, flush right) by highlighting the type and using these simple keyboard shortcuts:

Align Left:
Shift-Command-L
PC: Shift-Control-L

Align Right:
Shift-Command-R
PC: Shift-Control-R

Align Center:
Shift-Command-C
PC: Shift-Control-C

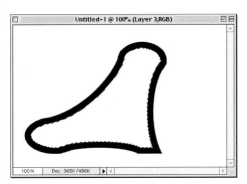

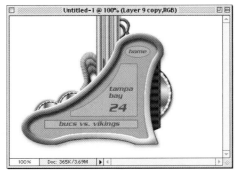

STEP SEVEN: In the Layers palette, click on the top layer in your stack, click on the Eye icon next to the Background layer to hide it, and from the Layers palette's pop-down menu, choose Merge Visible to put your structure on one layer. Hold the Command key (PC: Control key) and click once on this new layer to put a selection around it. Go under the Select menu, under Modify, and choose Contract. Choose 12 pixels, click OK, then press Delete (PC: Backspace).

STEP EIGHT: Now that you created the outline for your core interface, you can proceed with the technique on page 154 for beveling it. In the example above, I added a number of other interface elements taught in this chapter, including tubes, steel bars, and wires. I created the round knobs using the built-in copper gradient, but I pressed Shift-Command-U (PC: Shift-Control-U) to remove the copper color, and then added gray and white stripes.

Creating your own textures

If you want to create your own textures in Photoshop, here are a couple of tips that might help:

• The Clouds filter is a great place to start building your textures because it already has a texture.

• Many textures are built using the Add Noise filter as a base. Generally, you'd start by filling the Background layer with a color, and then running the Add Noise filter.

• Use Gradients as your base and build upon that. You can run filters like Polar Coordinates, Waves, Ripple, Glass, etc. on top of gradients to create your own custom textures.

• If you started with a noise background, try adding the Motion Blur filter to enhance your background.

• Use the Texturizer filter to add texture to flat colors or to enhance a noise background.

Adding Textures to Your Interface

After you create the core of your interface, you can add a texture to it by using this simple technique. You can create your own textures (from scratch in Photoshop) or use stock photography textures just as easily.

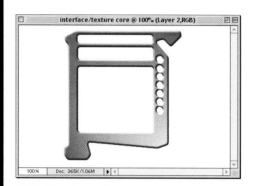

STEP ONE: Open the document containing your core interface.

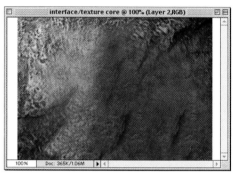

STEP TWO: Open the image texture that you'd like on your interface, and drag it into your interface document so that it appears on its own layer.

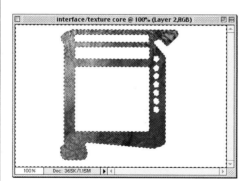

STEP THREE: In the Layers palette, hold the Command key (PC: Control key) and click directly on your interface layer to put a selection around it. Click on your texture layer and press Shift-Command-I (PC: Shift-Control-I) to inverse the selection. Press Delete (PC: Backspace) to remove the excess texture from around your interface. Press the letter "v" to switch to the Move tool.

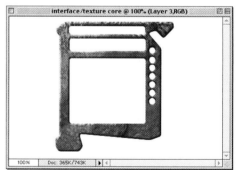

STEP FOUR: Start pressing Shift-+ (plus sign) to rotate through the layer blend modes in your Layers palette. Usually, Overlay mode looks best, but depending on the color of your texture, other blend modes, like Hard Light, Soft Light, or Multiply, may look better (I used Hard Light in this example). When it looks good, press Command-E (PC: Control-E) to merge the two layers together.

Adding Reflective Round Dials

In this tutorial, we're using the Airbrush tool again (but in a slightly different way) to create a highlight around an object to make it look shiny and rounded. This is another element we can use in our overall interface.

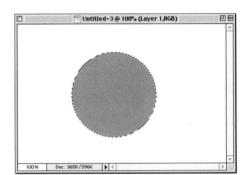

STEP ONE: Open a new document in RGB mode. Create a new layer by clicking on the New Layer icon at the bottom of the Layers palette. Using the Elliptical Marquee tool, draw a circular selection and fill it with 50% gray. Press the letter "d" to set your foreground color to black.

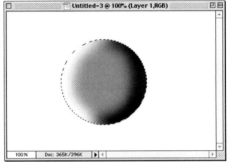

STEP TWO: Press the letter "j" to get the Airbrush tool. From the Options Bar, choose a large, soft brush and paint a black stroke around the right side of the circle. Then, switch your foreground color to white by pressing the letter "x," and using the same large, soft brush, paint a white stroke around the left side of the circle (as shown).

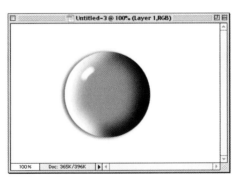

STEP THREE: In the brushes flyout menu, choose a smaller, hard-edged brush, and paint a tiny arc (in white) in the upper left-hand quadrant of your dial (as shown above). Add a drop shadow by choosing Drop Shadow from the Layer Style pop-up menu at the bottom of the Layers palette (it's the little *f* icon), then click OK.

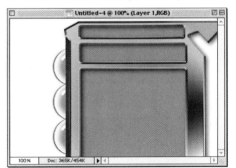

STEP FOUR: Drag this round button layer into your interface and place it behind your interface layer (as shown here). In this case, I made two more copies of the dial by holding Shift-Option-Command (PC: Shift-Alt-Control) and clicking-and-dragging downward. This makes copies of the button (holding the Shift key keeps them in line as you drag).

Selection super timesaver

If you've made a selection in Photoshop, there are a wide range of things you can do with that selection (besides dragging it around): you can feather it, save it, copy it to a layer, transform it, and so on. Well, you can access a list of the things that you're most likely to do with your selection by holding the Control key and clicking-and-holding inside your selected area (PC: Right-click your mouse). A pop-up contextual menu will appear with a list of commands that you can apply to your selection. This is a huge timesaver and keeps you from digging through menus while you work.

Changing the size of selections

Any time you have a selection in place, you can make that selection a few pixels larger or smaller by going under the Select menu, under Modify, and choosing Expand (to make your selection bigger) or Contract (to make your selection smaller). There's a weird thing about this function; when you make a large change either way, it doesn't keep the edges sharp and crisp—it tends to round (anti-alias) the edges a bit, so keep this in mind if you need to grow your selection by a large number of pixels. To see what I mean, draw a square selection, then go under the Select menu, under Modify, and choose Expand. Enter 15 (the maximum is 100) and click OK. Look at the edges of your selection—they're not square anymore, they're sort of rounded off at the corners. I haven't found a way around this; I try to keep my expansions to only 3 or 4 pixels, and it works just fine.

Embedding Objects into Your Interface

This is a quick trick for making an object appear as if it is embedded into your interface. It's an amazingly simple trick that is actually very effective.

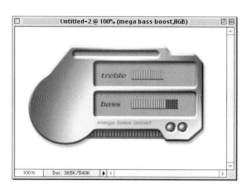

STEP ONE: Open the interface you're working on.

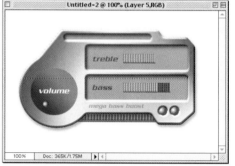

STEP TWO: Open the object you'd like to appear embedded into your interface (in this example, it's a blue volume knob), and use the Move tool to drag it into your interface document. It will appear on its own layer.

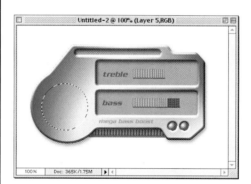

STEP THREE: Go to the Layers palette, and Command-click (PC: Control-click) directly on your object layer's name to put a selection around it. Now that your selection is active, you can hide this layer from view by clicking on the Eye icon in the first column next to your object layer. Don't deselect yet.

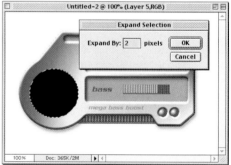

STEP FOUR: Create a new layer by clicking on the New Layer icon at the bottom of the Layers palette. Go under the Select menu, under Modify, and choose Expand. Enter 2 pixels and click OK. Set your foreground color to black by pressing the letter "d," then fill your selection with black by pressing Option-Delete (PC: Alt-Backspace).

STEP FIVE: Deselect by pressing Command-D (PC: Control-D). Make a duplicate of this black circle layer in the Layers palette by dragging it to the New Layer icon. Make white your foreground color by pressing the letter "x."

STEP SIX: Fill this duplicate layer with white by pressing Shift-Option-Delete (PC: Shift-Alt-Backspace). Now you should have the volume knob layer (which is hidden from view), a black circle on a layer above it, and a white circle on another layer above that.

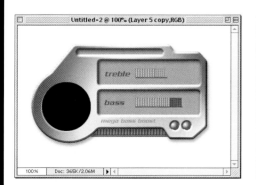

STEP SEVEN: Switch to the Move tool by pressing the letter "v," then press the Left Arrow key on your keyboard twice, and press the Down Arrow key twice to offset this white circle from the black circle below it. In the Layers palette, change the layer blend mode from Normal to Soft Light and your circles should look like they do above.

STEP EIGHT: Go back to your original object layer (in this example, the volume knob), and in the Layers palette, drag it to the top of the layer stack (so that it's the top layer) to complete the embedded effect.

Duplicating layers

There are a couple of different ways to duplicate layers and different reasons why you might choose one over the other. The most popular way to duplicate an existing layer is to open the Layers palette and drag the layer you want to duplicate to the New Layer icon at the bottom of the Layers palette, which immediately makes a duplicate and adds the word "copy" to the end of the layer's name to let you know it's a copy (how thoughtful).

If you want to rename the layer as you duplicate it, choose Duplicate Layer from the Layers palette's pop-down menu instead. A Duplicate Layer dialog will appear where you can type in the name that you want for your layer copy. Click OK and your newly named layer copy will appear in your Layers palette.

Quick steel bars

The method on the right shows you how to create your own custom gradient for making steel bars. But if you just need a quick steel bar, you can use the Copper gradient preset that's already in Photoshop's Gradient Picker. Just draw your thin rectangular selection, drag the Copper gradient within that selection, then press Shift-Command-U (PC: Shift-Control-U) to remove the copper color from the gradient, making it appear grayscale and giving you a really easy instant steel bar.

Steel Bars

Here's another one of those "must-know" elements that come in very handy when you're creating your interfaces. The technique is based totally on creating a gradient that looks like a metal bar.

STEP ONE: Open a new document in RGB mode. Create a new layer by clicking on the New Layer icon at the bottom of the Layers palette.

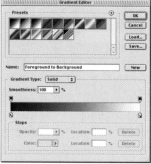

STEP TWO: Press the letter "g" to switch to the Gradient tool. Click once on the gradient sample up in the Options Bar to bring up the Gradient Editor (shown above).

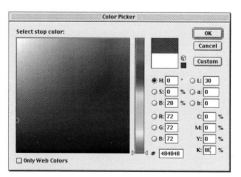

STEP THREE: Double-click on the black Color Stop on the left-hand side (under the black bar). When the Color Picker appears, under CMYK (on the bottom right side of the dialog) enter 0 for C, 0 for M, 0 for Y, and 80 for K (which is black).

STEP FOUR: Double-click on the right Color Stop. When the Color Picker appears, under CMYK (on the bottom right side of the dialog) enter 0 for C, 0 for M, 0 for Y, and 20 for K (black). Slide this gradient stop to the middle of the bar (as shown above).

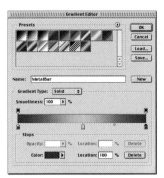

STEP FIVE: Click once on the left Color Stop, then hold the Option key (PC: Alt key), and click-and-drag the left (80% black) Color Stop to the right, passing over the middle stop and all the way to the right. This creates a duplicate of your left Color Stop. Your gradient should now have an 80% black stop on the left, a 20% black stop in the middle, and an 80% black stop at the right. Name your gradient, click the New button, then click OK.

QUICK TIP

When you're using a tool, you can temporarily switch to the Move tool by holding the Command key (PC: Control key). As long as you hold this key down, you'll have the Move tool. When you let go, it switches you back to the tool you were last using.

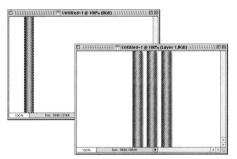

STEP SIX: Switch to the Rectangular Marquee tool by pressing the letter "m." Draw a thin rectangular selection, then drag your new gradient from left to right inside your selection to create your metal bar. If you want to create a weathered look, go under the Filter menu, under Brush Strokes, and choose Sprayed Strokes. Put your stroke length at 12, your Spray Radius at 1, then click OK. Create multiple bars and add them to your other interface elements.

Lighting Effects tips

We use the Lighting Effects filter quite a bit when we're creating interfaces and interface elements. Here are a few tips that will make using the Lighting Effects dialog even easier:

• Think of the Style pop-up menu at the top as a list of "presets," because that's exactly what they are.

• You can create your own styles (presets) by configuring the Lighting Effects the way you want, and clicking on the Save button at the top of the dialog just below the Style pop-up.

• To add another light, click-and-drag the Light icon into the preview, or hold the Option key (PC: Alt key) and click-and-drag a copy of your existing light.

• Press the Tab key to jump from one light to the next.

• To delete any light, click on it and press Delete (PC: Backspace).

It was about a year ago that I read about a study conducted by some huge university up north about people

Surfin' USA
Photoshop Web Effects

who created Web sites for a living. I can't remember the name of the university, but it was one with enough money to fund silly studies. They asked these Webmasters all sorts of questions about their education, background, their favorite game shows, blah, blah, blah, and then they got more specific about their Web design careers. What really caught my eye was the statistic about which graphics application they used to create their Web graphics. Of the 1,700 professional Webmasters, do you know what percentage said they used Adobe Photoshop for creating their Web graphics? You don't? Then you better look up that study. OK, OK, it's was 100%. Every single professional used Adobe Photoshop. You know what that told me? When I write a book, there had better be a chapter on designing Web graphics. See, that silly study really did pay off.

Creating new layers

There are a number of ways to create new layers. The quickest way is to click on the New Layer icon at the bottom of the Layers palette. No dialog box pops up to slow you down—you immediately get a new blank layer.

You can use the keyboard shortcut Shift-Command-N (PC: Shift-Control-N) to create a new layer and bring up the New Layer dialog box (so you can name your layer as you create it), but that's a bit slower.

If you're looking for the absolute slowest way to create a layer (if you're charging by the hour), you can go under the Layer menu, under New, and choose Layer.

You can also choose New Layer from the Layers palette pop-down menu if you're charging by the hour, but still have a deadline to meet.

Creating 3D Pill-Shaped Buttons

This style of 3D-looking button is usually created through a complicated series of channel operations, but here's a way, using the Airbrush, that's quicker and much easier. This technique for making objects look rounded works on almost any object, not just pill-shaped buttons. (But you knew that, didn't you?)

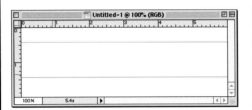

STEP ONE: Create a new layer by clicking on the New Layer icon at the bottom of the Layers palette. Make your rulers visible by pressing Command-R (PC: Control-R). Click-and-hold inside the top ruler and drag a guide down into your document, then drag out another guide approximately 1" past the first guide and release it. Press Shift-M until you have the Elliptical Marquee tool.

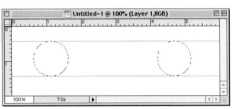

STEP TWO: Start on the left side of your image, hold the Shift key, and draw a circle between the two guides. Move over about 2", hold the Shift key again, start to draw your second circle, release the Shift key, press the Shift key again, and then finish drawing your circle (the first time you hold the Shift key lets you add to your existing selection; the second time you press it, it confines the selection to a perfect circle).

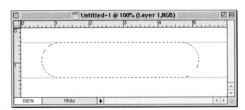

STEP THREE: Press Shift-M again to return to the Rectangular Marque tool. Hold the Shift key down and draw a rectangle starting at the top center of the left circle and ending at the bottom center of the right circle to complete the pill shape (as shown above). Press the letter "v" to switch to the Move tool and remove the guides by dragging them back up to the ruler.

STEP FOUR: Next, choose a new foreground color from the Color Picker. Fill the pill shape with your new foreground color by pressing Option-Delete (PC: Alt-Backspace). Press the letter "j" to switch to the Airbrush tool. In the Options Bar, lower the Pressure to 10%. Next, press the letter "d" to reset your Foreground color to black.

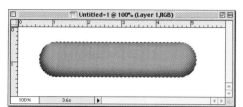

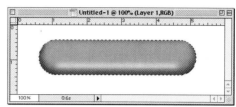

STEP FIVE: Go to the Brushes palette and choose a large, soft brush. We're going to use the Airbrush tool to paint a $^1/_3$" thick border inside the edges of the pill. Start by painting both round ends of the pill, then hold the shift key to draw a straight line across the bottom of the pill (as shown above). Paint a thin black line across the top—maybe $^1/_8$" deep (see above). You might have to paint over the areas a few times to make your Airbrush strokes dark enough to match the image above. Note: We haven't mentioned deselecting yet, so you should still see a "marching-ants" selection around the entire pill shape.

STEP SIX: Press the letter "x" to make your foreground color white. Now we're going to draw a white airbrushed line from left to right just above the black line you drew earlier at the bottom of the pill. Starting from the left side, click once, hold the shift key, and drag from left to right (as shown above), stopping before the end of the pill. Don't deselect yet.

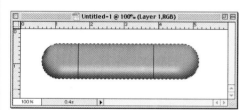

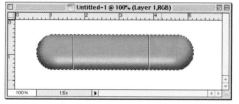

STEP SEVEN: Go to the Color Picker and choose a darker shade of the color you originally used for the pill shape. Switch to the Pencil tool by pressing Shift-B. About $^1/_3$ of the way from the left side of the pill, hold the Shift key and draw a straight pencil line from top to bottom. Go to the right side, about $^1/_3$ from the other end, and do the same thing (as shown above). Next, switch your foreground color to 50% gray. Draw two more lines (in gray) directly next to the two lines you just drew to make it look as if these lines are indented into the pill.

STEP EIGHT: Deselect by pressing Command-D (PC: Control-D) and add a drop shadow to your pill shape by going under the Layer menu, under Layer Style, and choosing Drop Shadow.

Hiding the marching ants

If you're working on a project, there are times where you need to have something selected, but it would help if you didn't have to see the "marching ants" selection border on the screen (like in Step Five at left). To keep your selection in place, but hide those annoying marching ants, press Command-H (PC: Control-H). Adobe now calls this command "Show Extras," but it probably should be called "Hide Selection" or "Hide Marching Ants"; but if they did name commands with such obvious names, then you wouldn't need this book, so now that I think of it, I really like that name. Show Extras. Yup, that works for me.

Getting your text to blend

In Step Nine on the right, I had you lower the opacity of your Type layer to 70% to help it blend better with the background. You can also experiment with layer blend modes and see how your type blends with the layer below it. You can choose a blend mode from the Layers palette, or you can rotate through the blend modes by pressing Shift-+ (the plus sign) to see which one looks best —just make sure that you don't have a tool selected that has a blend mode in the Options Bar because Shift-+ will change the tool's blend mode rather then changing the layer's blend mode.

STEP NINE: You can add text to your pill button if you'd like by using the Type tool. If you do, I recommend creating your text in white and then lowering the opacity setting of the text layer to around 70% (as shown above). Lowering the opacity on the text layer helps the text blend into the pill background rather than looking just pasted on top.

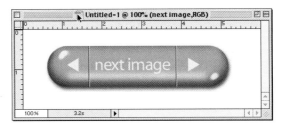

STEP TEN: We're going to add two white Airbrush strokes to give the button a more rounded plastic feel. First, press the letter "d" then "x" to set your foreground color to white. Then press the letter "j" to switch to the Airbrush tool. Choose a medium-sized, hard-edged brush from the brushes flyout menu in the Options Bar. Choose Layer 1 and add a little curved stroke to the top left corner of the pill, and add an even smaller half-curve to the bottom right corner (as shown above). Make the stroke once, and then go back over it in the opposite direction to make it more pronounced. These two little paint strokes can make all the difference in the world.

QUICK TIP

You can jump to the layer below your current layer in the Layers palette by pressing Command-Left Bracket (PC: Control-Left Bracket), or you can move to the layer above your current layer by pressing Command-Right Bracket (PC: Control-Right Bracket). Using these keyboard shortcuts, you can step up and down through your Layers palette.

Yummy Metal Web Buttons

In this day and age, if you have to make a Web button, it better be pretty slick. Here's a technique for making a yummy-looking, metallic-like, plastic, reflecto-looking thingy that is. . . well, pretty slick.

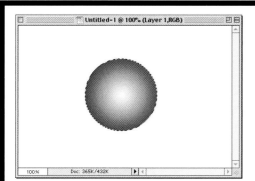

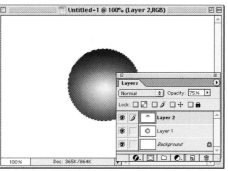

STEP ONE: Create a new document (RGB, 72 ppi). Create a new blank layer. Draw a circular selection using the Elliptical Marquee tool. Press "g" to switch to the Gradient tool. In the Options Bar, click on the downward-facing arrow for the Gradient Picker and choose Foreground to Background. Press "d" then "x" to set your foreground color to white. Click the Radial Gradient icon (it's the 2nd one) and drag a white to black gradient from the center of the selection to 1/4" past the edge.

STEP TWO: Create a new layer by clicking on the New Layer icon in the Layers palette, then in the Gradient Picker choose the Foreground to Transparent gradient. Press "d" to make black your foreground color. In the Options Bar choose the Linear Gradient (it's the first one). Drag the Gradient tool from the top of your selection to the middle to fill the top with black. In the Layers palette, lower the opacity to 75%. With your selection still in place, create a new layer.

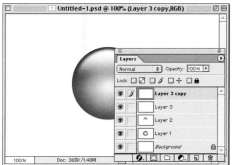

STEP THREE: Under the Select menu, under Modify, choose Contract. Enter 6 pixels and click OK. Press "x" to set your foreground color to white, then drag from the top of your selection through about 1/3 of your selected area. Press Command-D (PC: Control-D) to deselect. Under the Filter menu, under Blur, choose Gaussian Blur. Enter 3 pixels and click OK. Duplicate your top layer by dragging it to the New Layer icon. Press Command-T (PC: Control-T) to bring up Free Transform. Control-click (PC: Right-click) inside the bounding box, choose Rotate 180°, and press Enter. Press "v" to switch to the Move tool.

STEP FOUR: Drag this layer straight down almost to the edge. Lower the opacity to 60%. Go back to Layer 3 and bring up Free Transform. Hold the Shift key, grab the bottom right handle and shrink this highlight by 15%. Hide the Background layer and choose Merge Visible from the Layers palette's pop-up menu. Press Command-U (PC: Control-U) to bring up Hue/Saturation. Click the Colorize button and choose a color. Add a Drop Shadow and some type to complete. (Note: we used 6.0's Warp Text feature Bulge at +10% to make the type look rounded and added a drop shadow).

Making circular selections

When you draw a circular selection, by default, it draws from where you click your mouse button, but if you prefer, you can drag your circular selection from the center outward by holding the Option key (PC: Alt key) while you drag. Don't forget to add the Shift key if you want to keep your circle perfectly round as you drag.

3D Spherized Buttons

We use this quick, 30-second effect for both print and Web design. The beveled look to the edges comes from simply creating a gradient in one direction, shrinking the selection, and dragging the same gradient in the opposite direction. The 3D text effect within the button uses one of Photoshop's standard filters.

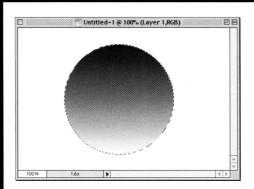

STEP ONE: Open a new document in RGB mode at 72 ppi. Create a new layer by clicking on the New Layer icon at the bottom of the Layers palette. Click-and-hold on the Rectangular Marquee tool and choose the Elliptical (round) Marquee tool from the flyout menu. Draw a circular selection. Press the letter "d" to reset your foreground and background colors to their defaults.

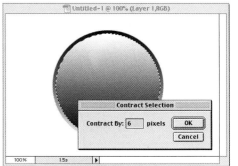

STEP TWO: Switch to the Gradient tool and drag a Foreground to Background gradient from the top of your circular selection to ⅛" past the bottom of the circle. Go under the Select menu, under Modify, and choose Contract. Enter 6 pixels and click OK. Using the Gradient tool, drag a gradient from the bottom of your circle to ⅛" past the top of your circle. Go under the Select menu, under Modify, and choose Contract. Enter 3 pixels.

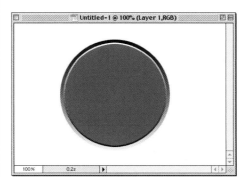

STEP THREE: Choose a new foreground color and press Option-Delete (PC: Alt-Backspace) to fill this selection with your new foreground color. Then go under the Select menu and choose Save Selection. When the dialog box appears, click OK. Press Command-D (PC: Control-D) to deselect.

STEP FOUR: Switch to the Type tool and create some white text that fits (size-wise) within the colored circle. Switch to the Move tool (press "v") to reposition your type. Go under the Layer menu, under Rasterize, and choose Type.

STEP FIVE: Go under the Select Menu and choose Load Selection. When the dialog box appears, make sure that Alpha 1 is selected and click OK.

QUICK TIP
You can also load a selection by going to the Channels palette, clicking on the Alpha channel you want to load as a selection, and dragging it to the selection icon at the bottom of the Channels palette. It's the first one from the left. Click back on the RGB channel to view the entire RGB image again with the loaded selection.

Make 'em big

Many designers prefer to create their Web graphics at a much larger physical size (like two- or three-times bigger) than the final size that the graphic will wind up being on the Web page. This is especially helpful when the final size is very small, like Web buttons—which would be hard to create from scratch at their actual size. If you decide to go this route, you can scale your object down to its final size by using Free Transform and sizing down before you save the file for the Web.

STEP SIX: Go under the Filter menu, under Distort, and choose Spherize. When the dialog appears, move the Amount slider to 100% and click OK. Deselect by pressing Command-D (PC: Control-D). Add a drop shadow to Layer 1 by going under the Layer menu, under Layer Style, and choosing Drop Shadow. Click OK to complete the effect.

What if your background isn't white?

In Step One of the technique on the right, I tell you to put the logo on a white background, but I don't tell you how to do that—that's what makes all of this so much fun... for me. (Note: I was going to leave it at that, but my wife just read this and insists that I tell you how, so here goes.)

If your logo doesn't appear on a white background, you have to select it using one of Photoshop's selection tools. If it's on a background that is one color, or a couple of similar colors, your best bet might be to click the Magic Wand once on the background to select it. That gives you the opposite of what you want (you've got the background selected, but you want the logo selected). To pull the ol' switch-a-roo, go under the Select menu and choose Inverse, which will then select the logo. Now create a new document and drag your logo into it. That's a best-case scenario, but hey, it's better than me leaving you with just that first brief paragraph.

Creating Web Backgrounds with Logos

If there's anything clients love, it's seeing their own logo tiled over and over again as the background of their Web page. It never fails—they lose their mind (and often complete control of their checkbook). Here's a quick way to turn their logo into a nonstop client/designer love fest.

STEP ONE: Open the logo that you want to appear as a tiled background. For best results, you want the logo to appear on a white background (as shown above).

STEP TWO: Go under the Image menu, under Adjust, and choose Levels. In the Levels dialog, drag the far left Output Levels slider to the right to lighten the overall image. Drag it further than you think you should (type has to be read clearly over this background, so don't be afraid to make it too light).

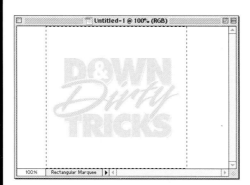

STEP THREE: Switch to the Rectangular Marquee tool by pressing the letter "m," hold the Shift key, then draw a perfectly square selection around your logo. Make your selection larger than your logo so that there's some space around it. While your square selection is still active, go under the Image menu and choose Crop to crop your image into a perfect square.

STEP FOUR: Now go under the Image menu, under Mode, and choose Indexed Color. Then save your image as a GIF, and when you designate this image as your background, it will tile over and over again, displaying the logo as the background of your page, yet it's light enough that it lets you easily see type placed over it. The capture above shows the background when placed into a Web authoring application.

Instant Recessed Buttons

This is one of those instant effects where Photoshop does all the work, courtesy of a setting within the Layer Effects Bevel and Emboss dialog box.

STEP ONE: Open the background image (or interface) where you want your recessed button to appear. Create a new layer by clicking on the New Layer icon at the bottom of the Layers palette.

STEP TWO: Set your foreground color to the color that you want your recessed button to be. Switch to the Elliptical Marquee tool by pressing Shift-M until you see the round selection tool appear in the Tool palette. Hold the Shift key and draw a small circular selection on the spot where you want your recessed button to appear.

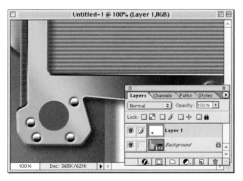

STEP THREE: Fill this selection with your foreground color by pressing Option-Delete (PC: Alt-Backspace). Deselect by pressing Command-D (PC: Control-D).

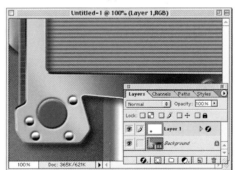

STEP FOUR: To make this flat-looking button look recessed, go under the Layer menu, under Layer Style, and choose Bevel and Emboss. Under the Style pop-up menu, change the Style to Pillow Emboss, and your button will immediately appear recessed into your background because this effect adds shadows and highlights that make it look instantly sunken in.

Makin' copies

After you create a Web button (or almost anything else on a layer), you can make duplicate copies super fast by using this shortcut: First, hold the Command key (PC: Control key) and click on the layer you want to duplicate (this puts a selection around everything on the layer). Then, hold Option-Command (PC: Alt-Control) and drag off copies as you need them. Yeah, baby!

How Web browsers display backgrounds

Just about everyone has a different sized monitor for their computer, and just about everyone sees your Web page in a different sized browser window (some have it fill their entire screen, but most leave it set at the default size the browser manufacturer specified). The point is that some people have a 21" monitor and some have a 15", and to make sure you never see a huge blank spot, browsers automatically tile (repeat vertically and horizontally) whatever sized image you use as a background. They tile like tiles on your kitchen floor (you do have tile, don't you? That carpet-in-the-kitchen thing gets really messy).

Because we know the browser is going to tile our background, filling every inch of visible space, we don't need to create huge backgrounds in Photoshop. Instead, we can create tiny little backgrounds that appear seamless when displayed on a page. This helps the file size stay small and the page load faster.

Creating Seamless Backgrounds

If you're creating a tiling background for a Web page, the last thing you want to see is a seam between tiles. Generally, you want the tiles to repeat as one big seamless background. Here's how to preview your background so that you can hide any seams before it's too late.

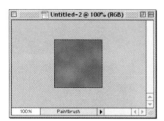

STEP ONE: Open the background that you want to use for your Web site. If you don't have a background handy, you can create one for now. Open a new document, 96 pixels by 96 pixels in RGB mode. Set your foreground color to dark blue, then go under the Filter menu, under Render, and choose Clouds. This creates a cloud pattern that you can use as a background.

STEP TWO: To see what a simple square background will actually look like when it tiles as a background on your Web page, go under the Filter menu, under Other, and choose Offset.

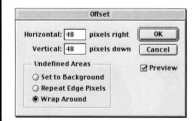

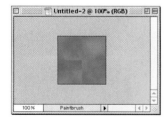

STEP THREE: When the Offset dialog appears, for the Horizontal and Vertical fields, enter values that are approximately half the size of your background image (in this case, my background image is 96 x 96 pixels, so I entered 48 for Horizontal and 48 for Vertical. If you don't get the exact number, it won't make a big difference, so don't sweat it).

STEP FOUR: For Undefined Areas choose Wrap Around, and make sure the Preview check box is turned on. Now take a look at your image on screen, and there you have it—that's what your background is going to look like when it tiles on your Web page. Chances are, you're going to see a very visible seam where one tile stops and the next starts. Click OK to apply the offset. In the next step, we hide the seam.

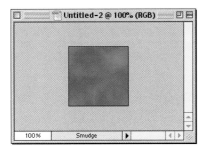

STEP FIVE: There are two popular ways to hide the visible seam. If the background image doesn't have a lot of detail (like the clouds background), you can use the Smudge tool (press Shift-R until you see a tool icon that looks like a finger smudging) to smudge over the seam. This should hide the seams from view. If the background is more detailed, you can use the Clone Stamp tool to clone over the seam (see the sidebar to the right if you're new to cloning with the Clone Stamp tool).

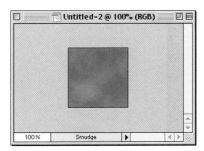

STEP SIX: After you hide the seam, you better check to see if you really got rid of it all. To do that, go back under the Filter menu, under Other, and choose Offset again. Your previous settings will still be there, and the Preview button will already be turned on, so just look at your image and see if you actually did remove the seams so that your background image looks seamless. If not, repeat Step Five (smudging or cloning), then run the Offset filter again to check for seams. Once your image is seamless, you're ready to save it as a background for your Web page.

QUICK TIP

In this particular case, the second time we opened the Offset dialog box, we actually needed to have the dialog box appear on screen so that we could see the preview. However, if you want to apply the last filter you used with the same settings, we would generally just press Command-F (PC: Control-F). There is a shortcut you can use that will open the dialog box with the same settings of your last used filter: it's Option-Command-F (PC: Alt-Control-F).

Using the Clone Stamp tool

To clone over a seam using the Clone Stamp tool, all you need to do is move to an area of your background just outside the seam, hold the Option key (PC: Alt key) and click once. This tells Photoshop that this is the area you want to clone from (this is referred to as "sampling"). Then, move over the seam, click-and-hold your mouse button, and start painting. As you paint, you'll notice that you have two cursors—one where you're painting and a target cursor showing you the area that you're cloning from. In just a few moments, you'll be able to clone over your seam.

Paint Bucket tricks

The Paint Bucket tool is probably my least favorite tool, because you can do almost everything it does using keyboard shortcuts instead of having to change tools. However, it does do two neat tricks:

(1) You can click on the Paint Bucket tool and in the Options Bar, there's a pop-up menu where you can choose your type of fill: either Foreground of Pattern. Using Pattern saves you a trip to the Fill dialog box (used in the trick on this page).

(2) You can use the Paint Bucket to change the color of the area that appears outside your canvas (you know, that gray area you see when you stretch your window out). If you want to change that color, drag your window out (or press the letter "f") to display the gray pasteboard area. Choose a new foreground color, then hold the Shift key and click once on the background to assign your foreground color as the new background.

Hi-tech Grids

This is a quick way to create grids that you can use for backgrounds in Web pages, as elements of interfaces, or just about anything that you can think of that you need to use a grid for.

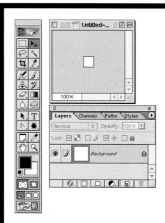

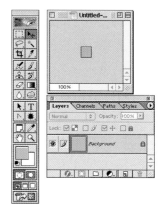

STEP ONE: Open a new document in RGB mode in the size that you want your grid squares to be (in the example here, I chose a 20 x 20-pixel square). Set your foreground color to the color that you want your grid lines to appear (I chose a vibrant green).

STEP TWO: Fill your document with your foreground color by pressing Option-Delete (PC: Alt-Backspace). Create a new layer by clicking on the New Layer icon at the bottom of the Layers palette.

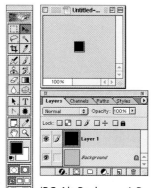

STEP THREE: Set your foreground color to the color that you want for your background. Fill your layer with that color by pressing Option-Delete (PC: Alt-Backspace). Press the letter "v" to switch to the Move tool. Press the Left Arrow key once then press the Up Arrow key once. Press Command-A (PC: Control-A) to Select All. Go under the Edit menu and choose Define Pattern. Name your pattern and click OK.

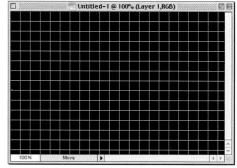

STEP FOUR: Now switch to the document where you want to apply your grid (or create a new one at the size you want). Go under the Edit menu and choose Fill. For Contents use Pattern. Click on the down-facing arrow next to the Custom Pattern sample and choose your new pattern from the bottom of the flyout Pattern Picker. Click OK to fill your image with your repeating grid.

Quick 3D Buttons

Need a quick 3D button but don't want that standard old radial gradient button that permeated the Web for about two years? Here's a quick way to start with a standard and give it a quick twist.

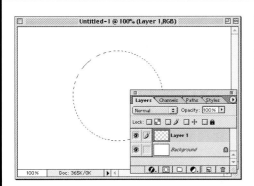

STEP ONE: Create a new blank document in RGB mode, then add a new layer by clicking on the New Layer icon at the bottom of the Layers palette. Switch to the Elliptical (round) Marquee tool, hold the Shift key, and draw a circular selection on this new layer. Make white your foreground color by pressing the letter "d" then the letter "x."

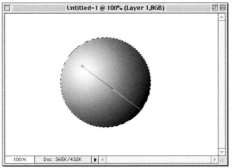

STEP TWO: Press the letter "g" to switch to the Gradient tool. Up in the Options Bar, choose the Radial Gradient (it's the second Gradient tool from the left) and make sure your gradient is set to Foreground to Background. Drag your gradient from just below the upper-left side of your circle down to the bottom-right side (as shown above). Don't deselect quite yet.

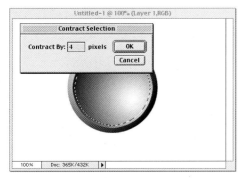

STEP THREE: Go under the Select menu, under Modify, and choose Contract. When the dialog box appears, choose 10 pixels and click OK. Your selection will shrink (contract) by 10 pixels. Go under the Edit menu, under Transform, and choose Rotate 180°. Go under the Select menu again, under Contract, but this time contract by only 4 pixels.

STEP FOUR: Go under the Edit menu, under Transform, and choose Rotate 180°. Press Command-U to bring up Hue/Saturation. Check the Colorize box and choose a color for your selected circle. Deselect by pressing Command-D (PC: Control-D). Go under the Layer menu, under Layer Style, and choose Drop Shadow to complete the effect.

Jumping to the tool you need

There are five ways to select tools:

(1) If the tool you want is visible in the Tool palette, you can click directly on it to switch to that tool.

(2) If the tool you want is not visible, you can click-and-hold on any tool that has a tiny black right-facing triangle in the bottom right-hand corner of the tool's icon. That tells you there are more related tools hidden, and if you click-and-hold, they will "fly out" on a menu for you to choose.

(3) You can select tools by pressing their keyboard equivalents. For example, for the Magic Wand tool, you just press the letter "w" (for Wand).

(4) If the tool you want is not visible, you can usually hold the Shift key and press the one-letter keyboard equivalent to rotate through related tools.

(5) If the tool you want isn't visible, you can also Option-click (PC: Alt-click) on the visible tool to rotate through the tools.

12

I put this chapter last for a very important reason: It's Chapter 12, and right after it is the Index, so I felt it belonged back here. But besides that, there were other reasons. Let's

12

Let's Get Ready to Rumble
Special Effects

face it, this is a Photoshop effects book. There are 100 Photoshop books that teach you what a pixel is, how to use the Lasso tool, and what the Radius slider in the Unsharp Mask filter does. But this book is different. It does some, all, or none of the following: (a) assumes you know those things, (b) it doesn't care if you know those things, (c) it assumes you'll buy a different book if you want to learn those things, and (d) it doesn't try to teach you those things because those things just aren't fun. They're useful. They're important, but they're not fun. Effects are fun. Effects are a blast. In fact, effects are special. That's why they're called special effects.Hey, that would make a great title for the last chapter of my book. Here are some of my very favorites, and I honestly hope that (a) they'll become some of your favorites, and (b) they'll make you lots of money, and (c) you decide to send me a percentage of your profits because after all, (d) we're like best friends forever now, right? Right! Go forth, and affect things in a special way.

Quick layer duplication

Want to make a copy of your active layer? Press Command-J and presto— you've got a copy.

You can also duplicate a layer by holding Option-Command (PC: Alt-Control) and dragging a copy.

Then, of course, there's the incredible molasses way (only to be used by those charging by the hour) of going under the Layer menu, or Layers palette pop-down menu, and choosing Duplicate Layer, which brings up a dialog box and wastes even more time. It's a bill-by-the-hour dream come true.

Quick Prism Starbursts

This is a twist on an effect that I learned from *Photoshop User's* Creative Director Doug Gornick for adding a photographic-style starburst to an image. The effect can be applied to reflective objects with dark backgrounds, resulting in some specular highlights.

STEP ONE:
Open a background image in RGB mode. Using the Pen tool draw a cross-shaped path with sharp points at 90° from one another, as shown above. Press the letter "d" than "x" to switch your foreground color to white. Switch to the Channels palette and create a new channel by clicking on the New Channel icon at the bottom of the palette (the channel will appear black).

STEP TWO:
Switch to the Paths palette. In the Paths palette pop-up menu, choose Fill Path. When the dialog box appears, set the Feather Radius to 1, and then click OK. Press Shift-M until the Elliptical Marquee tool appears in your Tool palette. Hold Shift-Option (PC: Shift-Alt) and draw a circular selection from the center of the cross outward.

STEP THREE:
Double-click the Quick Mask icon in the Tool palette. In the options dialog, make sure that Color Indicates Masked Areas is selected and click OK. Go under the Select menu and choose Load Selection. When the dialog box appears, choose Quick Mask as the channel to load and click OK. Switch to the Gradient tool, and in the Options Bar, choose the Radial Gradient (it's the second tool from the left). Draw a white to black gradient starting from the center (being white) and terminating at the outer limit of the circle (as black).

STEP FOUR:
Before deselecting, make sure your foreground color is set to white, go under the Edit menu, and choose Stroke. When the dialog box appears, set the width to 1 pixel, choose Center for Location, and click OK. Press the letter "q" again to return to normal mode. Fill the selection with the foreground color (should still be white) by pressing Option-Delete (PC: Alt-Backspace) to produce the effect shown here.

STEP FIVE: Return to the composite color preview by pressing Command-~ (tilde) (PC: Control-~). Switch to the Layers palette and create a new layer. Press Command-A (PC: Control-A) to select all. Press the letter "d" then press Option-Delete (PC: Alt-Backspace) to fill this layer with black. In the Layers palette, change the Layer mode from Normal to Lighten (the black should disappear). Go to the Select menu and choose Load Selection.

STEP SIX: When the dialog box appears, choose Alpha 1 and click OK. Go under the Filter menu, under Render, and choose Lens Flare. Center the flare in the preview box, enter 175 as the Brightness, and click OK. Now Deselect. Go to the Paths palette and click just below the Work Path to deactivate your path. The final step is to rotate the Lens Flare by drawing a rectangular selection around it, and then pressing Command-T (PC: Control-T). You can now rotate and scale the flare for a more realistic look.

QUICK TIP
You can view each color channel individually by pressing Command-1, Command-2, Command-3, and so on. (PC: Control-1, Control-2, Control-3, and so on). To view the composite RGB channel, press Command-Tilde (the tilde key is right above your Tab key, it looks like this: ~).

Selecting layers without using the Layers palette

Wouldn't it be great to be working on an image and, without even opening the Layers palette, click on an object right within your image and jump to the layer that the image is on? Well, believe it or not, there are three different ways to do just that:

(1) Click on the Move tool, and in the Options Bar, turn on Auto Select Layer. Now, whenever you click on an object, the layer that the object is on becomes instantly active.

(2) When you have the Move tool active, you can also hold the Control key (PC: Right-click) and click within your image and a pop-up list of layers will appear. Choose the one you want from the list and it becomes the active layer.

(3) If you don't have the Move tool selected, press Control-Command (PC: Alt-Control) and click in your image. You'll get the same contextual menu mentioned above.

Adding spot colors

For years, Photoshop only wanted you to do one of three things: Create a black-and-white image, a grayscale image, or a full-color image. However, back in Photoshop 5.0, Adobe introduced the ability to create spot color separations. To add a spot color to your grayscale image, make a selection of the area you want to have a spot color, then go to the Channels palette and from the pop-down menu choose New Spot Channel. When the dialog box appears, you can click on the color swatch and choose a Pantone color to be your spot channel.

You can also add an extra spot color (or bump plate) to a four-color CMYK image in a similar fashion (giving you four color plates and a fifth spot color plate when you run your separations). There's even a special format for saving your image with spot colors: It's an EPS format called DCS 2.0 (which stands for Desktop Color Separation). There's a lot more to creating spot color seps, but at this point (because we're dealing with Channels), I just wanted to mention that they were there. See, I care.

Dramatic Beam of Sunlight

This is a trick I used during the "Instructor Jam Session" at PhotoshopWorld, and I had so many comments about it, I thought I'd include it here. Although the effect makes use of channels, it's so simple, you don't really have to understand how channels work—just follow along, step-by-step.

STEP ONE: Open a background image that would be appropriate to have a beam of light shining in on it. (Note: this effect works in RGB color or Grayscale.)

STEP TWO: Go to the Channels palette and click the New Channel icon (found at the bottom of the Channels palette). A channel filled with black will appear. This is the channel we'll use to draw our beam of light, but before we start drawing, we have to see the underlying image.

STEP THREE: In the Channels palette, click in the first column just to the left of the RGB channel's thumbnail to make the RGB image visible behind your channel (this is how we're able to see the underlying image and put our beam of light in the right place).

STEP FOUR: Switch to the Polygonal Lasso toll (press Shift-L until it appears in the Tool palette), and select the area where you'd like your beam of light to fall. Draw your beam so it starts off small at the top and then grows larger as it hits the point you want to focus on.

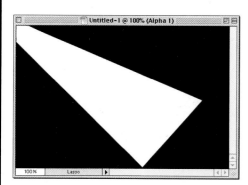

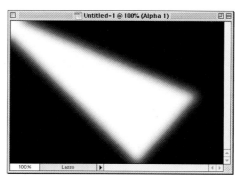

STEP FIVE: In the Channels palette, click the Eye icon next to the RGB channel's thumbnail again to hide the RGB image, leaving just the new channel visible. Make sure that you have your foreground color set to white. Press Option-Delete (PC: Alt-Backspace) to fill your selection with white. Now, press Command-D (PC: Control-D) to deselect.

STEP SIX: Go under the Filter menu, under Blur and choose Gaussian Blur. Enter 8 pixels (use 18 for high-res, 300-dpi images) and click OK to soften the beam of light.

STEP SEVEN: Go to the layers palette and click once on the Background layer. Now go under the Select menu and choose Load Selection. A dialog box will appear, and the channel you created with the beam of light (named Alpha 1) will appear in the Channel pop-up menu. Click OK to load this channel (selection) onto your background image.

STEP EIGHT: Go under the Select menu, and choose Inverse to select the background area (everything but the beam of light). Then go under the Image menu, under Adjust and choose Levels. We'll use Levels to darken the background. At the bottom of the Levels dialog box, drag the Right Output Levels slider to the left to darken the background (leaving the beam area untouched). Click OK. Don't Deselect yet.

CONTINUED

Running filters on CMYK images

The next time you convert a file to CMYK format, take a trip under the Filter menu and you'll find something that might surprise you. Many of the filters are grayed out (unavailable). Once you've converted to CMYK, you don't want to convert back to RGB to use these filters, because when you convert back to CMYK again, it's going to re-separate your image and cause untold horrors to your separation (OK, it's not that bad, but it's not a good thing to do).

Instead, here's a trick that lets you apply any filter to your CMYK images. Go to the Channels palette and click on a color channel (say Cyan for example). Now, look under the Filter menu—the filters are back, baby! You can now apply the filter to each individual CMYK channel. It takes a little longer, but it'll get the job done. Here's a tip to speed up the process: Run the filter on the Cyan channel, press Command-2 (PC: Control-2) to switch to the Magenta Channel, and then press Command-F (PC: Control-F) to run the filter again. Repeat this for the Yellow and Black channels.

Photoshop's "Client Presentation Mode"

When it's time for me to show a client the final image (or an on-screen proof along the way), I don't like them to see the application running, just the image.

One reason is that I've had clients say, "Hey, is that Photoshop? My next door neighbor Earl has Photoshop on his home computer and he does some really neat stuff." At this point, I start to cringe because you can tell he's thinking "Hey, my neighbor could do this for me, and I'd save a bundle."

Secondly, it puts the client's focus on the image, and not the software surrounding it (which can be distracting), and third, it just looks more professional.

To get into what I call "Presentation mode" press f-f-Tab (press the letter "f" twice, then the Tab key once). This centers your image on screen, puts a black background behind your image, and hides Photoshop's menus and palettes. It looks great.

When you're done and your client steps away, just press f-Tab to get all your goodies back.

STEP NINE: Go under the Select menu again, and choose Inverse to inverse the selection again (so now we're going to affect the beam, rather than the background). Next, go under the View menu and choose Show Extras. This leaves your selection in place, but hides the annoying "marching ants" selection border so that we can see the effect in the next step clearly as we bring it into the image.

STEP TEN: To complete the effect, press Command-L (PC: Control-L) to bring up the Levels dialog box again. This time, slide the LEFT Output Levels slider to the right and as you slide, you'll start to see the ray of sunlight appear in your image. When you feel it's bright enough, click OK. Press Command-D (PC: Control-D) to deselect and view the final effect.

QUICK TIP
The keyboard shortcut for inversing your current selection is Shift-Command-I (PC: Shift-Control-I). Don't confuse **Inverse** *(which swaps the selected area for its opposite) and* **Invert** *(Command-I [PC: Control-I]), which turns your image into a negative of itself.*

Instant Lightning Bolts

It doesn't get much down-and-dirtier than this. In just a few simple steps, you can create realistic lightning bolts and add them to your images. This effect works best when added to an existing background image, but it's just as easy to create it starting with a blank background.

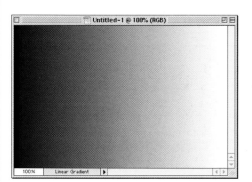

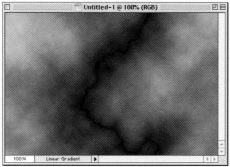

STEP ONE: Open a background image. Create a new layer. Press the letter "d" on your keyboard to set your foreground color to black. Fill this new layer with a black to white gradient by using the Foreground to Background gradient and dragging the Gradient tool from the left edge of the image to the right edge.

STEP TWO: Go under the Filter menu, under Render, and choose Difference Clouds (this will render a random texture similar to clouds). Press Command-I (PC: Control-I) to invert the image.

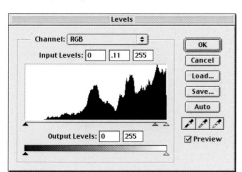

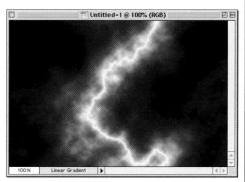

STEP THREE: Open the Levels dialog box by pressing Command-L (PC: Control-L) and slide the middle Input Levels triangle (under the histogram) to the far right until the lightning effect appears. Click OK. To bring this lightning effect into your background image you must change the layer mode of the lightning layer. To do this, go to the Layers palette, click-and-hold on the pop-up menu near the top left of the palette, and change the mode from Normal to Screen.

STEP FOUR: If you want to colorize your lightning, first change the layer mode (on the Layers palette pop-up menu) back to normal. Then press Command-U (PC: Control-U) to open the Hue/Saturation dialog box. Check the Colorize box in the lower right-hand corner, then slide the saturation slider down to 25. Use the Hue slider to change the color to any hue you'd like, then click OK. You can now change the layer mode from Normal back to Screen to complete the effect.

Don't like the lightning pattern? Request a new one

One of the great things about the Clouds filter is that the pattern it generates is totally random, so if you do the effect at left and don't like the way your lightning spikes look, just start from scratch and redo your clouds filter. Each time you do it, you'll get a different cloud effect and a different set of spikes in your lightning.

Change your view anytime

When you open a filter dialog, or any dialog like Levels or Curves, most of your menus are grayed out while you're in that dialog. However, one menu that's almost always available is your View menu. Your keyboard shortcuts for accessing View menu items also still work, even though you're in a dialog box.

Try it for yourself: Open an image, bring up the Gaussian Blur filter dialog, then look at the menu bar up top. View is still available, you can just reach out and choose a new view or use the keyboard shortcut of your choice.

Creating Metal Rivets

This effect is popular both in print and on the Web. It comes in handy for a variety of projects, and it is especially well suited for high-tech interface design. A similar effect was used in the promotional posters for the movie *Wild Wild West* starring Will Smith.

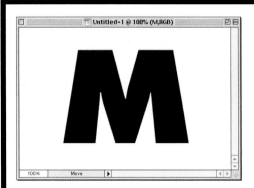

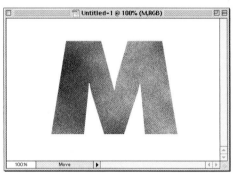

STEP ONE: For this example, we're going to start with a 72-ppi document in RGB mode. Next, create the image that you want to have rivets (in this instance, I used a capital M in the font Futura Extra Bold, but any thick bold font will do). Go under the Layer menu, under Rasterize and choose Type to convert your type into an image layer. First, we'll give our type some metal texture.

STEP TWO: In the Layers palette, turn on Lock Transparent Pixels for your text layer. Press the letter "d" to reset your foreground color to black. Then go under the Filter menu, under Render and choose Clouds. Next, go under the Filter menu again, under Noise, and choose Add Noise. Set the Amount to 10%, Distribution to Gaussian, check the Monochromatic box, and click OK.

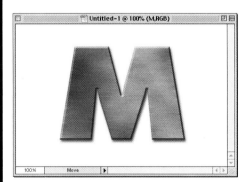

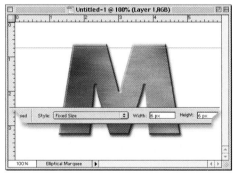

STEP THREE: To give your type a weathered, steel effect, go under the Filter menu, under Blur, and choose Motion Blur. In the Motion Blur dialog, for Angle choose 0, for Amount choose 24, then click OK. To add a bevel to the letter, go under the Layer menu, under Layer Style, and choose Bevel and Emboss. Increase the depth to 300. Then, in the list of Layer Styles on the left side of the dialog box, click the check box beside Drop Shadow to apply a soft drop shadow behind your letter, then click OK. Now, on to the rivets.

STEP FOUR: Press Command-R (PC: Control-R) to make your rulers visible. Click on the top ruler and drag a guide out to where you want the TOP of your first row of rivets to appear. Create a new layer by clicking on the New Layer icon in the Layers palette. Get the Elliptical (round) Marquee tool. In its Options Bar, change the Style from Normal to Fixed Size (as shown above). Set both your Width and Height to 6 pixels. Now when you click this tool, it will automatically draw a 6 x 6-pixel circular selection (pretty slick, eh?).

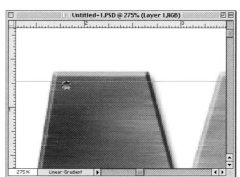

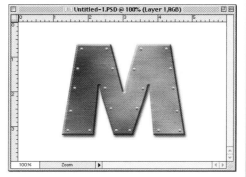

STEP FIVE: You need to zoom in pretty close to build your rivets, so press Command-+ (PC: Control-+) a couple of times to increase the magnification of your image. Next, with the Elliptical Marquee tool selected, click once directly on the guide where you want the top of your first rivet to appear. A 6 x 6-pixel circular selection will appear.

STEP SIX: Press the letter "g" to switch to the Gradient tool. In its Options bar, make sure the Gradient chosen is Foreground to Background. Then take the Gradient tool, start at the top of your 6 x 6-pixel circular selection and drag to the bottom of the circle and release. This creates a black to white gradient inside the circle. Don't deselect yet.

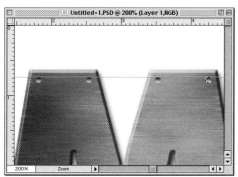

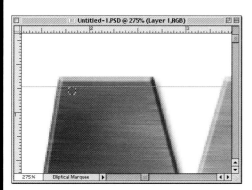

STEP SEVEN: Hold Shift-Option-Command (PC: Shift-Alt-Control), click on your circle gradient, and drag to your right to make a copy of it. Place this rivet copy where you'd like it, then repeat the process for as many rivets as you need. You can "drag-copy" the last rivet you created and start the process again at the bottom of the letter, just drag out another guide to use for alignment purposes.

STEP EIGHT: You can also drag-copy more rivets to go up the sides of the letter using the same process (just don't hold Shift). Deselect by pressing Command-D (PC: Control-D). Zoom back out to 100% view by double-clicking on the Zoom tool in the Tool palette. To give the rivets a more realistic effect, press Command-I (PC: Control-I) to invert the rivets and complete the effect. If you want some variations, continue on to the next page for two optional versions.

How to navigate your image when you're zoomed in close

When you've zoomed in on an image (as we have in the effect at the left), trying to navigate using the scroll bars is frustrating at best, because when you're zoomed in really close, even a small move with the scroll bar can move the area you're working on totally out of the image window. Instead, when you've zoomed in, hold the Spacebar and your cursor will temporarily change to the Hand tool, and you can click-and-drag around your image. This is an ideal way to move quickly around your zoomed image, without the frustration of the scroll bars. When you release the Spacebar, you immediately switch back to the tool you were using.

How to copy a flattened version in a multilayered document

When you make a selection on a layer and press Command-C (PC: Control-C), it copies the selected area from that layer into memory. But did you know that you can copy from all your visible layers (as if it was a flattened image), by adding Shift to that keyboard shortcut? That's right. To do that press Shift-Command-C (PC: Shift-Control-C), and it captures everything inside your selected area as if it was a flattened background image.

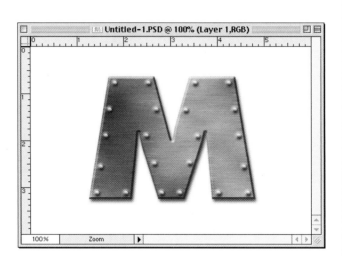

RIVET OPTION #1: For a raised rivet effect, go under the Layer menu, under Layer Style, and choose Bevel and Emboss. For Style, choose Outer Bevel, lower the Depth to 50%, and click OK to create the effect shown above.

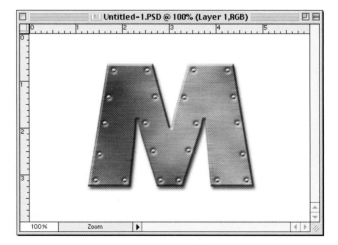

RIVET OPTION #2: For a sunken-in rivet effect, go under the Layer menu, under Layer Style, and choose Bevel and Emboss. Change the Style setting to Pillow Emboss, then click OK to create the rivet effect shown above.

QUICK TIP
To remove a Layer Effect from a Layer, click on the effect's name in the Layers palette and drag it into the trash can at the bottom of the Layers palette.

To hide a currently applied Layer Effect from view, in the Layers palette, click on the Eye icon next to the effect you want to hide. To reveal it again, click in the column where the Eye used to appear.

Metal Stamp Effect

This tip lets you create some type and have it appear to pop up from a background image, as though it was stamped into the background. This effect used to be accomplished by using channels, but here's a way to get the same effect without using channels, and it's quick and easy.

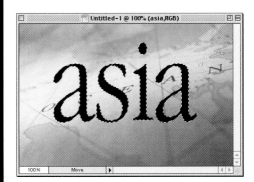

STEP ONE: Open a background image. Using the Type tool, create the type that you want to pop up from the background. Position the type as you want it, then go to the Layers palette and Command-click (PC: Control-click) on the Type layer's name to put a selection around your type.

STEP TWO: Now that your type is selected, you can drag the Type layer into the trash can at the bottom of the Layers palette. This deletes the layer, but leaves an active selection in the shape of your type.

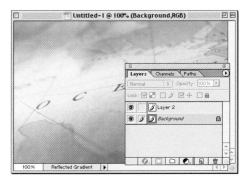

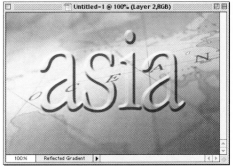

STEP THREE: Now press Command-J (PC: Control-J) to take the area under your selection (on the Background layer) and put it on its own layer.

STEP FOUR: Go under the Layer menu, under Layer Style, and choose Bevel and Emboss. Under Style choose Emboss. Increase the Depth to 300 and click OK to complete the effect. Note: depending how dark/light the background image is, you might want to darken/lighten your type layer using the Output Levels sliders at the bottom of the Levels dialog box.

Selecting just one letter, rather than the whole word

We've been using the Command-click (PC: Control-click) on the layer's name trick to put a selection around your type throughout this book. But that puts a selection around all your text. What if you want just one letter or two? You can do it, but first you have to rasterize your Type layer by going under the Layer menu, under Rasterize, and choosing Type. You might be tempted to try selecting the letter with the Magic Wand tool, but don't—it'll leave behind little edge pixels if you move the type. Instead, try this: Draw a very loose selection around the letter or letters that you want to select (don't touch the edges of the letter, just make a loose selection). Hold the Command key and press on of the arrow keys on your keyboard. Your letter will be immediately selected with no messy edge pixels, so now you can colorize it, move it, or do whatever.

Setting shades of gray

Photoshop is such an incredibly powerful program that surely there would be a little slider or pop-up menu for creating shades of gray, right? Well, there is one, it's just a bit hidden. Go under the Window menu and choose Show Color to bring up the Color palette. In the pop-down menu, choose Grayscale Slider. A slider will appear that goes from 0% to 100% and you can slide it to the percentage of gray that you want.

Another popular way, though a bit more cumbersome, is to click on the Foreground color swatch and in the CMYK fields of the Color Picker, enter 0 for Cyan, Magenta, and Yellow. Under Black, enter 40 and click OK. This gives you a shade of gray without any CMY in it, whereas the Color palette gives you a gray color build, with percentages of Cyan, Magenta, and Yellow in your gray.

Water Drops

This is a quick effect inspired by a product shot I saw in the Hammacher Schlemmer gift catalog. In their product shot for these cool-looking dive watches, they had two wristwatches crisscrossed over a gray gradient background covered with water droplets. Here's how to recreate a similar style effect.

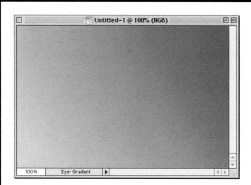

STEP ONE: Open a new document and fill the Background layer with a gradient that goes from 70% black to 20% black at a 45° angle (as shown above). Create a new blank layer by clicking on the New Layer icon at the bottom of the Layers palette. Press the letter "d" then the letter "x" to set your foreground color to white, then fill this new layer with white by pressing Option-Delete (PC: Alt-Backspace).

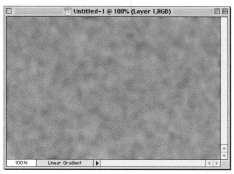

STEP TWO: Go under the Filter menu, under Noise, and choose Add Noise. For amount, enter 400%. For Distribution choose Gaussian, check Monochromatic, and click OK. Then under the Filter menu, under Blur, choose Gaussian Blur. Add a 5-pixel blur, and click OK.

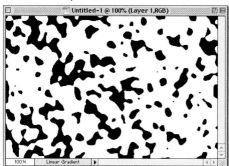

STEP THREE: Go under the Image menu, under Adjust, and choose Threshold. When the dialog box appears, drag the slider slightly to the right until rounded spots start to appear. When the spots look fairly large, click OK. Press Command-F (PC: Control-F) to add another 5-pixel Gaussian Blur.

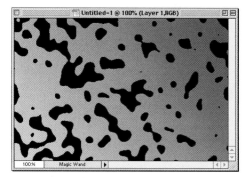

STEP FOUR: Go to Threshold again and move the slider towards the right until you have even bigger raindrop-looking spots. Switch to the Magic Wand tool and click it once on any white area surrounding your spots to select the white areas, then press Delete (PC: Backspace). Deselect by pressing Command-D (PC: Control-D).

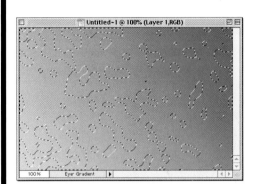

STEP FIVE: Hold the Command key (PC: Control key), and in the Layers palette, click on Layer 1 to select the spots. Press the letter "g" to switch to the gradient tool and drag the same 70% to 20% gradient through your water drops (your selection will still be visible on screen. Don't deselect yet).

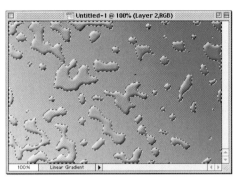

STEP SIX: Go under the Layer menu, under Layer Style, and choose Bevel and Emboss. When the dialog box appears, in the Shading section increase the Highlight Opacity to 100% and click OK (Note: for high-res images you may need to increase the Size amount to 8 or 9).

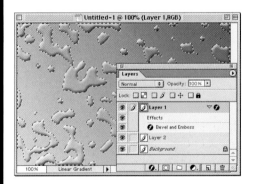

STEP SEVEN: Create a new blank layer and drag it below your water spots layer. Click on the water spots layer and press Command-E (PC: Control-E) to merge your water spots layer with your blank layer (this keeps the effect on the spots, but removes the effect from any further changes).

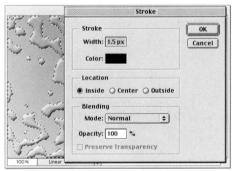

STEP EIGHT: Press the letter "d" to reset your foreground color to black. Then go under the Edit menu and choose Stroke. When the dialog box appears, enter 1.5 pixels for Width, choose Inside for Location, and click OK to stroke your water spots with a black stroke. Don't deselect quite yet.

Why you don't always want to merge down

By default, each Layer Effect has a blend mode chosen for it. For example, the Drop Shadow filter has the Multiply mode chosen because it helps the shadow look better when printed. That's all well and good, but there is sometimes a downside that occurs when you merge layers together.

You have to remember, blend modes determine how a layer interacts with the layer beneath it. In normal mode, it doesn't interact, it covers whatever is beneath it (unless you lower the opacity of the layer, of course). So, when Adobe assigned these modes to Layer Effects, they react to objects on the layers beneath them, and when you merge down layer by layer, often you'll lose part or all of the effect. There are two ways around this: (1) don't merge layer by layer— flatten the whole image at once by choosing Flatten Image from the pop-down menu; and (2) hide any layers you don't want merged, then choose Merge Visible from the pop-down menu.

CONTINUED

Apply changes to multiple layers

There are a number of changes and transformations you can apply to multiple layers at once. The first step is to go to the Layers palette and link together the layers that you want to affect. This is done by clicking in the second column beside each layer you want to link. A tiny link icon will appear indicating that the layer is now linked to your currently active layer. Once that's done, whatever transformation (like scaling or rotating) you do to your active layer will also affect all your linked layers.

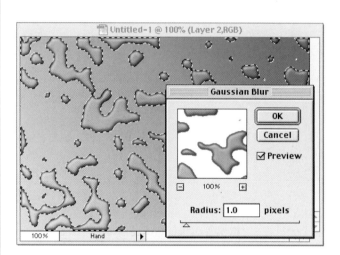

STEP NINE: Go under the Filter menu, under Blur, and choose Gaussian Blur. Add a 1-pixel blur and click OK. Deselect by pressing Command-D (PC: Control-D). Sometimes, this effect creates too many water spots, but you can easily eliminate some by using the Eraser tool on the water spots layer.

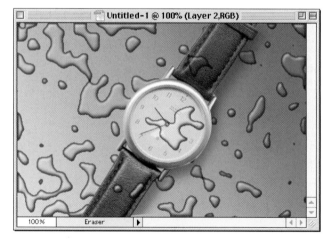

STEP TEN: Now open your product shot image and drag it onto the water drops image. Add a soft drop shadow by going under the Layer menu, under Layer Style, and choosing Drop Shadow. Lastly, go to the water spots layer, use the Lasso tool to draw a loose selection around a few drops, then press Command-J (PC: Control-J) to put them on their own layer above your product. Change the layer mode of these new drops to Hard Light to make them appear transparent (as shown on the watch face above) and switch to the Move tool to position them over your object to complete the effect.

QUICK TIP
Anytime you're in a Filter dialog, you can increase or decrease the value in the selected field by pressing the Up/Down Arrow keys on your keyboard.

Chiseled Edge Effect

What's different about this particular torn edge effect is the fact that you're making the edge appear more chiseled than just merely torn like a piece of paper. Although we're using this effect on a marble texture, the technique works on almost any texture or even a solid color fill (as long as the color isn't black).

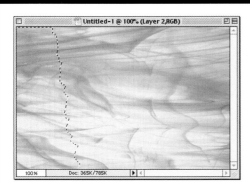

STEP ONE: Open a background texture. Press the letter "L" to switch to the Lasso tool. Hold the mouse button down and click where you'd like your chiseled edge to begin. With the mouse button still held, draw a jagged selection from top to bottom. When you get to the bottom of the image, drag the lasso to the left of your image (you can actually go outside the image to draw a straight line along the edge). With the mouse button still down, move your mouse up to the top of your image, and finally, over to the right where you started. Release the mouse to close the selection.

STEP TWO: Press Command-J (PC: Control-J) to put this jagged selection on its own layer. Next, click once on the Background layer in the Layers palette, press Command-A (PC: Control-A) to select the entire background, and then press Delete (PC: Backspace). Press Command-D (PC: Control-D) to deselect. Click back on Layer 1. Make a copy of Layer 1 by dragging it to the New Layer icon at the bottom of the Layers palette.

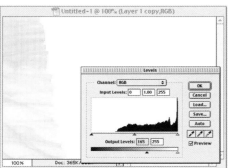

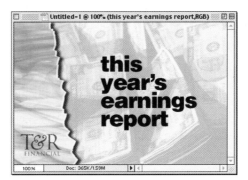

STEP THREE: Click back on Layer 1. Press Command-L (PC: Control-L) to bring up the Levels dialog. Drag the bottom left Output Levels slider to the right until the number reads at least 165 and click OK. Press the letter "v" to switch to the Move tool.

STEP FOUR: Press the Right Arrow key on your keyboard six times to move this lighter layer to the right a bit. Go under the Layer menu, under Layer Style, and choose Drop Shadow. Set the Distance to 7, Angle to 171, and click OK. In this example, I added a money background layer and some type.

Detaching a Layer Effect from its layer

When you apply a Layer Effect, the effect is attached directly to your layer. So if you apply a Layer Effects Drop Shadow to a Type layer, that shadow is attached to your Type layer. If you'd like to separate that drop shadow onto its own layer, you can go under the Layer menu, under Layer Style, and choose Create Layers. When you do this, a new layer is created which contains just the effect (in this case, it would contain the drop shadow). If you try this when you've applied a Bevel and Emboss Layer Effect, it separates the highlights to one layer and the shadows to another. However, in the case of Bevel and Emboss, they're still grouped with the original layer as a clipping group. To remove the clipping group, press Shift-Command-G (PC: Shift-Control-G). You will see that you now have three separate layers.

Viewing only your active layer and hiding the rest

If you have a multilayered document, you can look at just the layer you're working on (or any one layer for that matter) by holding the Option key (PC: Alt key) and clicking on the Eye icon in the first column next to it in the Layers palette. This immediately hides all other layers from view, leaving only your chosen layer visible (and any Layer Styles you have applied to other layers). To show all the layers again, hold the Option key (PC: Alt key) and click on the Eye icon again for your layer, and the rest will instantly reappear.

Multicolor Glow

Although we're doing this effect on type, this really isn't a type trick, because you can apply this multi-color glow to any object on a layer. This is an easy technique, thanks to Photoshop's Layer Effects and a few little tweaks by you.

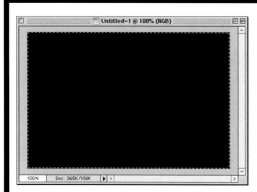

STEP ONE: Open a new document in RGB mode. Press the letter "d" to set your foreground color to black, and fill your background with black by pressing Option-Delete (PC: Alt-Backspace).

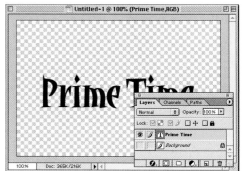

STEP TWO: Using the Type tool, create your type. It will appear on a layer above the background, but because they're both black, you'll have to hide the background layer to see your type. So click on the Eye icon next to your Background layer to hide it from view. Position your type as you'd like (shown above) and then click in the column where the Eye icon used to be to make your black background visible again.

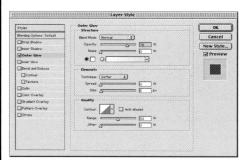

STEP THREE: Go under the Layer menu, under Layer Style, and choose Outer Glow. When the dialog box appears, click on the light yellow (OK, I admit it—it's beige. Yecch!) color swatch, and when the Color Picker appears, choose white as your color and click OK. In the Outer Glow dialog box, change the Blend Mode to Normal and click OK to apply a white glow to your letters.

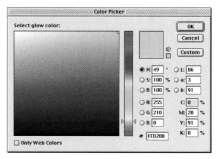

STEP FOUR: In the Layers palette, make a copy of your Type layer by dragging it to the New Layer icon at the bottom of the Layers palette. Drag this copy layer below your original Type layer. Then double-click directly on the little f that appears right before the words Outer Glow (in your copy) to bring up the dialog box's current settings. Click on the white swatch and change the color to yellow.

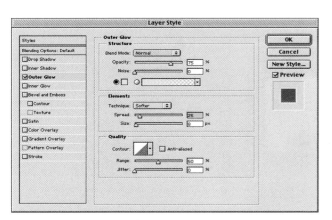

STEP FIVE: Increase the Size amount to 8, the Spread to 25, and click OK to apply a yellow glow that extends beyond your original white glow.

STEP SIX: Make a copy of this yellow glow Type layer (drag this layer to the New Layer icon at the bottom of the Layers palette). In the Layers palette, drag this new copy layer below your yellow Type layer. Double-click directly on the little *f* that appears right before the effect's name in the Layers palette to bring up its dialog box with its current settings. Click on the yellow swatch and change the color to purple. Increase the Size to 12 and click OK to apply a final glow. Now it appears that your glow starts with white (right around the letters) and then radiates to yellow, then to purple, creating a multicolored glow.

QUICK TIP
If there's a color in your image you want to use as a glow color, when you click on the color swatch in the Outer Glow dialog and the Color Picker appears, move your cursor outside the Color Picker, and click once within your image on the color you want for your glow.

Copying Layer Effects to other layers

After you apply a Layer Effect to a layer, you can apply that same effect (with the exact same settings) to any other layer. The slow sloth-like way is to go under the Layer menu, under Layer Style, and choose Copy Layer Style. Then go back to the Layers palette, click on the layer where you want the effects, then sloth your way back under the Layer menu, under Layer Style, and choose Paste Layer Style.

A much faster (and more fun) way is to hold the Control key (PC: right-click) and click-and-hold on your layer in the Layers palette. A pop-up menu will appear and you can choose Copy Layer Style. Then hold the Control key (PC: right-click) and click-and-hold on the layer in the Layers palette that you want to copy the effect to. Choose Paste Layer Style from the pop-up menu that appears. Try it once, and you'll never go digging under the Layer Style menu again.

The multiple undos keyboard shortcut

As I'm sure you know, Photoshop keeps track of your last 20 steps (by default) and at any time, you can undo your last 20 steps by going to the History palette and clicking on the point in time you want to jump back to (or you can move back one step at a time). I rarely do this, because there's a great keyboard shortcut that does it for me and I use it dozens of times a day. The standard Command-Z (PC: Control-Z) just undoes your last step, and if you press it again, it redoes your last step (toggling back and forth between undo and redo). But to have real multiple undo's on a keyboard shortcut, just press Option-Command-Z (PC: Alt-Control-Z), and every time you press it, it undoes the previous step (up to 20 by default).

Type on Fire!

This is my twist on the popular effect for setting your type on fire. I particularly like the way the fire looks when you get to Step Six; you could just stop the effect right there and have a pretty slick-looking white-hot effect, but I took it a few steps further to give you a little more flexibility (just in case).

STEP ONE: Open a new grayscale image (note: it must be grayscale at this point). Fill the Background layer with black. Make white your foreground color, then create your type. Rasterize your type by going under the Layer menu, under Rasterize, and choosing Type.

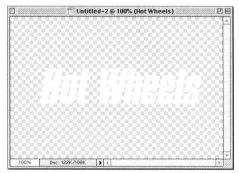

STEP TWO: Go under the Layer menu and choose Duplicate Layer. When the Duplicate Layer dialog appears, change your Destination to New at the bottom of the dialog and click OK. This will duplicate your text layer to a new document. We'll need this layer later in this technique.

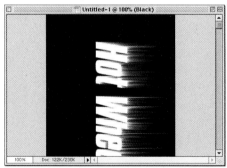

STEP THREE: Switch back to your original document. Merge your text layer with the background layer by pressing Command-E (PC: Control-E). Go under the Image menu, under Rotate Canvas, and choose 90° CW. Then go under the Filter menu, under Stylize, and choose Wind. In the Wind dialog box, make sure your chosen method is Wind and that your Direction is From the Left, and then click OK. Press Command-F (PC: Control-F) to run this same filter again with the exact same settings.

STEP FOUR: Go under the Image menu, under Rotate Canvas, and choose 90° CCW. Then, under the Filter menu, under Stylize, choose Diffuse. Make sure that it's set to Normal mode and click OK.

STEP FIVE: Go under the Filter menu, under Blur and choose Gaussian Blur. Enter 2 pixels, and click OK.

STEP SIX: Go under the Image menu, under Mode, and choose Indexed Color. Then go back under the Image menu, under Mode, and choose Color Table. In the Color Table dialog, choose Black Body in the Table pop-up menu at the top and click OK. Then go under the Image menu yet again, under Mode, and choose RGB.

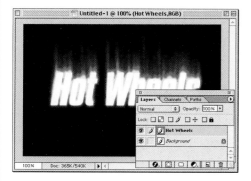

STEP SEVEN: Switch to the other document (the duplicate of our text layer—it might look blank if you have your transparency grid turned off because it's white text on a white background). Go under the Layer menu and choose Duplicate layer. When the Duplicate Layer dialog appears, change your destination to the name of your main document (the one with the fire) and click OK. Your text layer will appear in exactly the same place as it was earlier, before the duplication.

STEP EIGHT: Press the letter "d" to set your foreground color to black, then press Shift-Option-Delete (PC: Shift-Alt-Backspace) to fill your text with black. Lastly, go under the Filter menu, under Distort, and choose Ripple. In the Ripple dialog box, choose 27 for Amount, and for Size choose Large. Click OK to complete the effect.

Toggling your color spectrum

Toggling your color spectrum—that phrase just sounds like it would hurt, but actually, it's a trick for accessing colors in other modes while in the Color palette.

Open the Color palette, and you'll notice a color spectrum (looks like a multicolored gradient) running across the bottom of the palette. This is so you can visually click and choose a color, but if the color mode you want isn't the one that's currently displayed at the bottom of the palette, just Shift-click in the spectrum. Each time you do, it will toggle through the different color modes.

Resetting your foreground colors

The default color for your foreground is black, and the default color for your background is white. There are two ways to instantly reset your foreground and background colors to their default settings:

(1) If you look at the foreground/background swatches near the bottom of the Tool palette, you'll notice a little miniature version of the two color swatches just below and to the left. The top one's black, the one behind it is white. Click on it to reset your colors to their defaults.

(2) The other method is even faster. Press the letter "d" on your keyboard (it's easy to remember—just think "D for defaults").

A method I use often in the book for making your foreground color white is to press the letter "d" (which makes your foreground black) and then the letter "x," which swaps your foreground and background colors, making white your foreground color.

3D Plastic Effect

This is an easy way to create that smooth, rounded, almost plastic look on any object. In this example, I used type, but it works pretty much the same an any shape you draw.

STEP ONE: Open a new document. Choose a foreground color (I chose a violet shade) and fill your Background layer with that color by pressing Option-Delete (PC: Alt-Backspace). Set your foreground color to white by pressing the letter "d" then the letter "x." Click on the Type tool and create your text.

STEP TWO: In the Layers palette, change the mode of this Type layer form Normal to Overlay. Go under the Layer menu, under Rasterize, and choose Type.

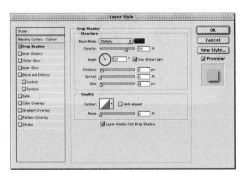

STEP THREE: Go under the Layer menu, under Layer Style, and choose Drop Shadow. When the dialog box appears, set the Angle to 121° and increase the Size to 8. Click on the black color swatch, and when the Color Picker appears, choose a slightly darker shade of color that you originally used to fill your Background layer, then click OK.

STEP FOUR: Go to the Layers palette, hold the Command key (PC: Control key), and click on your text layer's name to put a selection around your text. Go under the Select menu, under Modify, and choose Expand. Enter 2 pixels and click OK.

STEP FIVE: Switch to the Marquee tool by pressing the letter "m." Then press the Right Arrow key once and the Down Arrow key once to move your selection down and to the right. Now, go under the Edit menu and choose Copy Merged.

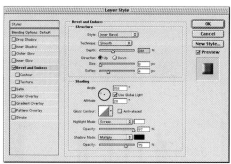

STEP SIX: Go under the Edit menu and choose Paste, and your type will reappear on its own layer. Go under the Layer menu, under Layer Style, and choose Bevel and Emboss. Increase the Depth to 381%, Size to 8, Soften to 4, and click OK.

STEP SEVEN: Press Command-L (PC: Control-L) to bring up the Levels dialog. Drag the top right Input Levels slider to the left until it reads 185 (this brightens the type). Go under the Filter menu, under Artistic, and choose Plastic Wrap. Set your Highlight Strength to 15, Detail to 9, Smoothness to 7, and click OK. Go under the Edit menu, and choose Fade Plastic Wrap.

STEP EIGHT: Lower the Opacity to 75 and click OK. In the Layers palette, click on the Background layer. Press "d" to set your foreground to black. Press Command-A (PC: Control-A) to select the entire background. Press Delete (PC: Backspace) to delete the background. Click on your top layer, then go under the Layer menu, under Layer Style, and choose Drop Shadow to complete the effect.

How to get undo on a slider

In the effect at the left, we use the Fade function after using the Plastic Wrap filter. I always think of the Fade filter as "Undo on a slider" because that's pretty much what it does.

The Fade command now appears in the Edit menu, (it used to be in the Filter menu in previous versions). It includes the name of your filter, so if you run a Gaussian Blur, the menu item will read, "Fade Gaussian Blur." When you choose it, a dialog box appears with a percentage slider. At 100%, you get the full 100% effect of the filter. As you slide it to the left, it starts to fade the amount of effect of the last filter. When you reach 0%, you've completely undone your filter, which is why it works like "undo on a slider."

It also has a keyboard shortcut: press Shift-Command-F (PC: Shift-Control-F). Cool tip: It's not just for filters (that's why they moved it to the Edit menu). Paint a brush stroke, then try "Fade Brushstroke." Pretty handy.

When copying an image, Photoshop can do the math

If you make a selection and copy that image into memory, Photoshop automatically knows the exact size, resolution, and color mode of that image. If you decide to put that copied selection into a new document, go under the File menu, choose New, and as soon as the dialog box appears, just press Return (or Enter), then choose Command-V (PC: Control-V) to paste your image. The new document will automatically be the exact right size, mode, and resolution to accommodate that image in your clipboard memory.

If you ever wind up manually slicing images for the Web (rather than using ImageReady's Slice function), this comes in awfully handy. Once you select an area for slicing, press this combination of shortcuts real fast, one after the other: Command-C, Command-N, Return, Command-V. (PC: Control-C, Control-N, Enter, Control-V). That copies your selection, opens the new dialog box, clicks OK, then pastes—all in about two seconds flat.

X-Files Glow Effect

This is how to create the original X-Files glow effect that was used when the series debuted. This effect could be recreated using the Layer Effects Outer Glow, but honestly, doing it this way is a great way to start understanding Channels and how they work, so it's really worth doing (plus, it looks cool).

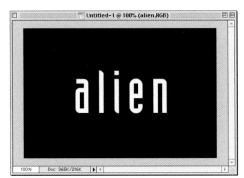

STEP ONE: Open a new document in RGB mode. Set your foreground to black by pressing the letter "d." Fill your background layer with black by pressing Option-Delete (PC: Alt-Backspace). Press the letter "x" to set white as your foreground color. Click on the Type tool and create your text (I used the font Industria Solid from Adobe).

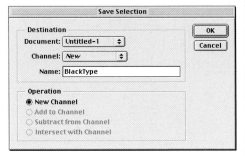

STEP TWO: Hold the Command key (PC: Control key), go to the Layers palette, and click once on your Type layer's name to add a selection around your type. Go under the Select menu and choose Save Selection. In the dialog, name the channel "Black Type" and click OK.

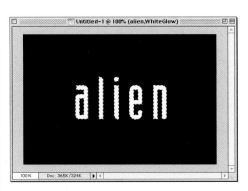

STEP THREE: Go to the Channels palette where you'll see your saved selection (named Black Type); its selection will still be active. Click on it. Then drag your Black Type channel to the New Channel icon at the bottom of the Channels palette to make a duplicate of this channel. Double-click on it and name it "White glow." Don't deselect yet.

STEP FOUR: Go under the Select menu, under Modify, and choose Expand. In the Expand dialog, choose 2 pixels and click OK. Fill this expanded selection with white by pressing Option-Delete (PC: Alt-Backspace). Press Command-D (PC: Control-D) to deselect. Go under the Filter menu, under Blur, and choose Gaussian Blur. Enter 2 pixels and click OK.

STEP FIVE: Make a duplicate of your White Glow channel by dragging it to the New Channel icon. Double-click on it and name it "Yellow Glow," then click OK. Command-click (PC: Control-click) on the Yellow Glow channel to load it as a selection. Go under the Select menu, under Modify, and choose Expand. In the dialog, choose 3 pixels and click OK. Fill this Yellow channel selection with white by pressing Option-Delete (PC: Alt-Backspace).

STEP SIX: Deselect by pressing Command-D (PC: Control-D). Go under the Filter menu, under Blur, and choose Gaussian Blur. Enter a 3-pixel blur and click OK. Drag your "Yellow Glow" channel to the New Channel icon to make a copy of it. Double-click on it, name it "Green Glow" and click OK. Command-click (PC: Control-click) on the Green Glow channel to load it as a selection. Go under the Select menu, under Modify, and choose Expand. In the dialog, choose 6 pixels and click OK.

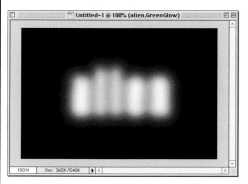

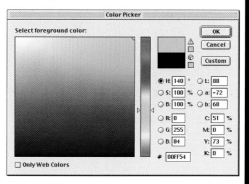

STEP SEVEN: Fill this Green channel selection with white by pressing Option-Delete (PC: Alt-Delete). Deselect by pressing Command-D (PC: Control-D). Go under the Filter menu, under Blur, and choose Gaussian Blur. Enter 10 pixels and click OK.

STEP EIGHT: Go the Layers palette and click once on the Type Layer. Delete your Type layer by dragging it to the trash can at the bottom of the Layers palette. Click on the Foreground color swatch and choose a bright green for your foreground color.

CONTINUED

What are those icons next to my colors (in Step Eight)?

If you choose a vibrant color and you see an upside down yield sign with an exclamation point inside it, that is a Gamut warning. This warning is for people who are taking this image to a printing press, and it warns them that the color they have chosen is outside the range (gamut) of what CMYK printing can print.

The little 3D cube is also a warning—this time, for Web designers. It's warning them that the color they have chosen is not a Web-safe color, and that color may dither to the next-closest Web-safe color when viewed by someone with a monitor that displays only 256 colors. Good luck finding some-one in the 21st century who can only display 256 colors, but hey, in case you're concerned, there's your warning.

Incidentally, the tiny color swatch under the warning icon shows you the nearest color in gamut (or the nearest Web-safe color). Click on that swatch to change to that color.

Doing this effect using Layers Effects

This technique could be achieved with the Layer Effects Outer Glow. You would start with a black background and black type on a layer above it (you'd have to hide your background layer from view to actually see your black type on a black background). After you position your type where you want it, make the background visible again.

You'll need two copies of your Type layer (for a total of three Type layers), so do that first. Then, add an Outer Glow Layer Effect to the top layer. Make the glow white, the Size 8, and the Spread 10.

On the next layer down, add another Outer Glow, but this time yellow, Size 15, and the Spread 18.

On the third layer down, add another Outer Glow, but this time green, Size 35, and Spread 22. That's it. It's easy, but you didn't learn anything (except how to glow). The other method takes a little more effort, but it's a great first step in under-standing channels, so it's well worth the extra time.

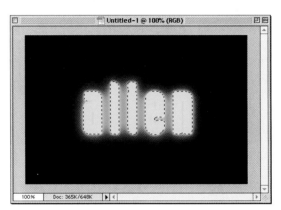

STEP NINE: Go under the Select menu and choose Load Selection. From the pop-up menu, choose Green Glow and click OK. Fill this selection with your foreground color (which should be green) by pressing Option-Delete (PC: Alt-Backspace). Choose Load Selection again, but this time, choose Yellow Glow from the pop-up menu. Change your foreground color to Yellow, and then fill the selection with yellow by pressing Option-Delete (PC: Alt-Backspace).

STEP TEN: Go under the Select menu and choose Load Selection. From the pop-up menu, choose White Glow and click OK. Switch your foreground color to white by pressing the letter "d" then the letter "x." Fill your selection with white by pressing Option-Delete (PC: Alt-Backspace). Choose Load Selection again. From the pop-up menu, choose Black Type and click OK. Press the letter "d" to set your foreground color to black, and then press Option-Delete (PC: Alt-Backspace) to complete the effect.

QUICK TIP

To lower the opacity of a layer, just type in the desired lightness on your keyboard. For example, if you want 80% opacity, type the number 8. For 70%, just type the number 7. If you want 56%, then type 56 very fast (if not, you'll get 50%, then 60% right after it).

Collaging with Screen Captures

I created this simple collage for a feature article on Photoshop 5.0 in *Photoshop User* magazine back in July of 1998. My goal was to create a graphic that would include stylized screen captures but would focus on the number 5. Here's how it was done (with lots of help from Photoshop's Layer Effects).

STEP ONE: Create a new document at 5" x 7" with a resolution of 72 ppi. Set the fore- ground color to a dark teal (like Pantone 328) and your background color to a light teal (like Pantone 320). Click on the Gradient tool and choose the Angle Gradient tool in the Options Bar (the center one of the five tools). Drag a Foreground to Background gradient from the middle of your document to the far right edge.

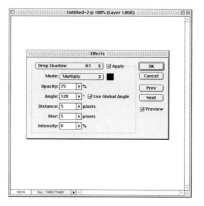

STEP TWO: Next, we'll take some screen captures of Photoshop 5.0's palettes (if you don't have 5.0 still installed, you can use 6.0's palettes). First, open a palette or dialog box of your choice and then take a screen capture while this palette or dialog box is open.

STEP THREE: Start off by making a selection around the dialog box or palette from your screen capture, switch to the Move tool (by pressing the letter "v") and drag this screen capture into your original docu- ment. (Both windows will have to be visible.) Next, invert the capture (creating a negative) by pressing Command-I (PC: Control-I). Your screen should look like the one shown above.

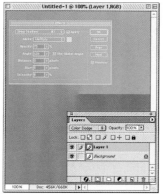

STEP FOUR: In the Layers palette, change the Layer mode (from the pop-up menu) from Normal to Color Dodge. This creates a transparent capture with white outlines (as shown above). Repeat Steps Two–Four for any additional screen captures you'd like.

CONTINUED

Using screen captures in print

Screen captures are low resolution by default, but you see us using them here in the book, and you've seen them in magazines, books, software packaging, and a host of other places in print. So what's the trick of getting enough resolution to go to press at 200-line screen? It's simple—make the screen captures much smaller when you import them into your page layout application (at least 50% smaller). That's the whole trick—shrink 'em. Not in Photoshop, in your page layout application (if you try to shrink them in Photoshop, believe it or not, they'll get fuzzy. Even if you reduce them just 5%, instant fuzz. You HAVE to do it in your page layout application).

There's a color separation secret, too. Before you convert to CMYK, set your Black Generation to Maximum (in your custom CMYK preferences) to force the black type to appear only on the black plate. It works wonders.

Creating screen captures on Macintosh

Press Shift-Command-3 to take a screen capture of your entire monitor image. This creates a file on your hard disk called "Picture 1." Go under Photoshop's File menu, choose Open, find "Picture 1" on your hard drive, and open this file. Press the letter "c" to get the Crop tool, and crop to the desired size. Now you can return to Step Three. *Note:* In Mac OS 8 and higher, you can use an alternate keyboard shortcut (Shift-Command-4) to select any portion of your screen (rather than the entire screen) to save as a screen capture (which will also be saved to your hard disk as "Picture 1").

STEP FIVE: After you add all the screen captures you want, arrange them to fill most of the screen. Go to the Layers palette and from the pop-down menu on the upper right choose Flatten Image. You should now have just a background layer.

STEP SIX: Now that you've flattened all the layers, you're going to apply a filter to the background. Go under the Filter menu, under Blur, and choose Radial Blur. When the dialog box appears, for Blur Method choose Zoom. Leave the Amount set at 10, and make sure the Quality Setting is set to Good. Click OK to apply this filter to your background.

STEP SEVEN: With the Radial Blur added, your image should now look similar to the capture above. Next, add some large text, like the words Multiple Undos, etc., in all caps. When each layer of text is complete, go under the Layer menu, under Rasterize, and choose Type. Next run a 1- or 2-pixel Gaussian Blur filter on each text block. Then lower the opacity on these text layers to 80%.

STEP EIGHT: Using the Type tool add the number 5. I used the font Goudy set at 400 points and filled it with a violet color (Pantone 253). In the next step, we're going to add three different special effects to our number 5 using Layer Effects (actually, when you're using more than one Layer Effects, it's called a Layer Style).

STEP NINE: Go under the Layer menu, under Layer Style, and choose Bevel and Emboss. Then click on the name Drop Shadow in the list of Layer Styles in the left column of the dialog box. In the Drop Shadow dialog, increase the Distance to 45, the Size to 20. Don't click OK yet.

STEP TEN: The third effect to add is an Outer Glow. You can jump right to it by clicking on the name Outer Glow in the list of Styles on the left of the dialog box. When it appears, change the glow color to white by clicking on the beige color swatch and choosing white from the Color Picker. Increase the Spread to 25, the Size to 25, and click OK to apply all three effects.

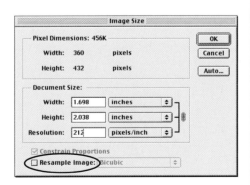

STEP ELEVEN: Our final step was to add the word "number" just to the left of the numeral 5 and then the words "is alive!" to the right of the numeral, both in white. We applied a drop shadow to both of these Type layers using the Layer Effects Drop Shadow with Distance set to 20 and Size set to 7.

STEP TWELVE: How did we get low-res screen captures to print crisp and clean in a magazine printed at 200-line screen? Read the sidebar on page 215 for how we did it. Hint: You can find out what size your image will shrink to at any given resolution by going into the Image Size dialog box, turning off "Resample Image" and typing in your desired resolution (as shown above).

Creating screen captures on a PC

Pressing Alt-Print Screen places a screen capture of your entire monitor image into Windows' clipboard memory. To get this screen capture into Photoshop, all you have to do is choose New from Photoshop's File menu and when the New Document dialog box appears, don't touch anything, just click OK. Then choose Paste from the edit menu and the screen capture from your clipboard memory will be pasted perfectly into your Photoshop document. Now you can return to Step Three.

How to move a layer to another document and have it appear in the exact same spot

There's a quick trick for duplicating a layer and having it appear in another document in the exact same position as in the original. In the Layers palette, click on the layer you want to duplicate, then in the Layers palette's pop-down menu, choose Duplicate Layer. When the dialog box appears, under Destination, choose your other document from the pop-up menu (or new if you want it to appear in a brand new document), and click OK. Your layer will be duplicated to its new document in the exact same spot as in the original.

Liquid Titanium

Because I don't see actual titanium every day (OK, any day), I'm not really sure if this is what the element titanium looks like, but I do know this, it makes a very cool name for a project, so I used it. It's much better than my original title, "Metallic thingy with lots of reflections and other liquidy-looking stuff."

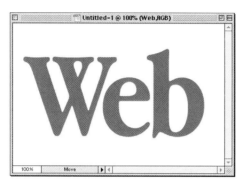

STEP ONE: Open a new document in RGB mode (72 ppi). Choose Pantone 646 for your foreground color (click on the Custom button in your Color Picker, then type 646 real fast). Use the Type tool to create some very large type (100 points or larger). Note: Serif fonts work better. When it's set, go under the Layer menu, under Rasterize, and choose Type.

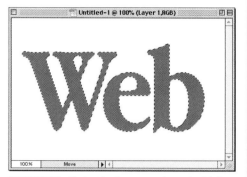

STEP TWO: Go to the Layers palette, hold the Command key (PC: Control Key) and click on your text layer to put a selection around your type. Create a new layer by clicking once on the New Layer icon at the bottom of the Layers palette.

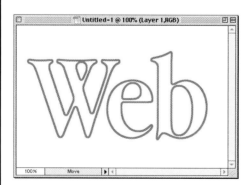

STEP THREE: Go under the Select menu, under Modify, and choose Contract. When the dialog box appears, enter 2 pixels and click OK. Set your foreground color to white by pressing the letter "d" then the letter "x." Fill your selection with white by pressing Option-Delete (PC: Alt-Backspace). Deselect your type by pressing Command-D (PC: Control-D).

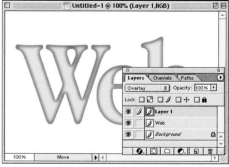

STEP FOUR: Go under the Filter menu, under Blur, and choose Gaussian Blur. Enter 3 pixels and click OK to blur your white type. Change this layer's blend mode from Normal to Overlay. Press Command-E (PC: Control-E) to merge your white blurry layer with your original type layer directly below it.

The limits of Bevel and Emboss

Photoshop's Bevel and Emboss Layers Effect works really well on low-res, 72-ppi images, but unfortunately when you're using high-res, 300-ppi images, the effect of the Bevel and Emboss filter is much less. For example, a depth of 20 gives a very thick, sharp inner bevel on a 72-ppi image, but the same setting of 20 on a 300-ppi image gives a softer, smaller bevel that seems to have about 30% to 40% of the intensity of the low-res version.

There's really no practical way around this in Photoshop, but if you want this type of bevel effect for high-res images, Alien Skin's EyeCandy collection of Photoshop plug-ins has an Inner Bevel filter that is first rate, and it works well on high-res images. Find out more at the Web site at www.alienskin.com.

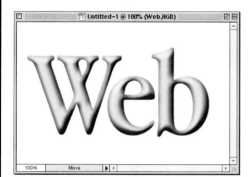

STEP FIVE: Go under the Layer menu, under Layer Style, and choose Bevel and Emboss. Increase the Size to 10, the Highlight Mode Opacity to 100%, and click OK. (Note: if you use a word with many letters, you might need to lower these figures to keep your letters from looking too messy. Just try to get them to look rounded as shown above).

STEP SIX: Go under the Filter menu, under Artistic, and choose Plastic Wrap. For Highlight Strength, enter 15; for Detail, enter 9; for Smoothness, enter 7; and then click OK.

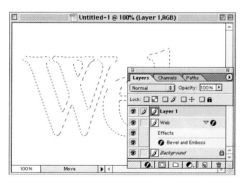

STEP SEVEN: Go to the Layers palette, hold the Command key (PC: Control Key), and click on your text layer to put a selection around your text. Create a new layer by clicking on the New Layer icon at the bottom of the Layers palette. Fill your selection with white by pressing Option-Delete (PC: Alt-Backspace). Deselect by pressing Command-D (PC: Control-D).

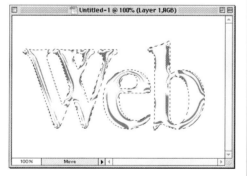

STEP EIGHT: Go under the Filter menu, under Sketch, and choose Chrome. When the Chrome dialog box appears, enter 10 for Detail and 10 for Smoothness and click OK. Change the layer mode for this layer from Normal to Multiply, and lower the opacity to 75%. Hide your background Layer (click on the Eye icon), then choose Merge Visible from the Layers palette's pop-down menu.
CONTINUED

We used this effect on the cover

If this effect looks familiar, it should—we used it for the word "Dirty" on the cover (actually, the amazing Felix Nelson did the cover, but I helped by looking at it often and saying stuff like, "Wow, that looks cool. Keep going!"). He customized my effect a bit by adding gradient fills in the initial type (rather than the solid blue Pantone 646 fill). He created a custom linear gradient that went from Pantone 285 on the left, to 100% Cyan in the middle, to white on the right. He applied this gradient to each character individually. His other tweak was adding multiple Plastic Wrap filters (rather than just the one I applied here) and adding multiple Unsharp Masks (rather than just my one).

For the word "Tricks," he used the Instant Chrome effect (from the Metallic and Chrome chapter of this book). Again, he added more Unsharp Masking, and he broke up the image into a bevel layer and an inner type layer, and applied a slightly different curve to each one. He can't just let well enough alone. You shouldn't either.

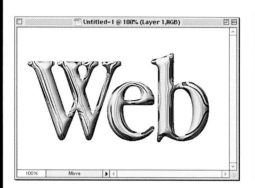

STEP NINE: Go under the Filter menu, under Sharpen, and choose Unsharp Mask. Increase the Amount to 500. Set the Radius at 1, and Threshold at 4, then click OK to add a shiny metallic-like shine to your type.

STEP TEN: Complete the effect by going under the Layer menu, under Layer Style, and choosing Drop Shadow. If you want to take this a step further and go for the liquidy effect, remove the drop shadow by going to the Layers palette, clicking on the Drop Shadow Layer Effects, and dragging it to the trash can at the bottom of the Layers palette.

STEP ELEVEN: Go to the Layers palette, hold the Command key (PC: Control-Key), and click on your text layer to put a selection around your text. Go under the Select menu, under Modify, and choose Contract. When the dialog box appears, enter 5 pixels and click OK.

STEP TWELVE: Complete the effect by going under the Select menu and choosing Feather. Enter 3 pixels and then hit the Delete key (PC: Backspace) to make the inside of your letters look transparent, while keeping the edges at 100%. Place your type over a background (as shown above) so that you can really see the glassy, liquidy nature of the effect. That's it!

NOTES

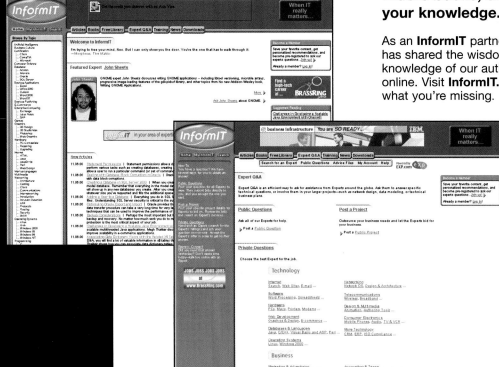